Conversational Realities *Revisited*:

Life, Language, Body and World

John Shotter

Second Edition of:
Conversational Realities: Constructing Life through Language,
first published by Sage Publications, London, 1993

Taos Institute Publications, 2008

COVER ART: Original painting by Hannah Cooperrider
and reproduced with permission for this book cover.

Taos Institute Publications
Chagrin Falls, Ohio

Library of Congress Catalog Card Number: 2008921981

ISBN: 0-9712312-5-7
ISBN: 978-0-9712312-5-2

Printed in the USA and in the UK

TAOS INSTITUTE Publications

Taos Institute Publications

The Taos Institute is a nonprofit organization dedicated to the development of social constructionist theory and practices for purposes of world benefit. Constructionist theory and practice locates the source of meaning, value and action in communicative relations among people. Chief importance is placed on relational process and its outcomes for the welfare of all. Taos Institute Publications offers contributions to cutting-edge theory and practice in social construction. These books are designed for scholars, practitioners, students and the openly curious. The **Focus Book Series** provides brief introductions and overviews that illuminate theories, concepts and useful practices. The **Books for Professionals Series** provides in-depth works, focusing on recent developments in theory and practice. Books in both series are particularly relevant to social scientists and to practitioners concerned with individual, family, organizational, community and societal change.

Kenneth J. Gergen
President, Board of Directors
The Taos Institute

For information about the Taos Institute and social constructionism
visit: www.taosinstitute.net

Taos Institute Publications

Focus Book Series

The Appreciative Organization, Revised Edition (2008) by Harlene Anderson, David Cooperrider, Ken Gergen, Mary Gergen, Sheila McNamee, Jane Watkins, and Diana Whitney

Appreciative Inquiry: A Positive Approach to Building Cooperative Capacity, (2005) By Frank Barrett and Ronald Fry

Dynamic Relationships: Unleashing the Power of Apprecitive Inquiry in Daily Living, (2005) by Jacqueline Stavros and Cheri B. Torres

Appreciative Sharing of Knowledge: Leveraging Knowledge Management for Strategic Change, (2004) by Tojo Thatchekery

Social Construction: Entering the Dialogue, (2004) by Kenneth J. Gergen and Mary Gergen

The Appreciative Organization, (2001) by Harlene Anderson, David Cooperrider, Ken Gergen, Mary Gergen, Sheila McNamee, and Diana Whitney

Appreciative Leaders: In the Eye of the Beholder, (2001) Edited by Marge Schiller, Bea Mah Holland, and Deanna Riley

Experience AI: A Practitioner's Guide to Integrating Appreciative Inquiry and Experiential Learning, (2001) by Miriam Ricketts and Jim Willis

Books for Professionals Series

Conversational Realities Revisited*: Life, Language, Body and World,* (2008) by John Shotter

Horizons in Buddhist Psychology: Practice, Research and Theory, (2006) edited by Maurits Kwee, Kenneth J. Gergen and Fusako Koshikawa

Therapeutic Realities: Collaboration, Oppression and Relational Flow, (2005) by Kenneth J. Gergen

SocioDynamic Counselling: A Practical Guide to Meaning Making, (2004) by R. Vance Peavy

Experiential Exercises in Social Construction – A Fieldbook for Creating Change, (2004) by Robert Cottor, Alan Asher, Judith Levin, Cindy Weiser

Dialogues About a New Psychology, (2004) by Jan Smedslund

TABLE OF CONTENTS:

From the Preface to the First Edition:

Although the aim of this book is to give voice to many topics covered by other books in this series on social constructionism, it also goes a step further: it attempts to describe crucial features of the conversational world, or worlds, within which we have our being. For conversation is not just *one* of our many activities in *the* world. On the contrary, we constitute both ourselves and our worlds in our conversational activities. For us, they are foundational. They constitute the usually ignored background within which are lives are rooted. But they need not remain so. For, from within our conversational activities themselves, we can draw attention to certain of their crucially important features that would otherwise escape our notice. Thus we can come to grasp aspects of their nature *through* talk itself, even when a vision of it as a whole, in theory, is denied us.

Second thoughts, the reason for a Second, 'Revisited' Edition:

The style of this second edition of this book is different from the first, and there is a reason for it. My intellectual life in academic psychology and in the communication discipline has been spent in giving expression to a tension I have felt between the pressures one feels as a professional academic, and what one feels is crying out for expression as an ordinary individual among all other such ordinary individuals – namely, the need for us all as ordinary people to gain control over the conditions determining the nature of our lives together (see the biographical account of my work (Shotter, 2005) published in Yancy and Hadley (2005)) .

As a professional academic, one feels compelled to conform oneself to the requirements (and thus to the limitations) of one's discipline. This has its positive side, for others of good will and tremendous intelligence and commitment have trodden the path before one, and there is no shortage of further projects on the horizon to contemplate. Indeed, if one is just concerned to further one's career, the way ahead is often quite clear. Also, there are standards, high standards, to be maintained, if the enrichment and refinement of the discipline is to be sustained. And this means, as Kuhn (1962) pointed out, that important nuances and interconnections between things, that would not otherwise be unnoticed, often come to light. As a vocation, a calling, the pursuit of a discipline can be enthralling.

But in the middle of all this excitement the question still nags: Is one in fact *doing justice* to the phenomena before one's eyes, before one's ears, in one's everyday life? Is there something crucial one is still *missing*?

I have always felt that there is: that there is something to do with creativity, novelty, and uniqueness that I have still not understood, something mysterious at the heart of how we make sense to each other, that has still not been adequately expressed in any of our social, behavioural, or human sciences. And it is this that has lead me to the rather special and peculiar 'take' on our inquiries into the events occurring between us with our lives together that I want to present in this book – and I will say more about that special 'take' later. But let me say straight away here, it involves something of a return to the "social ecology" I thought of myself as pursuing in my *Social Accountability and Selfhood* book (Shotter,1984)

****

Beginning in the Social Sciences in the discipline of psychology, but finally (and more happily) ending up within the communication discipline, I made quite a number of new starts along the way: rat psychology, behaviourism, mathematical psychology, computer simulation, developmental psychology, social psychology, communication, and so on. Within this odyssey, social constructionism lasted the longest. The claim that words have no meaning *in themselves*, nor is their meaning a matter of them occurring *in a context*, nor is it solely a matter of a speaker's *intentions*, but that meanings are created by, with, and for people in their collaborative meetings with each other, are all very important claims.

But now that I have 'retired' from academic life, and turned at last to working more with practitioners, with people who have to face new and unique circumstances every day and who have to work 'in the moment' to do what seems to them to be for the best, I find myself better able to appreciate their needs more clearly. As a consequence, I now feel that much more needs to be said. General claims are not enough. Practice is *not* a matter of applying theories! And the enrichment and development of better practices is not merely a matter of discovering better theories! Much more complex issues are at stake.

So although social constructionism is now clearly established in academe as a central approach in the social and behavioural sciences, this means – let me emphasize – that as such, as an academic enterprise, it still emphasizes the need for the readers of its texts to be schooled in relevant disciplines with their associated *language games* (Wittgenstein, 1953) – to put the issue in academic terms! And central to every discipline are *authorities*, the masters of the disciplinary discourses, so to speak, and it is in *their* terms that all the rest of us must learn to talk (and write) if we want to qualify as serious professionals within the discipline. In other words, this still leaves us as ordinary, everyday individuals subjected to academic authorities.

But even more important that this, it leaves us also with a special language – a vocabulary of terms and their contexts of use – oriented toward the goals and concerns of academics. Now it is important to realize that the goals and concerns of academics (no matter what the *content* of their talk or texts might be) are of very largely of a linguistic kind: academics are not often themselves directly engaged in the practices, or with the practitioners, they study. They are mainly responsible to, and responsive to, their academic colleagues. Hence most academic social constructionists are, of necessity, concerned with participating in arguments and debates occurring inside academic classrooms, seminar rooms, or conference halls (Shotter & Lannamann, 2002).

Given its situation within academe, along with the pressure on it to adopt scientific forms of reasoning, it is thus not surprising that much social constructionist inquiry emphasizes linguistic issues – linguistic representations, theoretical or conceptual terms, etc. – and much energy is spent in seminar room arguments as to whether such terms are essentialist, reductive, or contain hidden realist assumptions, and so on.

Indeed, it is worth remembering that, classically, science assumed that successful action depended on the accuracy of one's representation (one's theory) of reality, and that an accurate representation is a sufficient guide to practical action. Inquiry was thus concerned to arrive at a *true* theory – where implicit here is the idea that a true theory correctly 'pictured' reality or corresponded with it (a least in its *ideal* characteristics).

Social constructionism questioned not only the idea of an already well defined reality 'out there' awaiting our description of it, but also the very idea of 'truth as accuracy'. Instead of our actions giving rise to linguistic representations, it reversed the arrow, so to speak, and suggested that our linguistic representations give rise to our realities. In other words, it reversed *one* of the major assumptions of classical science.

There are, however, two other major assumptions that it did not reverse: 1) one is the assumption that a linguistic representation is a sufficient guide to practical action; and 2) the other is the assumption that a representation exerts its shaping influence on our actions in terms of its patterning, its *order*. Both these assumptions are aspects of the overall assumption that a language is a self-contained system with its own structure (or grammar) that puts limits on how its elements can be sequenced into representations.

It is this central focus almost solely on language, and on the importance of our ways of talking, which has worried me. It has, as I see it, misled some students of social constructionism into thinking that if they are to change their relations to the others and othernesses around them, all they need to do is to change the language they use, the ways of talking they adopt, and desired changes will occur. This, I think, is a serious mistake. Clearly, our ways of talking *are* very influential in shaping our actions. But there are, as I shall show below, good reasons for assuming that it is not simply by choosing to construct different linguistic representations of a circumstance that we can come to act differently in relation to it; something much deeper and less open to our deliberation and choice is at issue.

Rather than to do with our minds and ways of thinking, it is much to do with our bodies and our ways of acting; perceptual rather than cognitive changes are crucial. It is our spontaneous bodily reactions to events occurring around us that have come to be of central importance in the approach I have adopted in this *revisited* version of *Conversational Realities*.

****

In a moment I will begin to outline some of the central features of the more *bodily* less cognitive approach to the relation of our talk to our actions that I have adopted in this book. But for the moment, let me point out that in my 1993 books (Shotter, 1993a, 1993b), although drawing upon much the same material from Wittgenstein and Bakhtin (and many others) that I also draw on here, at that time I turned to rhetoric and to an emphasis on persuasive language – whereas now, as will be clear in a moment, I have de-emphasized this aspect of language use. My earlier turn to rhetoric, however, was very much in line with a view being proposed by Rorty (1989):

> "A liberal society is one whose ideals can be fulfilled by persuasion rather than force, by reform rather than revolution, by free and open encounters of present and other linguistic practices with suggestions for new practices... It is a society whose hero is the strong poet and the revolutionary because it recognizes that it is what it is, has the morality that it has, speaks the language that it does, not because it approximates the will of God or the nature of man but because certain poets and revolutionaries of the past spoke as they did" (pp.60-61).

But as I see it now, this approach still leaves each of us, no matter how much we may each be concerned to do the best in each unique moment of our lives, seemingly *dependent* on the authoritative words of others, especially on the words of certain of our predecessors. This makes it difficult for us to act – and especially difficult for us to *justify* to others how we act – *in our own terms*.

This, I think, is what makes this new version of *Conversational Realities* distinctive: it focuses on spontaneously expressed, unique, bodily activities, on unique events – on what Bakhtin (1993) calls "once-occurrent events of Being" – and on the *social* influences shaping such unique events. Such a focus brings the importance of the unique experiences of unique individuals back into the picture; the role of the individual author is important too. Indeed, if individuals are to act in ways appropriate to their own unique circumstances, then their capacity to act in creative, once-off ways is crucial.

Almost all current approaches within the social contructionist movement – those focussing on rhetoric, on metatheory, on narrative, and even on various forms of autobiographical and more literary forms of writing – suggest that if we want to talk to those around us in meaningful ways, then we *must* call on already existing vocabularies (Rorty, 1989), or social conventions (Gergen, 1999). A failure to do so makes our utterances literally senseless, open to any accidental meaning others happen to put on them. This, however, leaves us unable to express *unique* things. Everything happens in everyday life, as Garfinkel (1967) so nicely puts it, "for 'another first time'" (p.9): not just simply in our meetings with strangers, but even someone we love, that we have lived with for many years, can still surprise us, can still require us to respond to their *uniqueness*. In psychotherapy and in organizations too, we continually meet new situations that we cannot simply place – without crucial distortions and reductions – into already existing categories.

So, although we may *explain* our actions *after the fact* by saying that we 'followed a principle', this is to reduce the complex exploratory struggle involved in finding a way to 'go on' in a never-previously-encountered circumstance to a set of instructions for those coming after us to follow. The retrospective stories we tell others about our actions inevitably miss out our reasons for why we nearly did something else at each step in the process, but as we began to take these steps, a sense of their inappropriateness arose in us.

If we are to move beyond these difficulties with academic versions of social constructionism – its tendency to look for *retrospective*, *orderly* accounts of and for our activities – and to move more toward *in the moment* accounts of the actual activities and processes occurring between us in our collaborative creations of meaning together, then, I think, we have to carry the processes of critique opened up by social constructionism even further. We have to delve even more deeply into the unnoticed assumptions still hidden in many of our everyday practices of communication and inquiry.

****

> "... if the body had been easier to understand, nobody would have thought that we had a mind" (Rorty, 1979, p.239).

I said above that in my 1993 books, my thought was to turn to rhetoric, to persuasive language, but as I worked through that thought, I began to ask myself: what is it that makes some kinds of language persuasive, that is, more 'touching', more 'moving', etc., and why is it that so much academic language 'leaves us cold'? And I began to see that, for me, this question was closely related to my concern with "joint action" (Shotter, 1980) and the dialogical (Bakhtin, 1981, 1916). In other words, to put it briefly, I saw that it was tied up with people being able to influence each other's behaviour directly and immediately in a bodily fashion, unmediated by any deliberative system of thought. It was the centrality of bodily responsiveness, our involvement as a whole person in the world around us, and the possibility that *that* offered us for uniquely new beginnings, that I had been missing.

As Vygotsky (1986) put it long ago: "The general law of development says that awareness and deliberate control appear only during a very advanced stage in the development of a mental function, after it has been used and practiced unconsciously and spontaneously. In order to subject a function to intellectual and volitional control, we must first possess it" (p.168) – our spontaneous, unthought out, living bodily responses are basic to the whole new approach I want to offer.

This, I think, is where we can find our new beginnings, both the new beginning we must make every time we encounter a new and unique situation in our daily lives, and where we can also find new beginnings for our practical inquiries. As Wittgenstein (1980) puts it: "The origin and primitive form of the language game is a reaction; only from this can more complicated forms develop. Language – I want to say – is a refinement, 'in the beginning was the deed'[Goethe]" (p.31). Where, by the word "primitive" here, Wittgenstein (1981) says that it means "that this sort of behaviour is *pre-linguistic*: that a language-game is based *on it*, that it is the prototype of a way of thinking and not the result of thought" (no.541). In other words, we can find in such spontaneously elicited reactions, the beginnings of uniquely new ways of acting – something that is quite impossible to achieve by the application of rational thought (which can only function by drawing on the already known and shared).

****

> "Our attitude to what is alive and to what is dead, is not the same. All our reactions are different" (Wittgenstein, 1953, no.284).

Thus, central to the new, more practical approach to social constructionism that I want to offer in this second, 'revisited' edition of *Conversational Realities*, is a focus on the *spontaneous*, *expressive-responsivity* of growing and living forms: they are both responsive and expressive to each other, *and*, responsive to, and expressive of, the othernesses (the 'things') in their surroundings. Indeed, to an extent I want to return in it more toward the *social ecological* approach to our inquiries that I first introduced in my book *Social Accountability and Selfhood* (Shotter, 1984). For it is in the fluid back and forth flow of living, interdependent activity – activity that is always inseparably intertwined, as in an ecology, in with all the other activities occurring in its surroundings – that a certain, special kind of understanding becomes available to us. It is this *dialogically-structured* (Bakhtin, 1984, 1986) form of understanding that was quite unrecognized in the mechanistic account of our relations to our surroundings which we inherited from Descartes. And that mechanistic, *monological* (Bakhtin, 1984) form of understanding is, if not explicit, then still implicitly hidden, in almost all our academic disciplines today.

Our bodily reactions to events occurring around us, and the anticipations in terms of which we orient to such events, count for little in classical forms of scientific inquiry. Clearly, they are implicitly present – for obviously, scientists unable, bodily, to distinguish between what they were expecting to happen as a result of their manipulations and what actually happens would be unable to do experiments – but the fact is, theories, ideas, and forms of thought are the focal topics of our critical discussions. This means that little significance is attached to whether the movements, behaviour, or activities being studied are the movements of dead or of living things.

Influenced by both Wittgenstein (1953) and Bakhtin (1986), however, I want to suggest that while we can come to an understanding of dead forms or states of affairs in terms of objective, general, explanatory theories representing the sequence of events supposed to have caused their present state, a quite different form of engaged, responsive understanding becomes available to us with living forms – if, that is, *we can engage ourselves in a 'living', flowing interaction with them over an extended period of time.* For they can, as a consequence of our actions toward them, spontaneously express crucially contingent 'replies' back toward us, thus 'setting the scene', so to speak, for how we should continue our efforts to make sense to them, in a way that is quite impossible for dead forms. It is this possibility, of coming to a unique, never before encountered understanding within such an exchange, that make our relations to living forms so special.

It is this possibility of entering into a *living-relation* with living forms that makes these two kinds of understanding so very different from each other. While we can study already completed, dead forms *at a distance*, seeking to understand the pattern of *past* events that caused them to come into existence, if we can enter into a (close and personal) relationship with a living form and, in making ourselves open to its movements, we can find ourselves not only *spontaneously responding* to it, but spontaneously responding to it *in anticipation* of what it might do next. In other words, instead of seeking to explain a present activity in terms the past, we can directly understand it in terms of its *meaning* for us, i.e., in terms of what, for us, it 'relates to' or 'points to' beyond itself, especially in terms of its point for us in the future.

To contrast this kind of spontaneous understanding with the kind of *representational-referential* understanding more well known to us in our conscious reflections as intellectual and academic individuals, we can, following Bakhtin (1986), call it a *relationally-responsive* form of understanding. Instead of the *rhetorically-responsive* version of social constructionism that I offered in the first edition of *Conversational Realities*, it is this *relationally-responsive* form of understanding that I now want to outline below, as it is this kind of understanding I now think relevant to practitioners.

For, as I see it now, our practical talk-entwined activities – according what the others and othernesses in our practical circumstances will allow us to do – continually *make and re-make relationships*, but as they do so, they also *make and re-make realities*. But the realities they make are of a *relational*, not of a Cartesian, kind, i.e., they are not composed of independent elements that can easily be arranged into new patterns; they are only open to changes of a very different kind (the practical implications of this shift are explored extensively below).

****

Thus now, instead of it being a book oriented toward arguments with other academics, I want to eliminate a number of chapters I now think irrelevant to practical issues, to present a number of relevant new chapters, and to reworking a number of original ones to make them more relevant to practical concerns.

Strangely, this does not make it a less intellectually demanding book. Quite the opposite. Tick-box, recipe books for practitioners may be demanded by the focus groups set up by publishers concerned solely with sales, but they demean in their simplicity and self-deception all concerned with their production. The task of understanding how to develop a mode of inquiry appropriate to events always occurring for *another next first time*, is a task of a most unusual kind. Some, but not many, have appreciated its special nature. Thus we are not wholly without a number of brilliant and committed guides. Among a number of others not mentioned here, we shall find the work of Wittgenstein (1953); Bakhtin (1981, 1984, 1986, 1993); Polanyi (1958, 1967); Voloshinov (1986, 1987); Vygotsky (1986, 1978); Garfinkel (1967, 2002, 2004); and Merleau-Ponty (1962, 1968), of especial importance.

To sum up then: the central focus of this book is now on our spontaneously responsive, living bodily activity, and on the fact that this activity is also expressive to others. In other words, it is on events that 'just happen' to us, rather then on those of our activities we perform deliberately and self-consciously. This leads us to take *meetings* of one kind or another as our focal events. Everything of importance to us in this book occurs in the developmental unfolding of the dynamic relations occurring in the meetings between us and the others and othernesses around us. What makes these meetings so special, is that, due to the fact that living processes grow and develop irreversibly in time, something unique and novel – an 'it' that characterizes each particular meeting – is always created between them when two or more such beings meet. If we are to do *justice* to the unique but complex circumstances of our own everyday lives in the world today, it is the unique nature of this 'it' that we must somehow grasp without 'stripping it down' to fit it into already well-known categories or frameworks. This is the aim of all the chapters that now follow in this book.

****

I must add one more introductory remark about the style of writing I employ in this book, for it also is of a special kind. As I mentioned above, the explorations that follow are all to do with attempting to understand – to 'get inside' – the developing nature of the invisible but complex dynamical events (occurring mainly in, over, or through time) that constitute the unique and distinctive 'it' characterizing the meetings in which we are (or can be) involved. Such events do not necessarily have a rhythm or a repetitive pattern, but they do, nonetheless, have a unique, distinctive *temporal contour* (Stern, 2002; Whorf, 1956). It is the writer's task (sometimes) to portray that contour in an effective manner. As Merleau-Ponty (1970) describes it, the writer's task is to reactivate

> "the original operation of language with the deliberate aim of acquiring and putting into circulation not just the statistical and common aspects of the world, but its very manner of touching and inserting itself into the individual's experience. It cannot therefore be content with the established and current significations. Just as the painter and the musician make use of objects, colours, and sounds in order to reveal the relations between the elements of the world in a living unity... so the writer takes everyday language and makes it deliver the prelogical participation of landscapes, dwellings, localities, and gestures, of men among themselves and with us. In literature, ideas, as in music and painting, are not the 'ideas of the intellect'; they are never quite detached from what the author sees; they are transparent, as unchallengeable as persons, but not definable. What has been called Proust's Platonism is an attempt at an integral expression of the perceived or lived world. For this reason, the writer's work is a work of language rather than of 'thought'. Its task is to produce a system of signs whose internal articulation reproduces the contours of experience; the reliefs and sweeping lines of these contours in turn generate a syntax in depth, a mode of composition and recital which breaks the mould of the world and everyday language and refashions it" (pp.24-25, my emphasis).

I am aware that readers have not found my writing 'easy to understand': "What is he writing *about*?," they ask. But, in line with Merleau-Ponty's comment above – that it is the writer's task is to reactivate the original operation of language and to reproduce in readers the contours of experience – the peculiar task of the chapters in this book is: (1) Not only to provide a dynamic portrayal of a practice of inquiry 'on the hoof', so to speak, by proving a range of exemplars of it in action. (2) But also to provide a dynamic portrayal – to *show* whilst also talking *about* it – of what our everyday world must be like for us from within the middle of our action for us to be able to do what we do within it.

As we shall see, when seen in this *dynamic-relational* aspect, the world in which we perform our activities is a very different kind of world than that assumed in our current, taken-for-granted, forms of thought. Descartes (1968) decided "to speak only of what would happen in a new world, if God were to create, somewhere in imaginary space, enough matter to compose it, and if he were to agitate diversely and confusedly the different parts of this matter, so that he created a chaos as disordered as the poets could ever imagine, and afterwards did no more than to lend his usual preserving action to nature, and to let her act according to his established laws" (p.62). In other words, he decided to exclude from his vision, his view of things, *all the already existing relations at work in his participation in his surroundings*, and to adopt an approach appropriate to our making "ourselves, as it were, masters and possessors of nature" (p.78). And it is this vision – of fundamental elements of matter moving according to discoverable laws – that has (in many spheres, successfully) driven our inquiries in our modernist times.

But our everyday world of our actions, the world we *ecologically* share and participate in with all the others and othernesses around us, cannot be like this. As we shall see, in finding ourselves *chiasmicly* intertwined (see Merleau-Ponty, 1968, chap. 4) in with events and activities unfolding in our surroundings, rather than exerting our manipulative actions on something 'over there', rather than having to think *about* such events, we have to act and think *with* them. Indeed, this is the case, not only if we want to participate in a more *socially ecological* appropriate fashion in our everyday world, but even in our Cartesian attempts to gain mastery over our surroundings. We depend on the inherent relations with the others and othernesses around us, the relations that Descartes ignored, to be who we are, and to do what we do. I cannot be me without you, and without all the others and othernesses around us.

Introduction:

A RELATIONALLY-RESPONSIVE VERSION OF SOCIAL CONSTRUCTIONISM

"The primary human reality is persons in conversation" (Harré, 1983, p.58).

"Conversation flows on, the application and interpretation of words, and only in its course do words have their meaning" (Wittgenstein, 1981, no.135).

"Conversation, understood widely enough, is the form of human transactions in general" (MacIntyre, 1981, p.197).

"If we see knowing not as having an essence, to be described by scientists or philosophers, but rather as a right, by current standards, to believe, then we are well on the way to seeing conversation as the ultimate context within which knowledge is to be understood" (Rorty, 1980, p.389).

In what follows, our talk (and our writing) about talk will begin to take a dialogical or a conversational turn. Instead of taking it for granted that we understand another person's speech simply by grasping the inner ideas they have supposedly put into their words, that picture of how we understand each other will come to be seen as the exception rather than the rule. Most of the time, we shall come to realize, we do not fully understand what another person says. Indeed, in practice, completely shared understandings occur only occasionally, if they occur at all. And when they do, it is by people testing and checking each other's talk, by them questioning and challenging it, reformulating and elaborating it, and so on. For in practice, shared understandings are developed or negotiated between participants over a period of time, in the course of an ongoing conversation (Garfinkel, 1967). But if people are not simply putting their ideas into words, what are they usually doing in their talk? Primarily, it seems, people are *responding* to each other's utterances in an attempt to link their practical activities in with those of the others around them; and in these attempts at coordinating their activities, they are constructing one or another kind of social *relationship* (Mills, 1940). It is the character of these conversationally developed and developing relations, and the events occurring within them, that are coming to be seen as of much greater importance than the shared ideas to which they might (or might not) give rise. For, it is from within the dynamically sustained context of these actively constructed relations that what is talked about gets its meaning. Thus, instead of focussing immediately upon how individuals come to know the objects and entities in the world around them, we are becoming more interested in how people first develop and sustain certain *ways* of relating themselves to each other in their talk, and then, from within these ways of talking, make sense of their surroundings.

For, although our surroundings may stay materially the same at any one moment in time, how we make sense of them, what we select for attention or to act upon, how we connect those various events, dispersed in time and space, and together attribute significance to them, very much depends upon our use of language. In other words, instead of understanding our thoughts and ideas being presented to us as if *visually*, like we see bounded, material objects, in an instant, we are coming to talk of them as having more the quality of an extended sequence of commands or instructions as to how to 'orchestrate' our inner acts of understanding. In this, the sequential variations, the always unfinished, unfolding temporal contours of an activity are crucial, rather than finished, pictureable, spatial shapes.

Indeed, as I shall argue below, it is as if our thoughts are like commands or instructions that are presented to us dialogically or conversationally by the *voice* of an other, one who responds to each phase of our action by indicating to us a next feature to which we should attend (see the chapters in Part I). Thus, instead of in visual and ocular metaphors, we are coming to make sense of our talk much more in terms of metaphors drawn from the realm of talk itself.

Thus, as I claimed in the new Preface to this 'revisited' edition of CR, it is actually within the ongoing realm of our talk intertwined activities – then and there, in the moment-by-moment unfolding course of their expression – that everything of importance to us in our understanding of how communication works, is to be found. Our words have no meaning *in themselves*, nor is it a matter of them occurring *in a context*, nor is it a matter of a speaker's *intentions*. Meaning is created by, with, and for people in their collaborative meetings with each other. And it is this that we shall begin to explore further below.

Verbally constructed relationships and our disciplinary practices

We can perhaps see the importance of such verbally constructed relationships if we begin by taking an extreme case: what happens at a certain moment in a relationship, when one person says to another: "I love you." Quite apart from its function as a statement of fact, such a statement can function (if appropriately responded to by the other) to reconstitute the whole character of the speaker's relation to the person to whom it is addressed. Indeed – and this is especially important – the changed relationship acts back upon the speaker to change the nature of the speaker too. For not only will the speaker now take on new duties (in exchange for new rights) regarding the person of the other, but what he or she will notice and care about in the other will also change: she or he will be changed in their moral sensibility, in their very being, in the kind of person they are. What they anticipate of each other will also change. While the speaker was solely responsible for trying to initiate the 'creation' by the couple of a new form of their relationship, and in that sense, made the disclosure out of the blue, in another sense, the speaker will not have acted out of the blue at all. They will have acted at a crucial moment in the changing context of their developing relationship. Usually, he or she will have noticed certain incipient tendencies in their relationship with and to the other: the other might have spent more than a usual time gazing at them, or, is disconcerted by their presence, and so on. And they have decided that when in the right situation – when in an appropriate interactive position in relation to the other, at the right *interactive moment* – to risk making their declaration. For, unless the whole enterprise is bungled, its meaning, its unique meaning for those involved, will be apparent *within* the flow of activity in which it appears. The words "I love you" will then draw their power – to change the whole character of the future flow of essentially conversational activity between the partners – very little from the words themselves: they merely function to make a crucial difference at a crucial moment, one that arises as a result of the history of its flow so far; thus their meaning is mostly in their use at that moment. But to use them thus, takes judgment; hence the speaker's feelings of apprehension and risk.

However, if managed well, the 'declaration of love' works to create a whole new kind of relationship with the other. Where, from within that new kind of relationship, a new kind of 'reality' becomes apparent – for those in love which each other attach a quite different kind of significance to even small tendencies in each other's actions: the lover, enraptured by the loved one, finds them to be a source of "ceaselessly unforeseen originality" (Barthes, 1978, p.34). For being in love is more than just being friends. It is distinctive in that we feel suddenly seized by passions that wrench us right out of the mundane flow of everyday life. We are transported into another, special reality, in which things happen in seemingly extraordinary ways. Thus, just as "the world of the happy man is different from that of the unhapppy man" (Wittgenstein, 1961, no.6.43), so the world of those in love is different from those who are not: (i) they are in control of themselves (or not) in different ways, (ii) they expect different things of, notice different things in, and have different motives regarding, each other, (iii) they also use different ways of judging each other's worth.

In other words, in their relationship, their way of being with each other is quite different from their ways of being with others. And it is against this new background, this new *structure of feeling* (Williams, 1977), that certain acts are judged by those within a love relationship as fitting or not. Thus as a result of their declarations of love for each other (assuming the initial declaration to have been reciprocated), they will expect different things of each other in the future. If they take their utterances seriously and are concerned about their (moral) implications, they will not now expect, for instance, often to be left alone, while the other goes off with other friends, and so on. Indeed, speakers not honouring the moral commitments implicit in their avowals can be shamed by being confronted with that fact by those to whom they addressed them.

While not perhaps so emotionally intense, nor quite so exclusive of others, many of our other activities in everyday life take place within the context of such conversationally developed relationships. Some are fleeting, others are more long term. Some are more open and disorderly than others; conversations among friends are less constrained than those in which we have to get some 'business' done; in some contexts – in offices, businesses, bureaucracies, educational establishments, etc. – knowing the order of talk required is a part of one's social competence as an adult. Indeed, so powerful is our talk in affecting our relations to others, that certain ways of talking take on an 'official' or 'sacrosanct' form, and one is sanctioned for talking 'against' them, so to speak. Thus Nietzsche's claim that "God is dead," is still regarded in many quarters as shocking. And certainly in the United States of America, it is not a taken for granted aspect of the daily world to which one could appeal in opposing some of the social policies being implemented currently by state legislatures under the control of the Christian Right. Within such groups, strong feelings are aroused by talk that undermines the 'basic' ways of talking they use in relating themselves to each other. Talk that undermines the boundaries between our categories of things in the world, undermines 'us', the stability of the kind of beings we take ourselves to be and the shape of the desires, impulses, and urges we have; thus such talk is dangerous (Douglas, 1966). It is not easy to question or to change our 'basic' ways of talking[1].

In the west, in our everyday, practical talk about ourselves, we take a great number of things for granted. And in our traditional forms inquiry into ourselves and the nature of our everyday social lives, in psychology and sociology and in social theory in general, we have codified these 'basic' ways of talking into a number of explicit assumptions: for instance, we take it that we are self-contained individuals, having minds that contain 'inner mental representations' of possible 'outer' circumstances, set over against other such similar individuals, and against a social and natural background lacking such a cognitive ability (Sampson, 1985, 1988).

Indeed, so 'ingrained' is this way of thinking about ourselves, that in our everyday conversations it is difficult for us intelligibility to talk about – and thus to imagine – ourselves in any other way. In fact, we hold each other to these forms of talk. To talk otherwise is considered a bit strange, it is as if one did not quite know what is involved in being a normal person. Indeed, these basic, taken-for-granted ways of talking are the source of our assumption that to understand something means 'having something like a picture of it in our heads'. And when, prior to the problem of attempting to explain it as a psychological process, we are faced with the problem of saying what understanding 'is', we say to ourselves, that is how it 'must' be – how else could it be? Yet, as the anthropologist Geertz (1979) remarks about this whole conception we have of ourselves: "however incorrigible it may seem to us, [it is] a rather peculiar idea within the context of the world's cultures" (p.229). Other peoples seem to have developed very different ways of accounting for themselves to each other – as Lienhardt (1961) reports of the Dinka, for instance: they seem to have "no such interior entity [as a 'mind'] to appear, on reflection, to stand between the experiencing self at any given moment and what is or has been an exterior influence upon the self" (p.149). Could it be that our talk of people as having "inner mental states," and of them as always understanding things in terms of such states, is less universal than we think?

Yet, as we have seen, it is 'basic' for us. It arises out of a whole set of, to an extent interlocking, everyday practices in terms of which we all live and make sense of our lives together. Thus, although new ways of talking can be proposed, unless a way of fitting them harmoniously in with those already existing can be found, difficulties will be raised.

In this regard, of particular interest to us as professional academics, are the disciplinary relationships we share with our professional colleagues. Although we have been used in the past to thinking of our disciplines as concerned with dispassionate knowledge, it is clear that this is only so in the centre of the discipline, so to speak. Those who operate there, who have passed their examinations well, who know not only how to draw upon certain already fixed meanings in an order of meanings but also how to critically reject all those that do not fit, find an orderly, tranquil world with everything in its expected place. But as Foucault (1972) points out, at the boundaries, as those on the margins of disciplines know to their cost, there are a whole range of *exclusionary practices* working to sustain the limited and orderly nature of its subject matter. "Within its own limits, every discipline recognizes true and false propositions, but it repulses a whole teratology of learning" (p.223). And so it has been in the history of psychology (Danziger, 1991). Each new approach in psychology has had to struggle in from the margins to a place in the centre. For, to those who currently occupy the centre, new approaches can often seem like dangerous monsters on the prowl around outside the discipline, intent, if allowed in, upon destroying any order so far achieved within it.

Thus, like friends posed on the brink of being lovers, can we (should we) risk shifting our disciplinary relations onto a new footing? While we might experience what we have never experienced before, we might also lose the basis of all the gains we have so far made. But also like the lovers above, perhaps the risk is not so great as feared. Perhaps we are only required to recognize what it is that we already doing in our relations to and with each other: to recognize and attend to how we ourselves do the work of making sense of ourselves and our world to each other, where before we thought 'mechanisms' beyond our control must be at work.

What is utterly new here, then, and quite against the grain of the whole western tradition of intellectual and academic inquiry – which is oriented toward the search for already existing but hidden patterns or orderings, repetitions or regularities, that can be used to predict and control events in one's surroundings – is a view of people as creative agents able to fashion between themselves, in the moment, the very orders within which they both see themselves as significantly involved, and which are used (as a matter of practical hermeneutics) as a context for rendering their own behaviour meaningful.

What is central to this 'revisited' edition of *Conversational Realities*: the 'first-time' nature of all our everyday understandings

This, then, is what it will be difficult to orient toward in what follows: it will be a matter of working on ourselves to change our expectations in our inquiries. Whereas in the past we have thought that hidden 'mechanisms' beyond our control must be at work in shaping and controlling our behaviour, and that it is our task to bring such mechanisms out into the light of day by providing a description of their 'workings' (an explanation), in what follows in this book, we will face a quite different task: We must *notice* what it is that we are already actually doing in our relations to and with each other; we must recognize and attend to how we ourselves in fact do the work of making sense of ourselves and our world to each other. If we can do this, then how our ways of making sense to each other *work*, i.e., how and why we take each step in the unfolding sequence of 'moves' we make in our interactions with each other, will become apparent to us. Thus if we want to convey to others the 'workings' of our actions, no further 'explanation' will be necessary. The detailed description will be enough.

But in our attempts to do this, to direct our attention in this way (as already mentioned in the Preface), we shall need to shift from a focus upon how we understand objects to how we understand each other – a shift of interest away from a world of separate, independent individuals to a world of interdependent, continuously unfolding processes; away from an interest in how events in the past lead to those occurring in the present to how our anticipations and expectations lead what we take the meaning of events occurring in the present moment to be; a shift in concern, in other words, from epistemology (with the gaining of objective knowledge) to one in practical hermeneutics, to do with our everyday, practical, embodied, meaningful relations with each other. In other words, a shift to a focus on our own *ontological skills* (Shotter, 1984), on our own ways of *relating* or *orienting* ourselves toward events occurring in our surroundings. And in focussing upon how we make use of different ways of talking, to construct different ways of relating ourselves to the others and othernesses around us, this book is concerned with a special dialogical or conversational version of *social constructionism* (Coulter, 1979, 1983, 1989; Gergen, 1982, 1985; Harré, 1983, 1986; Shotter, 1984, 1993), which focuses especially upon the role of our expectations and anticipations in our efforts to understand each other, an approach which, to repeat, I now call a *relationally-responsive* one.

I have called it this because I want to claim that our ability as individuals to speak representationally, i.e., to depict or describe a unique state of affairs (whether real or not), as we please, independently of the influences of our surroundings, is a very secondary use of language and is a way of talking that we makes use of only occasionally. As I see it, it arises out of our primarily speaking in a way that is both *related* to the others and othernesses around us, and is spontaneously *responsive* to them in ways determined by our relations to them. When this is the case, when we are in a *dialogically-structured* relation (Bakhtin, 1981, 1984) with those with whom we are interacting, our talk is not shaped by our following of pre-existing rules; it is inevitably unique and creative.

So, while it is undeniably possible to see repeated patterns, regularities, static shapes of forms within in our talk, it is also the case that – due to our ineradicable *spontaneous bodily responsiveness* to the unique events occurring in our surroundings – each occasion of our use of language, each of our utterances is unique. There is a "specific variability" (Voloshinov, 1984, p.69) always present in our language use, and it is in the uniqueness of this variability, its specific nature, that we can attempt to express our own unique meanings to each other. Thus, as Voloshinov (1984) puts it: "The basic task of understanding does not at all amount to recognizing the linguistic form used by the speaker as the familiar, 'that very same'... No, the task of understanding does not basically amount to recognizing the form used, but rather to understanding it in a particular, concrete context, to understanding its meaning in a particular utterance, i.e., it amounts to understanding its novelty and not to recognizing its identity" (p.68).

Thus, to move further away from the Cartesian idea that our activities are determined or governed by pre-existing rules, laws, or principles, and to move toward Wittgenstein's (1953) claim that: "the meaning of a word is its use in the language" (no.43), I shall want to argue that each of our utterances is a unique and creative use of language; and that norms, that 'proper ways of speaking' are brought in retrospectively, after the fact, and only then if necessary to clear up confusions and bewilderments, should they occur. As I see it, the meaning of an utterance, of a word in an utterance, is created only in the interplay between a speaker and listener as the utterance unfolds. A speaker's meaning is not 'in' the words used by the speaker, nor in the speaker's intentions, nor even in the speaker's words in this, that, or some other particular context; it is a "developing and developed event" (Garfinkel, 1967, p.40) that is realized and known, by all the parties involved in the interaction, only *from within* the unfolding course of the interaction producing it.

Thus we need to recognize that there is something at work *in our words in their speaking*, over and above what is there *in the patterns present in them once they have been spoken*. Due to our ineradicable spontaneous bodily responsiveness to the unique events occurring around us, there is a kind of *gestural meaning* immanent in our speech (Merleau-Ponty, 1962, p.179), expressed in the ways we body forth our utterances – in our choice of words, their pacing, intoning, their intertwining in with our other activities. And it is this that allows us to feel our way into the speaker's *relations* with his or her situation, for it is in the unfolding temporal shape of their utterances that they both allude to, 'touch on', or otherwise indirectly express the 'shape', so to speak of *their* situation, as well as 'pointing toward', or gesturing toward, what they anticipate as occurring next in their movement within it. And it is against our understanding of this background – where they are 'coming from' and where they are trying to 'get to' – that we can grasp the relevance of the 'facts' they are communicating to us.

This, however, must not be taken as meaning that there is a "body language" at work unrecognized in the background in the use of our words – that would be once again to put an emphasis on finished and static forms and patterns, and to ignore the workings of living, dynamical events uniquely unfolding in the moment of interaction. Indeed, it would be once again to see the process of understanding as merely a matter of transmitting and receiving information. But to repeat: we are not treating people here as primarily information transmitters, as putting their ideas into words and sending their ideas 'across' to others as the 'content' of their words. No. We are seeing people as primarily *responding* to each other's utterances in an attempt to link their practical activities in with those of the others around them, and in so doing constructing one or another kind of social *relationship* with them. Thus, with these *relational* aspects of interaction in mind, rather than transmitting information, communication is, in Wittgenstein's (1953) terms, primarily a matter of people becoming *oriented* in relation to each other, of them coming to know to 'know their way about' within each other's worlds, and of how 'to go on' with each other within the shared worlds constructed in their meetings.

Ongoing, responsive or transitional understandings within the ceaseless flow of conversation

A:"Who's talking to Whom here?"
B:"Who's Who?"
A:"He's the one talking to Whom?"
B:"Oh I thought Whom was Who?"
A:"No, it's the other way around."
B:"Thanks, I would have got it wrong."

The opacity of this little exchange between A and B (concocted with apologies to Abbott and Costello) becomes transparent, once one *orients* toward the words 'Who' and 'Whom' as being used as the names of actual individuals, rather than as relative pronouns (as we *normally expect*). It is our embodied, spontaneously expressed, taken-for-granted expectations to words in the course of their use that are at issue here.

In the past, we have talked of our words as exerting their influence on us in terms of them as having a *shape* or a *form* that can convey a particular *content* to us, by our being able to place them into an already existing framework or structure of some kind. We thus talked of *interpreting* their meaning or meanings. But if, as I claimed above, shared understandings are achieved in practice, step-by-step, by people testing and checking each other's talk, by them questioning and challenging it, reformulating and elaborating it, and so on, so as to *develop* or *negotiate* a shared understanding between them, over time, in the course of their ongoing talk-intertwined interactions – without them having to rely on making sense of each other's talk by placing it within an already determined framework of some kind, or by interpreting it according to some already existing conventions – then something very different from such a process of interpretation must be occurring. Transitory, or what we can call, following Bakhtin (1986), *responsive* understandings must be occurring to guide the next relevant step aimed at achieving a clearer understanding.

Thus we can now say a little more about the detailed structure of such 'developed and developing' interactions: To finally arrive at an understanding, as the result of a *negotiated development*, it is not necessary for each participant to fully and finally understand each speaker's utterance as it is uttered; the kind of understanding required *in practice*, is much more of a partial, transitional kind. As Bakhtin (1986) puts it, "all real and integral understanding is actively responsive, and constitutes nothing more than the initial preparatory stage of a response (in what ever form it may be actualized)" (p.69).

Indeed, to reinforce the comments already made above, about the importance of our anticipations in our active understanding of another's speech, Bakhtin (1981) remarks that: "The word in living conversation is directly, blatantly, oriented toward a future answer-word; it provokes an answer, anticipates it and structures itself in the answer's direction. Forming itself in an atmosphere of the already spoken, the word is at the same time determined by *that which has not yet been said but which is needed and in fact anticipated by the answering word.* Such is the situation of any living dialogue" (p.280, my emphasis).

In other words, initially at least, what matters above all in speech communication is that, as each speaker finishes their utterance, listeners who will become the next speaker must know how to 'go on' to contribute an intelligible response to that utterance, i.e., how, in Wittgenstein's (1953) sense outlined above, to *orient* toward it, to know how to place it in the speaker's unique scheme of things. If they can, and if the speaker finds what the new listener/speaker has to say is something they can also *orient* to – i.e., grasp it as both *relating* to the speaker's own situation and as also *relating* to, where the new listener/speaker is coming from and where they are also going to (their 'point') – then their exchange can continue to develop smoothly, i.e., routinely, in all its creative uniqueness, without any need for explanatory breaks.

In short, we can see a kind of three-step developmental process implicitly at work here: If it is A who has to understand B's utterances, we can see the process operating as follows:

(1) B expresses an utterance, X, to which A must respond;
(2) A responds to X by uttering Y;
(3) B, in continuing to respond in an unquestioning manner to Y with Z, shows or displays to A in Z that B finds Y satisfactory.

For example:

"B: Lethal Attraction III is on the movies tonight."
"A: Oh good, I wanted to see that."
"B: Yeh, so do I."
"A: Shall we go together?"
"B: Sure."

In stating the fact that the film was on, B is not seeming to want a 'date' with A, but that's how it all develops, and the 'meaning's of their interchange is developed between them. But to reiterate what was said above about the importance of our anticipations in all of this: it is in terms of the each speaker's anticipations of each listener's responses, that they will find each other's responses satisfactory, or not; and I presume that A and B here were entertaining such anticipations of each other's reactions, without either being prepared to take the risk of blurting them out loud.

Garfinkel (2004) puts the matter thus (again with A as listener to B as a speaker) : "A acts towards B as if the signs that B provides are not haphazardly given. When we say that A understands B we mean *only this:* that A detects an orderliness in these signs both with regard to sequence and meanings. The orderliness is assigned to B's activities by A. The 'validity' of A's conception of the signs generated by B are given in accordance with some regulative principle established for A when his return action evokes a counter action that somehow "fits" A's anticipations. Understanding means a mode of treatment of B by A that operates, as far as A sees it, under constant confirmation of A's anticipations of treatment from B" (p.184).

What Garfinkel is emphasizing here is that, whatever order or pattern is found to be at work in people's meetings with each other, it is initially an order *made* to exist as such by the actual participants themselves, and that if *they* cannot ultimately make such an order between them, then and only then do they begin to question the character of each other's participation in the meeting. In other words, it can only be seen as an order *retrospectively*. It is not an order present to the participants *prior to* their interaction. It is *constructed*, if at all, not as a crucial step in the process of communication itself, but as a consequence of communication – the process of communication being thus conducted in quite some other means than by a reliance on it. Indeed, most of our everyday meetings are not conducted according to pre-established orders, and any attempts to impose such a pre-established order, results in one or more of the other participants becoming irate (see Garfinkel's 1967 work reported in Chapter 1 below).

In other words, within or inside our everyday processes of communication, a lot goes on implicitly, unseen and unselfconsciously experienced within the ever-changing dynamics of the background flow of activity occurring in all our communications with each other. As such, it is not easily noticed or remarked on. About this situation, Wittgenstein (1953) notes: "it all goes by so quick, and [we] should like to see it as it were laid open to view" (no.435).

What this means in practice, though, is: (1) that without participants initially achieving an *orientation* toward each other's utterances, they cannot begin the collaborative process of developing shared understandings between them; (2) that only *momentary, unique meanings* understandings, understandings *from within* our meetings matter; (3) that while our words may be open to other interpretations by outsiders, *from within* our meetings with each other, single, unambiguous understandings can be constructed; (4) indeed, it is also only *from within* meetings in which participants are mutually oriented, that "specifically vague" (Garfinkel, 1967, pp.40-41)[2] forms of talk can be used, i.e., forms of talk that are open to being most precisely determined in the course of further talk – our use of images, metaphors, slang, etc., to have precise meanings in specific situations, depends also, of course, on our being appropriately oriented toward one another.

Summary

To summarize, then: The basic issue that I want to tackle in this book is to do with the question as to what counts as a useful outcome of inquiry *to practitioners*, to people actually at the point of contact with the reality of everyday affairs – (1) a retrospective, justificatory, reason-giving account of an already achieved outcome; or (2) a prospective, action guiding account of the detailed struggles required to achieve, develop, or construct that outcome for the very first time in practice? Where here by 'practitioners' I do not just mean professional researchers in business consultancies, psychotherapists, social workers, probation offices, mental health nurses, and the like, I also mean all the rest of us, ordinary everyday people in the street who are puzzled about what next to do for the best in their lives.

Conventional research portrays practitioners, and all the rest of us in our daily lives – if we are not acting impulsively and heedlessly – as adopting a course of action by first reflecting on possibilities and then as choosing amongst them. It fails to portray us as already caught up in ongoing processes *from within* which we must express – in the face of both the constraints and limited resources it offers them – recognizable, legitimate, and above all, successful (in relation to already existing criteria) actions and utterances. In other words, to portray us in this way is, as Garfinkel (1967) puts it, to portray us as "judgmental dopes" (pp.67-68), i.e., as people who are unable to take the complexity of our practical lives into account and to make judgements about them as they unfold.

In 'going on' within a world that we are creating as we move on within it, as participants in a world still in the making, we are not able to reflectively articulate to others the character of those aspects of it that are not yet completed. In being performed for yet another first time, while we *anticipate* that others *will*, sooner or later understand us, we can never be sure: we know what we are trying to do; we know why we are trying to do it; but what we don't know until we have succeeded in our attempts to make sense to the others around us, is *what* our saying and doing has said and done.

Standard, mainstream scientific research approaches the already made social world both as a finished and complete world but as a world still not well understood by us, and reflects on it with the aim of mastering its reproduction, i.e., of making it for a second time, of copying it. It fails to capture what it is to which actors have to attend in their first time creative developments of this world, how they can from within their participation within it, further develop it and refine it to accord more with their own needs, rather than with needs imposed on them by unknown influences outside of their control. It fails, in other words, to take account of the enormous grasp of detail available to us in our ways of knowing how to make sense of the myiad events occurring around us, and our embodied ways of spontaneously reacting to them. We need some other way of making sense of our first-time activities than having to describe them within already shared and pre-existing categories, thus to treat them as no different from previous, already performed activities. It is the main task of this 'revisited' version of *Conversational Realities*, to try to outline what is required – not to *explain* our first-time, uniquely creative activities accurately – but to do justice to *portrayals* of them.

It is our embodied feelings – and the embodied anticipations and expectations to which they spontaneously give rise – that are neglected in the theories of many social scientific theorist. But it is just these *contingent, action guiding feelings* (which are ill served if they just called 'emotions') that work both to guide our next actions and as the 'momentary standards' against which our more explicit formulations are judged for their adequacy and appropriateness. In fact, I want to claim along with Wittgenstein (1980, II) that:

> "We judge an action according to its background within human life... The background is the bustle of life. And our *concept points to something within this bustle*... Not what *one* man is doing now, but the whole hurly-burly, is the background against which we see an action, and it determines our judgment, our concepts, and our reactions" (nos. 624-9, my emphasis).

In other words, whereas in the past we sought a theoretical or causal *explanation* to dispel our puzzlement as to next how to act, Wittgenstein's suggestion is that with respect to human affairs, this is unnecessary: "We must do away with all explanation, and description alone must take its place... [The difficulties we face can be overcome] not by giving new information, but by arranging what we have always known" (no.109). By arranging what we already know in such a way that we can produce "just that understanding which consists in 'seeing connections'" (no.122), we can overcome those orientational and relational difficulties that have the form of: "I don't know my way about" (no.123).

It is with these remarks of Wittgenstein's above in mind – that the new concepts we need to introduce must to point towards events occurring within the general background 'bustle' of our everyday human lives together – that we can turn to the next two chapters: Chapter one is aimed at discussing the embodied, conversational nature of this *background* activity – for, to the extent that everything we do and say both draws its possibility from and returns in its realization to this background, all our social constructions must be *situated* in it, i.e., our 'constructions' must draw on the 'provisions' it affords. Chapter two explores the consequences of situating social constructionist studies, not only in our shared conversation intertwined activities together, but also in the very *moment of meeting* between two or more persons. In other words, as mentioned in the Preface, I want to explore what is involved in conducting our studies from within an unceasing flow of turbulent but nonetheless formative, embodied, social activity.

Chapter One

THE CONVERSATIONAL BACKGROUND TO SOCIAL LIFE:

BEYOND REPRESENTATIONALISM

> "The human sciences, when dealing with what is representation (in either conscious or unconscious form), find themselves treating as their object what is in fact their condition of possibility... They proceed from that which is given to representation to that which renders representation possible, but which is still representation... On the horizon of any human science, there is the project of bringing man's consciousness back to its real conditions, of restoring it to the contents and forms that brought it into being, and elude us within in it..." (Foucault, 1970, p.364).

One of the aims of formulating a relationally-responsive version of social constructionism corresponds with that mentioned above by Foucault: it can confront us with the 'real' socio-historical and socio-cultural conditions of our lives, the background conditions making the current nature of our consciousnesses possible – where, of course, in the view taken in this book, all attempts to characterize them as such, i.e., as the 'real' conditions of our lives, can of course be contested. But if this is the case, if the background conditions of our lives can be responded to in different ways, then we must cease thinking of the 'reality' within which we live our lives, i.e., what we talk of as that reality, as homogeneous, as everywhere the same for everyone. Different people in different positions at different moments will live in what they formulate as different realities. Thus we must begin to rethink what we talk of as 'reality': we must begin to think of it as being differentiated and heterogeneous, as dynamic, as continually developing and changing, as consisting in many different regions and moments, all in constant intertwined motion, all with many different kinds of events occurring within them.

Thus we can begin to think of social reality at large as a dynamic ecology, as a continuously turbulent flow of ongoing, intertwined social activities, containing within it at least two basic kinds of activity: A set of relatively stable centres of *institutionalized*, well ordered, self-reproducing activity, sustained by those within them being accountable to each other for their actions (Mills, 1940; Scott & Lyman, 1968; Shotter, 1984) in terms of codified versions of order, i.e., social conventions, created in previous interactions – but, with the forms of accountability being used to sustain them being themselves continuously open to contest and change (Billig, 1987; MacIntyre, 1981). But we can also imagine these diverse regions or moments of institutionalized order being separated from each other by zones or regions of much more disorderly, institutionally unaccountable, chaotic activity. Where it is in the meetings occurring in these more unaccountable, marginal regions – on the edge of chaos, away from the orderly centres of social life – that the events of interest to us occur.

In fact, as we move away from a modern toward a more postmodern (or premodern!) world to confront the times in which we live, we begin to realize that our reality is often a much more disorderly, fragmented, and heterogeneous affair than we had previously thought[3]. Thus, if uncertainty, vagueness, and ambiguity are *real* features of much of the world in which we live, *and*, how we 'construct' or 'specify' these features further influences the nature of our own future lives together, then their contested nature should come as no surprise to us: for what is at stake *is* which of a possible plurality of future next steps should we take for the best? *Whose* version points towards a best future for us? Clearly, there is a political aspect present in all our meetings with the others and othernesses around us.

Knowing of the third kind: knowing "from-within"

As I have already mentioned, it is a part of the relationally-responsive version of social constructionism being introduced here to argue that the importance of these contests inheres, not simply in their outcomes, but in the way in which the vocabularies and forms of talk at issue are *interwoven* into the practices in which our relations to the others and othernesses around us are conducted. For such forms or styles of talk are constitutive of different possible styles of our social lives together, especially our institutionalized forms of social life. Thus an important change occurs, not simply when one or another side in an institution wins an argument, but when such an opportunity is used to change the style of future forms of discussion, i.e., the permitted forms of talk within that institution. For instance, the move begun in the seventeenth century during the Enlightenment – to talk less about our lives in religious and more in secular terms, less in terms of 'souls' and the 'human spirit' and more in terms of 'brains' and 'minds', less in terms of God's will and more in terms of natural mechanisms – was, and still is, just as important for the new ways of talking and the new forms of social relationship (and new forms of contest) it introduced, as for any of the particular conclusions so far reached. Indeed, within the sphere of our socio-psychological interests here, these 'Enlightenment' forms of talk are clearly still of prime importance to us. Although now, perhaps, they are more important for what they have attempted to prohibit, to exclude, or to marginalize (Foucault, 1972) than for what they privileged as central.

Thus in pursuing the project of restoring to consciousness, i.e., kind of consciousness, an understanding of the conditions of its own possibility, I want to argue that present in the conversational background to our lives are many other forms of talk, with their own peculiar properties, currently without a 'voice' in the ongoing contests within this sphere. If they were to gain a voice, it could change our lives; the form or style of our consciousnesses could become very different from how it is currently manifested.

Indeed, it is one of the major claims explored in this book, that an important, special *third kind* of knowledge, embodied in the conversational background to our lives, has remained 'unvoiced' in our socio-psychological debates so far: a special kind of knowledge – to do with how *to be* a person of this or that particular kind not only both according to the culture into which one develops as a child, but also to the kind of exchange in which one is currently involved. It is a kind of knowing that cannot be finalized or formalized in a set of proven theoretical statements, nor need it be to be applied; for it shows itself only in the dynamics of our interactions with each other. Thus it is not theoretical knowledge (a "knowing-that" in Ryle's (1949) terminology) for it is a knowing, a knowledge-in-practice. Nor is it merely knowledge of a craft of skill (a "knowing-how"), for it is joint knowledge, knowledge-held-in-common with others; it is an intersubjectively shared form of knowing. Thus it is a third kind of knowledge, *sui generis*, that cannot be reduced to either of the other two, the kind of knowledge one has *from within* a situation, a group, social institution, or society; it is what we might call a "knowing-from[4]." Bernstein (1983) has called it a "practical-moral knowledge."

Elsewhere, I have discussed the nature of this special third kind of knowledge extensively (Shotter, 1984, 1993a). This volume explores various of its implications further in certain different spheres of psychology and our conversational lives together, as well as other, more general implications of its nature. Specifically, these studies address the question of how it is that we come to experience ourselves, our world, and our language, in the particular ways that (at the moment) we do, and how we might also come to experience all these entities differently.

Why, for instance, do we currently simply take it for granted that we each have minds within our heads, and that they work in terms of inner mental representations which resemble in some way the structure of the external world? Why do we feel that we live our social lives within certain, independently existing social structures, and act within them as if according to rules? Why do we think that the best way to make sense of our lives and to act for the best, is in terms of theoretical formulations provided us by experts (rather than in terms of more practical, everyday forms of knowledge)? And also, why do we feel that our language works, primarily by us using it accurately to represent and to refer to things and states of affairs in the circumstances surrounding us, rather than our using it influence each other's and our own bodily behaviour? In other words, why do we feel *impelled* or *compelled* to talk about ourselves as we do?

What is it in the conversational background to our lives that shapes our passions, our impulses, our taken-for-granted spontaneous responses to events occurring around us, and leads us to talk about ourselves and our world as we do – thus to 'construct' all our social relations along individualistic and instrumental dimensions, and our psychology in terms only of mental representations – while preventing us from noticing the consequences, the *unintended consquences*, of our so doing?

This also, I want to argue, is a consequence of our *joint action*. While there are many activities in which we as individuals know what we are doing and why, in joint action we can remain deeply ignorant as to what exactly it is that we are doing. This is because in such joint activity, people must, in their spontaneously responsive reactions to those around them, interlace what they do in with the activities of others. In such circumstances we remain ignorant of quite what we are doing, not because the 'plans' or 'scripts', etc., supposedly in us somewhere informing our conduct are too deeply buried to bring out easily into the light of day, but because they are not the major influences on our conduct[5]. The actions of others determine our conduct just as much as anything within ourselves. As a result, the overall outcome of the exchange is simply not up to us. In fact, it cannot be traced back to the intentions of any individuals. Thus rather than being experienced as a product of those actually producing it, it is experienced as an event which just happens, naturally, and we then feel impelled to seek its 'natural' causes (see its properties as set out in Chapter 2).

'Eternalizing' the ideology of the day

As I mentioned in the Introduction, it is very difficult to reorient ourselves away from thinking in this way, to turn away from thinking that hidden 'mechanisms' beyond our control must be at work in shaping and controlling our behaviour, and to orient ourselves toward noticing that it is we, in our relations to and with each other, that are in fact doing the work of making sense of ourselves – and our world – to each other. While, as a result of our own experiences in our upbringing we can learn to think in terms of inner mental pictures as a special skill, my suggestion is that no such already existing but hidden mechanisms, working in terms of inner mental representations, are *always* at work in our everyday exchanges with each other. As I argued in the Introduction, each of our everyday utterances makes a unique and creative use of language, and norms are only brought in 'after the fact', if necessary, to clear up confusions and bewilderments, should they occur.

In this connection, Rorty (1980) has argued that "the attempt (which has defined traditional philosophy) to explicate 'rationality' and 'objectivity' in terms of conditions of accurate representation is a self-deceptive effort to eternalize the normal discourse[6] of the day, and that, since the Greeks, philosophy's self-image has been dominated by this attempt" (p.11). Where, by the phrase 'eternalizing the normal discourse of the day', Rorty wants to suggest that in seeking, retrospectively, *to explain* the order or orders we observe in our everyday social lives together, we feel the need to do so in terms of an appeal to a certain fundamental, already existing 'essence' of some kind – perhaps to a 'spirit' or to a 'God', or perhaps to basic rules, conventions, or principles. In short, to a crucial 'something' beyond history or our daily social lives together[7], eternally present.

But how might we make sense of this 'something'? Central to his argument here, is the claim that: "It is pictures rather than propositions, metaphors rather than statements, which determine most of our philosophical convictions. The picture which holds traditional philosophy captive is that of the mind as a great mirror, containing various representations – some accurate, some not – and capable of being studied by pure, nonempirical methods. Without the notion of the mind as a mirror, the notion of knowledge as accuracy of representation would not have suggested itself" (p.12). In other words, in our attempts to make the unfamiliar familiar to us, we use metaphors; but then we very easily forget their metaphorical status and, as he put it in a later book, we "literalize" them (Rorty, 1989, 44)[8], i.e., begin to treat the unfamiliar 'mind' as if it *really* is in actually a mirror, a computer, an organ of calculation, etc., etc. But in so doing, we act like obsessive-compulsives, or fetishists, driven to perform actions irrelevant to our real needs, in order to obtain a satisfaction of certain perverse desires. And it is in our constant appeals to *rules* or to the *plans*, *beliefs*, *intentions*, or *wishes* of individuals in explaining why their talk, and other actions, take the 'shape' that they do, that we continually legitimate the particular, self-deceptive ideology implicit in normal discourse of the day when there is in fact no need to do this.

But as we shall see, such an individualistic, representationalistic, and intentionalistic ideology works as a way of talking that benefits certain social groups to the detriment of others. Thus, in originally calling the version of social constructionism displayed in the studies below a rhetorically-responsive version, I wanted to call attention to the fact that central to it is an attitude towards the nature of language which contrasts markedly with the "normal discourse of the day" in this regard: the taken-for-granted nature of language as a referential-representational system or as a code of meaningful signs. That stance, it can be argued (Harris, 1980, 1982; Voloshinov, 1973) – in which language is treated as a systematic object of thought, structured as if according to rules, or, as an objective system of differences (Saussure, 1960) – arose out the study of *already spoken words*, after all contest over their speaking has ceased[9].

By contrast, the studies in this book, display an interest in the contested activity of *words in their speaking*, in our *struggles* with language, i.e., in the practicalities and tensions at work in our use of them as means or as 'tools' in our efforts to communicative effectively in our everyday affairs, and in particular, an interest in their formative or 'shaping' function, and the 'resistances' they meet, in such processes[10].

Thus the stance I take in all the studies below is that, in an everyday process involving a myriad of spontaneous, responsive, practical, unselfconscious, but contested interactions, we unknowingly 'shape' or 'construct' between ourselves as already mentioned, not only a sense of our own identities, but also a sense of our own 'social worlds'. Or, to put it another way, that plane upon which we talk about what we think of as the orderly, accountable, self-evidently knowable and controllable characteristics of both ourselves (as autonomous individual persons) and our world, is constructed upon another, lower plane, in a set of unacknowledged and unintended, disorderly, conversational forms of interaction involving struggles between ourselves and others.

Historically, it is upon the more orderly, accountable plane – conducted in terms of certain 'basic' ways of talking – that we have attempted to construct and establish yet more orderly, or institutionalized ways of talking, i.e., disciplinary discourses, supposedly 'rational' bodies of speech or writing. Where, in Foucault's (1972) terms, such discourses are "practices that systematically form the objects of which they speak" (p.49), i.e., form them as objects of rational contemplation and debate, thus to establish the modern "human sciences" (Foucault, 1970) and the academic departments in which they are taught as disciplines, i.e., established and institutionalized as professions.

While the modern academic disciplines, along with the human sciences, were founded as disciplines in the optimism of the nineteenth century, the conditions making this possible were a product of the Enlightenment of the seventeenth century, and it will be useful here just to list what some of these conditions were. The very notion being enlightened – simply stated as the attempt to live one's life in the light of reason, not a victim of the mere opinions and prejudices of others – was that of people being able to be self-determining in the conduct of their own lives, rather than having their lives determined by others in authority over them.

Indeed, it was a movement in which a certain middle to upper class group – known as the *philosophes*, the first secular (and semi-professional) group of intellectuals powerful enough to challenge the clergy – questioned the legitimacy of the clergy's right to decree society's 'basic' ways of talking. New, secular ways of warranting claims to truth were fashioned (Gergen, 1989), ways that subverted the traditional authority of the priests. Central to these new ways were the following features: (1) the elaboration of a special, 'analytic' way of 'seeing', based in observation, which it was claimed, worked to reveal the hidden, systematic order of things underlying mere appearances; (2) the idea of language as being a shared *code* closely linking words to things; (3) the idea that the knowledge gained through this special form of observation could be symbolically formulated in terms of representations (which resembled in their form of order, the order of that hidden reality); (4) the idea of the world as already a mechanism, or an orderly system, whose principles of operation it was our task to discover; (5) the idea of individuals as containing wholly within themselves the resources required for the making of such discoveries; where (6) the new forms of knowledge could be formed without drawing upon previous, historical or traditional forms of knowledge – thus we had, besides a lack of interest in history, the denigration of traditional knowledge, practical knowledge, and rhetoric as 'mere' rhetoric. They also held (as we now realize) a wholly inadequate view of society, of it as a mere, homogeneous aggregate of individuals. A view which made it possible for them to dream that, if only we could arrive at an appropriate form of enlightened self-knowledge, then society itself could be controlled, through the prediction and control of the behaviour of individuals, and thus 'improved'.

It is against this background that, as Foucault (1970) points out, the 'human sciences' of sociology, psychology, and those disciplines concerned with the analysis of literature and mythology, emerged. For within these special disciplines, 'man' is not just

> "that living being with a peculiar form (a somewhat special physiology and an almost unique autonomy); he is that living being who, from within the life to which he entirely belongs and by which he is traversed in his whole being, *constitutes representations by means of which he lives,* and on the basis of which he possesses that strange capacity of being able to represent to himself precisely that life" (p.352, my emphasis).

Thus the subject matter of the human sciences is – as has finally become obvious with the emergence of *cognitive science* along with its concern with mental representations, as the central arena of current debate from out of the more heterogeneous arena of the *behavioural sciences* – not language itself as such, but a certain form or kind of human being: that which is formed within a certain set of established discourses to do with how we *represent* ourselves to ourselves. Where the discourses in question, let it be said, are of an ideological nature, in that they were first formulated by the philosophes (as a group) according to *their* interests – interests, let it be said, that they hoped would be shared by everyone, but in the first instance, *their* interests nonetheless, an interest in the overthrow of history and traditions.

It is my purpose in the essays that follow, of course, to question the norms that sustain these discourses in existence, to attempt to reveal their more disorderly, conversational origins, and to show how – in the transition from everyday conversation to the forming of disciplinary discourses – ideological processes working to benefit certain groups over others were, *and still are*, at play.

Psychology as a moral not a natural science

Turning now to professional, academic psychology, we can begin by remarking that, in our "official doctrines" (Ryle, 1949) it is thought 'natural', so to speak, to think of ourselves as possessing within ourselves something we call our "mind" – a supposed internal, secular organ of thought which mediates between us and the external reality surrounding us. And furthermore, it is also 'natural' to think that as such, our minds have their own discoverable, natural *principles of operation* which owe nothing either to history or to society for their nature. Thus, it is the task of a natural scientific psychology, of course, to discover what these principles are. Thus, within the ideology of the day, there is no necessity for professional psychologists to justify their projects or programmes of research; they appear to be 'obviously' of the correct form.

This conception of 'mind' is, however, I think, a myth: our talk *of* our minds leads us to experience ourselves as talking *about* our minds, i.e., to talking amongst ourselves as if our 'minds' exist as the real things underlying our behaviour. So the attempt to discover, scientifically, their principles of operation, seems unquestionably a good thing to do. But, I claim, there is no such 'underlying reality' to be found, and the belief that there is has led psychology into a number of dangerous mistakes. And in this chapter, I want to explore just one of them, the one which I think is the most central and the most dangerous: The failure to take account of the fact that in our everyday social life together, we do not find it easy to relate ourselves to each other in ways which are both intelligible (and legitimate), and which also are appropriate to *'our'* (unique) circumstances; and the fact that on occasions at least, we none the less do succeed in doing so.

Attention to the actual, empirical details of such transactions reveals a complex but uncertain process of testing and checking, of negotiating the form of the relationship in terms of a whole great range of, essentially, *ethical* issues – issues to do with judgments about matters of care, concern, and respect, about justice, entitlements, etc. For in our social lives together, the fact is, we all have a part to play in a major, two-part, corporate responsibility: that of *both* maintaining in existence the communicative 'currency', so to speak, in terms of which we conduct all our social transactions, *and* that of developing and updating it to cope with changes in our surroundings as they occur. This is what is involved in us maintaining a certain civility amongst ourselves within our social lives together. For our ways and means of 'making sense' to (and with) one another have not been given us as a 'natural' endowment, nor do they simply of themselves endure; what is possible between us, is what we (and our predecessors) have 'made' possible.

It is this responsibility that modern psychology has ignored, and which has led it, mistakenly, to give professional support to the individualistic view that: "'I' can still be 'me' without 'you'" – a view which, as I shall show in the next chapter, renders most of our actual social life 'rationally-invisible', i.e., beyond rational discussion and debate. But more than this. In ignoring this two-part responsibility, and the whole unnoticed background of spontaneously responsive, embodied, living activity within which in the past it has been played out, modern academic psychology can now, most dangerously, (mis)lead us into eradicating altogether those informal arenas and moments of meeting in which we sustain and further update this unnoticed but essential background to our lives together.

Thus, against the claim that psychology is 'naturally' a natural science, requiring for its conduct the same methods of inquiry of the other, morally neutral, natural sciences, I wish to differ, and to claim (see also Shotter, 1975, 1984, 1993b) that it is not a natural but a *moral* science, and that this gives it an entirely new character. The major change introduced is this: we must abandon the attempt simply to *discover* and *explain* our supposed 'natural' natures, and turn to a study of how we actually do treat each other as being, within the context of our everyday, conversation intertwined, communal activities – a change which leads us on into a concern with 'making', with processes of 'social construction' (Harré, 1979, 1983; Gergen, 1982, 1985; Shotter 1975, 1984, 1993a & b; Shotter and Gergen, 1988).

Thus, what I want to do in the rest of this introductory chapter, is to discuss two issues: (1) One is to explore why we are so attached to (in fact, 'entrapped' by) this myth of a 'naturally principled' mind, and other such similar myths to do with its supposed 'contents', e.g., 'ideas', 'intentions', 'desires', etc., and the power of a certain kind of systematic writing in creating and sustain such myths; and (2) the other is to explore the nature of an alternative set of assumptions in terms of which to orient psychological investigations, a set of alternatives which gives just as much if not more of a place to our 'makings' as to our 'findings'.

Textual realities and the myths of mind

Why do we seem so 'fixated', so to speak, upon the idea that there *must be*, somewhere in everyone, a 'mind', working upon some already existing or 'natural' systematic principles that, with the appropriate methods, can be discovered? Similarly, why are we so passionately convinced that there must be a single, well ordered 'reality' to be discovered underlying appearances, as well as an 'objective' viewpoint, in terms of which it can be characterized? There are, I think, at least two main reasons, both to do with our concern with rational systems inherited from the Enlightenment, already broached above. Let me discuss these reasons in turn.

(1) Firstly: as I have already partially mentioned but must now elaborate, ever since the ancient Greeks, people in the West have believed that 'reality' is to be found '*behind* appearances'. Thus it has long been thought that a very special power resides in the nature of reflective or theoretical thought:

it can penetrate through the surface forms of things and activities to grasp the nature of an underlying, deeper 'form of order', a more basic order from which all human thought and activity *must* in fact spring. Thus society at large has accepted it as a legitimate task of a certain special group of people – at first called priests, then scholars, and now philosophers, scientists, or just intellectuals – to attempt to articulate the nature of this deeper order. It seeking this deeper order, they face the questions of: *Where* is this special underlying order to be found? And, *how* is it to be made visible?

In the West, we first looked for this deeper order unsuccessfully in religious and metaphysical systems. But then, during the Enlightenment, having lost faith in "the spirit of systems," we adopted in our investigations, says Cassirer (1951, p.vii), "the systematizing spirit." And this, I think, is still the implicit project in modern psychology that we inherited from the Enlightenment: the task of 'discovering' a supposedly neutral set of underlying 'mental' principles upon which the rest of life should, rationally, be based. Few of us now, however, possess the intellectual, or, the moral confidence (passion) still to accept this aim in good faith. Yet, although we cannot entirely give up the belief that there must be some worth in the effort to think seriously about life's choices, we find it very difficult to devise alternatives: We keep finding ourselves as if 'entrapped' within an invisible maze, from which there is no escape – this is because, within our professional academic practices, when conducted as systematic enterprises within logical frameworks (as they are currently conducted), there isn't!

(2) This brings me to the second of my two reasons as to why we find it so difficult to formulate intelligible, alternative accounts of everyday ways of making sense of ourselves: In fulfilling our responsibilities as competent and professional academics, we must *write* systematic, objective texts, for we run the risk of being accounted incompetent if we do not. We cannot write literature, novels, poems, or plays. To do so would be seen as our not conforming to the proper methodological discipline required of us. Until recently, we have taken such neutral systematic texts for granted as a neutral means to use how we please. This, I now want to claim, is a mistake, and now we must also study their influence, and what cannot be expressed within such textual forms, what they exclude.

But why should a concern with the nature of the literary and rhetorical devices constituting the structure of a systematic, decontextualized text now be of such concern to scientific psychologists?

Because theorists, in attempting to represent the open, vague, and temporally changing nature of the world as closed, well-defined, and orderly, make use of certain textual and rhetorical strategies to construct within their text *a closed and finalized set of intralinguistic references* – thinking that an open, vague, an not wholly style of writing cannot possibly represent 'the facts' accurately. But we have not yet properly, however, appreciated the nature of the social processes involved in this achievement.

Whereas, the fact is that, in moving from an ordinary conversational use of language, in which meanings are left vague and open to further specification, to the construction of a systematic textual discourse, in which meanings are closed and specified precisely, a major change in our relations to each other is involved. For there is a transition from a reliance on particular, practical, and utterly unique meanings, negotiated 'on the spot' in relation to the immediate context, to a reliance upon links with a certain body of *already determined meanings* – a body of special, interpretative resources into which only properly trained professional readers have been 'educated' – in making sense of such texts[11]. Being able to make reference to already determined meanings in such texts allows a decrease of reference within them to what 'is' actually present in the 'situation' of the talk, and a consequent increase of reference to what it 'might be' about. But to be able to talk in this way, as a professional participant in a disciplinary discourse, one must develop *methods* for *warranting* in the course of one's talk, one's claims about what 'might be' *as being* what 'is'. It is by the use of such rhetorical devices – as reference to 'special methods of investigation', 'objective evidence', 'special methods of proof', 'independent witnesses', etc. – that those with competence in such procedures can construct their statements as 'factual statements', and claim authority for them as revealing a special 'true' reality behind appearances, without any reference to the everyday context of their claims[12].

But this process can also produce, and for us in the social sciences often does produce, what Ossorio (1981) has called, *ex post facto fact fallacies*: the fallacious retrospective claim that, for present events to be as they are, their causes *must* have been of a certain kind. Someone who has already studied the general nature of this fallacy in relation to scientific affairs is Ludwick Fleck (1979). He comments upon its general nature as follows:

> "... once a statement is published it constitutes part of the social forces which form concepts and create habits of thought. Together with all other statements it determines 'what cannot be thought of in any other way'... There emerges a closed, harmonious system within which the logical origin of individual elements can no longer be traced" (p. 37).

In attempting retrospectively to understand the origins and development (and the current movement) of our thought, we describe their nature within our now to an extent finished and systematic schematisms. But in doing so "we can no longer express the previously incomplete thoughts with these now finished concepts" (Fleck, 1979, p. 80).

But the trouble is, once 'inside' such systems, it is extremely difficult to escape from them. We can, as Stolzenberg (1978) puts it, become "entrapped" in the following sense: that "an objective demonstration that certain of the beliefs are incorrect" can exist, but "certain of the attitudes and habits of thought prevent this from being recognized" (p.224). This, I think, is the trap within which we have ensnared ourselves in our systematic academic thought about ourselves and our psychology. But it means that our scientifically acquired knowledge of the world and ourselves is not determined by our's or the world's 'natures' to anything like the degree we have believed (and hoped) in the past; but instead, our knowledge is influenced by the 'ways', the literary and textual means, we have used in formulating our concerns.

To go further: it means that we have spent our time researching into myths of our own making – the myths of 'mind', of 'an already ordered reality', and of 'objectivity' all being cases in point. How can we escape from this entrapment? By studying how it is that we come to entrap ourselves in the first place. We must study the parts played rhetorically by such terms in our talk. For, far from talk of 'mind', 'an ordered reality', and 'objectivity' being in contrast to rhetoric, in my view, they are a part of it. This is why I think that it is important to study the actual, empirical nature of our ordinary, everyday, nonprofessional, nontextual, conversational ways and means of making sense together: for we are 'talked into' our supposed 'realities' by its means.

Events within conversational realities

As I have already mentioned above, the essence of textual communication is its so-called *intertextuality*: the fact that it draws upon people's knowledge of a certain body of *already formulated* meanings in the making of its meanings - this is why texts can be understood without contexts, i.e., independently of immediate and local contexts. And it is also why, I think, experts can become trapped within systems of thought of their own making. But, as Garfinkel (1967) points out, in ordinary conversation people refuse to permit each other to understand what they are talking about in this way. A meaning unique and appropriate to the situation and to the people in it is developed. But that is not easy to negotiate. Thus, what precisely is 'being talked about' in a conversation, as we all in fact know from our own experience, is often at many points in the conversation necessarily unclear; we *must* offer each other opportunities to contribute to the making of agreed meanings.

In such a process, only gradually does 'the matter talked about' develop. Indeed, as Garfinkel (1967, p.40) puts it, it is a "developed and developing event" within the course of action that produces it. Thus as such, it is only "known by both parties [involved in its production] *from within* this development..." Here, I cannot emphasize too strongly the deep and revolutionary or strange nature of what Garfinkel is claiming here: the nature of the 'reality' occupied by conversational events, is at least as strange as any of the 'realities' discussed in modern physics. 'Making sense' of such an event from within a conversational reality, constructing a grasp of what is being 'talked about' from what is 'said', is not, according to Garfinkel, a simple 'one-pass' matter of an individual saying a sentence and a listener 'understanding' it. The events talked about are "specifically vague," that is, "not only do they not frame a clearly restricted set of possible determinations but the depicted events include as their essentially intended and sanctioned features an accompanying 'fringe' of determinations that are open with respect to internal relationships, relationships to other events, and relationships to retrospective and prospective possibilities" (Garfinkel, 1967, pp.40-41). Specifying or determining them sufficiently for the relevant practical purposes, involves a complex back-and-forth process of negotiation both between speaker and hearer, and between what has already been said and what currently is being said, the making use of tests and assumptions, the use of both the present context and the waiting for something said later to make clear what was meant earlier, and the use of many other "seen but unnoticed" (Garfinkel, 1967, p.36) background features of everyday scenes[13].

These strange temporal and spatial properties of conversational events, are in fact, Garfinkel claims, the properties of ordinary conversational talk.

> "For the purposes of *conducting their everyday affairs* persons refuse to permit each other to understand 'what they are really talking about' in this way. The anticipation that people *will* understand, the occasionality of expressions, the specific vagueness of references, the retrospective-prospective sense of a present occurrence, waiting for something later in order to see what was meant before, are sanctioned properties of common discourse. They furnish a background of seen but unnoticed features of common discourse whereby actual utterances are recognized as events of common, reasonable, understandable, plain talk" (p.40).

And as he says (1967):

> "People require these properties of discourse as conditions under which they are themselves entitled and entitle others to claim that they know what they are talking about, and that what they are saying is understandable and ought to be understood. In short, their seen but unnoticed presence is used to entitle persons to conduct their common conversational affairs without interference. Departures from such usages call forth immediate attempts to restore a right state of affairs" (pp.41-42).

We can thus begin to see why, when Garfinkel had his students try to talk to others as if single words should have already clear and determined meanings[14], it provoked a morally motivated anger in the student's victims. People felt that in some way their rights had been transgressed – and as Garfinkel shows, they had! In having other people's pre-established meanings imposed upon them, they had been deprived of their right to participate in the making of meanings relevant just to the situation they were in, to negotiate a properly *shared* outcome; they were unable to make a unique meaning appropriate to their own unique circumstances. Moral sanctions follow such transgressions, people feel aggrieved and attempt to sanction or 'punish' those who perpetrate them. Garfinkel's 'breaching' experiments are a very effective means for showing up our unnoticed, taken-for-granted, background expectations.

But if we take this view – that what is 'talked about' by *us* is developed from what is 'said' by *each* – what should we say about the nature of words and their meanings, if we are not to see them as having already determined meanings? Rather than *already* having a meaning, we perhaps should see the *use* of a word as a *means* (but only as *one* means among many others) in the social making of a meaning. To claim that they *must* already have a meaning of some kind, is yet again to ignore that special but unrecognized, third kind of knowledge to do with how we grasp 'what is being talked about' in a conversation in the course of all our talk 'about' it. Ignoring it, leads us to ignore the unique and very special 'developmental' nature of such conversational situations or events *and* the rights of the people within them. Indeed, to insist words have pre-determined meanings is to attempt to rob people of their rights, both to participate in developing a conversational topic with others, and to their own individual way of making that contribution. But even more than this is involved: it is to deprive one's culture of those conversational occasions or events in which people's individuality is constituted and reproduced. It is also to substitute the authority of professional texts in warranting claims to truth (on the basis as we now see of the unwarranted claim that they give us access to an independent, extralinguistic reality), for the *good reasons* we ordinarily give one another in our more informal conversations and debates. But, if we cannot find the foundations we require for an academic psychology in the writings of philosophers, or the researches of our scientists, where can we find them?

The foundations of psychology: in principles of mind, or, in everyday, conversational realities?

The move from a referential-representational view of language to a relationally-responsive view, entails also the move from a decontextualized concern with a theoretical-explanatory psychology of mind, to a 'situated' concern with the practical-descriptive psychology of socio-moral relations I mentioned earlier. For 'mind' as such, ceases to be something to be explained, and becomes instead a rhetorical device, something we *talk of* at various different times for various different purposes. And what we require are ways of critically describing those purposes – where, a *critical* description is one alive to the ideological biases inherent in the normal discourses of the day, i.e., alive to the fact that we are not always correct in our 'theories' as to why it is that we talk about ourselves as we do. Such a change, however, a change to a critical practical-descriptive approach, entails a change in what we take the *foundations* of our discipline to be.

As we know, our Cartesian tradition has it that our investigations must, if they are to be accounted intellectually respectable, possess foundations in explicitly stated, self-evidently true, propositional statements. And to deny this (as indeed Rorty (1980) has done) seems to open the door to an 'anything goes', relativistic chaos. It seems as if there is nothing at all in terms of which claims to knowledge can be judged. This, however, is simply not the case. For let me state again what seems to me to be the undeniable empirical fact which a natural scientific psychology has consistently ignored: the fact that our daily lives are not rooted in written texts or in contemplative reflection, but in oral encounter and reciprocal speech. In other words, we live our daily social lives within an ambience of conversation, discussion, argumentation, negotiation, criticism and justification; much of it to do with problems of intelligibility and the legitimation of claims to truth. Anybody wanting to deny it will immediately confront us with an empirical example of its truth. And it is this 'rooting' of all our activities in our involvements with those around us, which prevents an 'anything goes' chaos. Truth is something we arrive at the constant checking out our claims in the face of challenges from all those around us, not something we depart from.

But only if we possess a certain kind of *common sense*, a special kind of ethical sensibility, that we gradually came to embody in the course of our growth from childhood to adulthood, to do with sensing or feeling what the people around us are trying to do in their actions, can we qualify for involvement in such an activity. If we lacked that sensibility, that embodied capacity to judge our own (or another person's) relations, i.e., our (their) *orientation*, to the topic of our (their) talk, then we would be denied our right to act freely in our society; our autonomous status would be denied us. We would be treated as some kind of *dope*, unable to tailor our actions (or how others were tailoring their's) in ways proportionate to our (their) circumstances. Yet this is exactly how, as social science theorists, we have often treated people in our theories: as not in fact using their judgment at all in acting, but as just 'following rules'. We ignore what seems to be the fact of that matter: that people themselves create and sustain the orders at work in their relations with the others and othernesses around them. As a consequence of this neglect, as Garfinkel (1967) points out, is that we mislead ourselves "about the nature and conditions of stable actions. This occurs by making out the member of the society to be a judgmental dope of a cultural or psychological sort... [Where] by 'cultural dope' I refer to the man-in-the-sociologist's-society who produces the stable features of the society by acting in compliance with preestablished and legitimate alternatives of action that the common culture provides. The 'psychological dope' is the man-in-the-psychologist's-society who produces the stable features of the society by choices among alternative courses of action that are compelled on the grounds of psychiatric biography, conditioning history, and the variables of mental functioning. The common feature in the use of these 'models of man' is the fact that courses of common sense rationalities of judgment which involve the person's use of common sense knowledge of social structures over the temporal 'succession' of here and now situations, are treated as epiphenomenal" (pp.67-68). In other words, instead of being treated as always being accomplished *for another first time*, they are treated always as a repeat of something that has already been achieved previously.

It is our embodied feelings – and the embodied anticipations and expectations to which they spontaneously give rise – that are neglected in the theories of many social scientific theorist. But it is just these *contingent feelings* (which are not properly called emotions) that work as the 'momentary standards' against which our more explicit formulations are judged for their adequacy and appropriateness. Although, I hasten to add, that it does not determine them all in an instant, nor is all the *possible* background bustle and hurly-burly of life present 'in' an instant either. The character of our judgments, our concepts, and our reactions are all present to us only in terms of their unfolding temporal contours. To this extent, the foundations of our lives never cease being open to contest.

But it is this claim – that the roots or foundations of our actions are to be found generally *within* the unfolding dynamics of ordinary people's everyday activities (including the uncompleted "tendencies" to action they contain), and not within certain, already ordered principles of mind – that we professional academics have found, and still do find, difficult to stomach. For it means that anything we propose depends for its acceptance, just as much (if not more) upon the common, collective, but 'disorderly', *embodied* sensibility of people in society at large, as upon the refined, systematic, and self-consciously formulated notions of academics and intellectuals. But what this means, is that in the growth of a noncognitive, non-Cartesian, relationally-responsive, social constructionist approach to psychology as a *moral science*, an obvious next step is a growing interest, not in the mind or the brain, *but in the living body* – or more correctly, in the spontaneously expressed, unreflective bodily activities of the whole person. For paradoxical though it may be to say it, it is in sensuous bodily activities, I think, that ideas start, not in 'the mind'. Such sensuous or feelingful activities are both the *terminus a quo* and *terminus ad quem* of all our social constructions (Shotter, 1993a).

Conclusions

The relationally-responsive social constructionist stance I shall take, then, marks a radical departure from the 'analytic' aims of the Enlightenment: the dream of discovering the 'real', already existing, orderly principles underlying our behaviour, either in the 'minds' of individuals, or, in the 'rules' regulating a systematic, social order. In fact, the 'realist' rhetoric legitimating that project seems to authorize a way of talking 'about' certain 'entities', or 'structures' – such as 'the mind', or 'society', and other supposedly 'objectively real things'

– when no such orderly 'things' or 'structures' in fact actually exist. Indeed, it makes no distinction between a peoples's 'social reality' – understood, currently, in terms of who and what they are to themselves, as the inhabitants of a western, liberal, individualistic, scientistic culture – and the forms of 'reality' with which they might make contact, from within such social realities. Such a rhetoric makes it appear as if one's task is merely that of describing as accurately as possible how one has 'observed' the social world, or, a person's mentality, to be. But this form of 'analysis' as such is only of use here if we all already know perfectly well what the orderly 'it' *is*, that is being analyzed. But in our talk about such contested concepts as 'minds' or 'subjectivities', or 'cultures', 'histories', or 'societies', etc., this is not the case. These are 'political or contested objects' whose function, very largely, is in the constitution of different forms of social relations. Thus it is not surprising that different people have different 'views' as to what their supposed orderly nature *should* be, and express their views in the different 'images' they employ (Shotter, 1975).

In the relationally-responsive social constructionist view I am proposing here, such 'political objects' as these exist only to the extent that they play a part within a conversation. That is, a 'tradition of argumentation' structured in their terms works to bring a certain form of human being into existence – where, "... to imagine a language is to imagine a form of life" (Wittgenstein, 1953, no.19). In other words, *accounting* for ourselves by talk of such 'inner entities' as 'thoughts', 'motives', 'memories', and such like, allows us to structure and manage our *individualistic* forms of life, and to create certain forms of social institutions, not available to those lacking such a 'language of mind' (see Whorf on the native-american Hopi, Ch.7). This, indeed, *is* the nature of *our* 'social reality'; we sustain and manage it through such forms of talk.

But when we academics treat ordinary people's everyday talk *of* their 'thoughts', 'memories', 'perceptions', 'motives', 'needs', and 'desires', and such, uncritically, as ordinary people themselves treat it – in short, as talk *about* their 'minds'– then we fail to take into account "the contents and forms that brought it [such talk] into being" (Foucault, 1970, p.364). In such talk, in a social constructionist view, people are not making a *reference* to the nature of their already existing minds, but are taking part in a contested (or at least contestable) process, a tradition of argumentation, in which they are still struggling over the constitution of their own mental make-up. At a personal level, the whole lexicon of 'mind' and 'mental activity' terms provides a set of rhetorical resources or devices for use by them to serve their own personal interests in that struggle; while at a social level, it is a way of talking that serves to sustain, and perhaps develop further, our own western form of social life and personhood. If we want to change it, we must engage in argument, where, as Billig *et al* (1988) suggest, "one of the goals of social action or of social reform is to win a present argument, in order to change the agenda of argumentation" (p.149) – and this is the task in which, in contest with individualistic cognitivists, social constructionists are now engaged.

Chapter Two

SITUATING SOCIAL CONSTRUCTIONISM:

KNOWING FROM *WITHIN* 'THE INTERACTIVE MOMENT'

"... 'the matter talked about' as a developing and developed event over the course of the action that produced it, as both the process and the product [is] known *from within* this development by both parties, each for himself as well as on behalf of the other" (Garfinkel, 1967, p.40).

In this chapter I want to explore further the consequences of situating social constructionist studies not only in a conversational background or context, but also in the moment of meeting between two or more persons. That is, I want to explore what is involved in conducting our studies from within a continually ongoing flow of differentiated, turbulent but formative, social activity – where (to repeat Wittgenstein's phrase quoted in the previous chapter) our concerns will be to with "point[ing] to something within this bustle." In other words, our concern will be to bring aspects of the usually unnoticed background to our everyday activities into the foreground and to notice their *relations* to the initial focus of our concern. This is different from our usual way of proceeding with our inquiries.

Usually, once we have perceptually foregrounded an entity for study, we treat it as having its own isolated existence and ignore its relations to its background. It is unusual to treat it as only having its existence in virtue of its continued interaction with its background surroundings. But as the "I love you" example in the Introduction illustrated, words uttered in such contexts only draw their power from how they function to make a crucial difference at a crucial moment in that background flow of activity[15]. A possible difference arose as a result of the history of the flow of activity between the people involved, and the words uttered served to realize that possibility: they had their meaning mostly in their use only at that moment. Thus, in many such situations as this, what is being talked about (to refer to the Garfinkel quote above), is a developing and developed event, an event that is only properly known from within this development by those who are producing it. Crucial in such events are those points in a conversation when a 'gap' must be bridged: when either a change in speaking subject occurs, or when, to put it another way, what one person says or does must be accounted for, made sense of, or responded to in some way by an other (or by the person themselves).

In situating the kind of social constructionism I want to outline in this book, then, I want to emphasize a concern with investigating, and linguistically articulating, the nature of the background, common sense activities within which we live our daily lives[16]. Where it is that background: (1) from out of which all our activities emerge; (2) toward aspects of which (however mistakenly) they are all directed; (3) as well as against which, they are all judged as to their fittingness; and (4) upon which they all act back historically to modify. Thus the relationally-responsive version of social constructionism proposed here is not only directed towards an understanding of how we constitute (make) and reconstitute (remake) these usually unnoticed common sense activities, or ethos, but also, towards how we make and remake ourselves in the process. It is this dialectical emphasis upon *both* our making of, *and* our being made by, our own social realities, that is, I think, common to social constructionism in all its versions.

However, having situated our social constructionist studies within the bustle or hurly-burly of everyday social life, and having accepted that all the words we utter – if they are effective at all – function to make crucial differences at crucial moments – how should we talk or *tell* of the results of our investigations? For we can no longer claim to be presenting neutral 'pictures' of states of fixed, already existing states of affairs, awaiting our judgment as to their truth or falsity. The answer would seem to hinge upon what kind of activity in which we see ourselves as engaged, for we need to select different features for attention according to the end we have in view. As I mentioned in the previous chapter, in a social constructionist psychology, psychologists are not Olympian scientists looking down upon the society they are studying with no part to play within it themselves; they are engaged within a still developing tradition, a still developing cultures (or cultures). Thus they are taking part in a contested (or at least contestable) process, a struggle to do with the constitution of our own mental make-up. And crucial in that struggle is the 'basic' language ("vocabulary of motives" - Mills, 1940) in terms of which we *account* for ourselves, the terms in which we justify our actions to others when challenged by them to do so.

Thus in what follows, in response to question above as to how we might report the results of our investigations, instead of theories, I shall offer a number of *instructive statements*: they provide an *account* or a *portrayal* of a number of what I feel are crucial aspects in the nature of conversational exchanges.

Their function is not to represent a state of affairs, but to direct people's attention to crucial features of the larger situation within which the focal events of our concern make their appearance, features that 'show' connections between things that otherwise would go unnoticed. They have the form: 'attend to X if you want to grasp the crucial feature that gives you insight into the issue in question here'. They have their 'point' only in a context; they are important at just those points in the flow of everyday interaction, when the people involved sense that a change in the character of that form of life is at issue – hence their argumentative force. And that is how I intend my accounts to be read here: as suggesting a change in language in terms of which we currently conduct our debates in psychology about of own psychological nature.

In terming such accounts 'instructive', I want to call upon aspects of Vygotsky's (1978, 1986) important account of words as "psychological tools or instruments." Words function in this instrumental fashion when, for instance, others make use of various forms of talk, to draw our attention to features of our circumstances that otherwise would escape our notice, or, how to conduct ourselves in certain circumstances; they can instruct us in how to manage or organize our ways of perceiving and acting. As Vygotsky (1978) comments, in learning to coordinate their actions linguistically with the actions of those around them, "the child begins to perceive the world not only through his eyes but also through his speech" (p.32). And he goes on to show how the ways in which others can at first verbally instruct us can later become our own; as they verbally instructed us, so we can come to verbally instruct ourselves.

Thus, as Vygotsky (1986) notes, it is "the functional use of the word, or any other sign, as means of focusing one's attention, selecting distinctive features and analyzing and synthesizing them, that plays a central role in concept formation" (p.106); and he continues: "Learning to direct one's own mental processes with the aid of words or signs is an integral part of the process of concept formation" (p.108). I cannot emphasize strongly enough Vygotsky's account here of what he calls "the functional use of words." For, as he makes clear, the 'instructive' use of language I have outlined above – and especially its *self-instructive* use – is very different from its referential-representational function. And we shall find this crucial in what follows below, not only in elucidating the nature of a relationally-responsive, social constructionist psychology, and how such a psychology can function from within the everyday conversational background within which it is situated, but also in outlining the nature of a new, much more practical form of empirical inquiry than those currently driven by explanatory theory. For (in Chapter 3) we shall see how certain crucial terms (words) expressed in philosophical writing (particularly in Wittgenstein's and Bakhtin's writings) can both *sensitize* us to paying attention to, and *motivate* us into 'making or creating connections' between, features of our own activities that we would not otherwise notice.

The creation, from within self-other relations, of person-world relations

Above, I have mentioned the importance of our 'basic' ways of talking about ourselves and our world a number of times. What in particular I want to explore in this chapter, is how it is that, within the everyday, disorderly, practical, self-other relationships constituting the usually unnoticed background to our lives, we unknowingly construct between ourselves those orderly forms of (intralinguistic) relations I earlier called person-world relations. Where, what is special in such relations, to repeat, is that the orderly ways of talking constituting them, form our ways of accounting for and making sense of ourselves and our world, ways that are 'basic' in the sense that they form a lexicon of justificatory ultimates, so to speak (Mills, 1940): a whole taken-for-granted vocabulary of things and processes we talk of being the 'basic' nature of both ourselves and the world in which we live.

Although I shall argue here that the character or style of our 'basic' person-world relations is both 'produced by' and 'contained in' our self-other relations, clearly, because it is a matter of *joint action*, it is *as if* they are 'given' us by an 'external' agency. We have no awareness of our own involvement in their construction. It is as if our person-world relations are independent of, or 'orthogonal' to, our self-other relationships. Like the movements of the wineglass upon the *Ouija* board, people (and peoples) seem to lack any individual sense of responsibility for such socially produced outcomes – a fact that will concern us more in a moment, when we turn to a fuller discussion of "joint action" below. Yet, none the less, it is from within this relationally-responsive, two-way flow of living, embodied, sensuously channelled, activities and practices occurring between self and others that, I suggest, all the other dimensions of the person-world polarity that are significant for us originate and are formed.

The two-way process involved may be diagrammed as in figure 1 below, as a process in which an agency, rooted in a background and making use of the resources it provides, acts back upon that background to give or to lend it further form or structure:

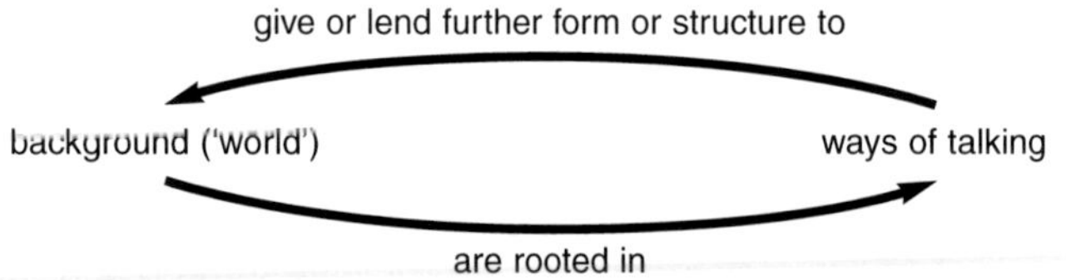

Figure 1

In such a two-way process, we can see our self-other, background activities as, on the one hand, formative of the routine, everyday, person-world ways of talking that we, as ordinary persons, make use of in normatively[17] accounting for ourselves and our world, to others in the 'social realities' we occupy. On the other hand, to the extent that our accountable forms of talk and activity emerge from out of such background activities, these forms can also be seen as 'rooted' in them, i.e., they provide shared the 'structures of feeling' in terms of which accountable formulations may be judged as appropriate or not (see note 2). It is because our accountable forms of talk still remain functionally embedded in the conversational background from out of which they have perceptually emerged, that our accounting can and does come to an end, ultimately – in an agreed justification that is 'felt' to be right by all.

In terms of exactly the same two-way process again – but now with our everyday, accountable activities as their basis – we can also see how our special, disciplinary forms of life may be developed, along with what is 'felt' to be right within them. Where we are 'schooled' in such feelings from our reading of (and being examined in) the appropriate disciplinary texts. With one such *feeling* in the social and behavioural sciences being, at the moment, the feeling that it is crucial to attempt to *explain* our 'external' worlds only in terms of particular kinds of objectively and theoretically identifiable entities – an account is called 'merely' descriptive is sensed as inadequate. For until recently, in thinking that if only we could stand upon the shoulders of giants, we could see to the far reaches of our forms of life, we have felt it reasonable to argue that certain of our special modes of being – especially those to do with theoretical physics and the mathematics of the cosmos – give us the opportunity of 'seeing' the whole. Reformulating the issue, however, in terms of a basis in structures of feeling, situated within a context, suggests that it is impossible to articulate the nature of the whole from the point of view of just a specialized part of it. That is just to offer a selected dimension. More that a view of a single systematic order of connectedness is required.

Thus, it is from within our status as ordinary persons, as we move about over the whole differentiated, background landscape of our lives, crossing from one institutional centre to another, experiencing the crossing of boundaries, the differences between the centre from the margins, and the margins from the centre, and so on, that we must attempt our account of it. Drawing upon the knowledge we already possess, what we need is an account or portrayal of our everyday life activities, in the ordinary sense of the term 'account' or a 'portrayal': as simply a narration of a circumstance or a state of affairs. Something which in its telling 'moves' us this way and that through the current 'terrain' of personhood, so to speak, sufficiently for us to gain a conceptual grasp of the whole, even though we lack a vantage point from which to view it – it is a view 'from the inside', much as we get to know the street-plan of a city, by living within it, rather than from seeing it all at once from an external standpoint. It is a grasp which allows us to 'see' all the different aspects of a person as if arrayed within a 'landscape', all in relation to one another, from all the standpoints within it[18]. As already mentioned in the Introduction, we want to 'know our way about' (Wittgenstein, 1953) inside our own socially constructed realities.

Let me turn here, then, to the issue of how people account to the others around them, both for themselves and for the general character of their surroundings: As we have already seen, in the earlier discussion of Geertz's

(1983) and Leinhardt's (1961) respective accounts of Western and Dinka forms of consciousness (in Chap.1) , people within different socio-historical groups seem to account for themselves, and their world, in very different ways. And as we saw carlier, much of what *we* experience as a part of *ourselves*, as an aspect of our agency under our own control, the Dinka experience as a presence in their surroundings, acting upon them from without. One feels that talk of an *ethos*, of finding ourselves embedded in a structure of feeling, would be more immediately intelligible to them than it is to us.

To reinforce the point, we might also compare how we experience the problematic relation of ourselves to our world, with how Whorf (1956) claims the seeming nature of that relation to be for the native american Hopi: While "... we are dimly aware that we carry about with us a whole imaginary space, full of mental surrogates... The Hopi thought-world has no such imaginary space... [A Hopi 'naturally'] suppose[s] that his thought (or he himself) traffics with the [thing] that he is thinking about" (p.150). Thus, where *we* 'plan' for the future, by drawing up a theoretical schematism, placing representations of things in their proper relation to each other ahead of time, thus to get it right when we apply the plan in practice, the *Hopi* 'prepare' for the future in quite a different way. For them, the present moment, in carrying forward the 'impress' of past activities, makes the carrying forward of yet further 'impresses' possible. Thus, for them, repetitions, the cumulative outcomes of innumerable small contributory (often ritual) acts, are not lost, but are stored up as a power in their surroundings, a power that will hold over into later events. Something that we in the West try to do, perhaps, when, by chanting at football matches, we try to build up a 'charge' to carry our team through to greater efforts; although we possess much less vocabulary than they for justifying and explaining the efficacy of such practices to those who might challenge them. But as for the Hopi, so for the Dinka: in the ordinary run of affairs, their world would seem to be a much more spiritually charged and chargeable place than ours. Later, in Chapter 6, I will return to Whorf's (1956) account of the Hopi's in-the-moment sensibility and relate it to Daniel Stern's (2004) account of *the present moment*.

How the Dinka and the Hopi experience their world is, perhaps, to an extent how things might appear to us if we were solely engaged in *practical* affairs, and faced the task of formulating the nature of such affairs exclusively from within our conduct of them – without ever being able to 'view' them, or talk of them, retrospectively, from an 'external' third-person point of view, thus to 'explain' them within a theoretical context.

In other words, their [the Dinka and the Hopi] ways of 'being ordinary', embodied as they are in their ways of speaking, in their social institutions and ways of doing things, in their tools and implements, along with their ways of judging the rightness of things, provide a background ethos that determines, not only what counts as real for them, but also a whole range of other things and categories they find strange or extra-ordinary. In the same way, our background ethos also determines for us, not only (1) our own ways of being ordinary, but also, in particular, what we think of as (2) the imaginary, the nonexistent, the impossible, the extraordinary, as well as (3) a whole range of things we do not even notice that we do not even notice[19] – things, events, and situations which, to invert a phrase of Garfinkel's (1967, p.vii), are rendered "rationally-*in*visible" to us. In other words, strangely, there is a whole range of things, events, and situations which our ways of perceiving, acting, talking, and evaluating *fail* to make visibly-rational to us, and in so doing, make it all but impossible for us to submit them to rational discourse and debate.

In our case, it is precisely the third sphere of activity I mentioned above – the unordered, diffuse, back and forth flow of practical, sensuous activity - that has long remained 'rationally-invisible' to us. And it is to the peculiar qualities of that sphere of activity that I will now turn.

"Joint action" and conversational realities

Turning to that third sphere of events, it is clear that the activity of interest to us, occurs in a zone of indeterminacy, a zone of uncertainty somewhere between the other two polarities mentioned above, upon which we have focussed our attention in the past. It occurs in a zone between (1) *actions*, i.e., what I as an individual 'do', and (2) *events*, i.e., that merely seems to 'happen' to, in, or around me, outside of my agency as an individual to control, and as such, does not seem amenable to characterization at all. Yet this, however, is not entirely the case. Indeed, it is its very lack of specificity, its lack of any pre-determined order, and thus its openness to being specified or determined by those involved in it, that is its central defining feature[20]. Here, I shall call activity in this third sphere, in this zone of uncertainty: "joint action" (Shotter, 1984); while later, in Chapter 3, in discussing Bakhtin's (1981, 1984, 1986, 1993) work, I will call it "dialogically-structured" activity; while toward the end of this book, in accord with Merleau-Ponty's (1968) account, I will begin to speak of it as *chiasmicly-structured.*

Joint action comes into being when, in their meetings with each other, people's activities become spontaneously and responsively intertwined or entangled[21] with those of the others around them. In such an intertwining, some very strange events occur – when after a time of mutual influence the participants separate again, they can no longer be simply described as before. Although they may still retain their identity, they can no longer be thought of as unchanged in their being, their way of being in the world. They will have come to embody different ways of perceiving, thinking, talking, acting, and valuing; they will now have changed in their *ontological skills* (Shotter,

1984), i.e., in how they now experience and respond to their surroundings in a spontaneous and unproblematic fashion. They will have learnt how *to be* certain kinds of person, e.g., how to be a mathematician (with a sensitivity, say, to patterns among numbers), a painter (with a sensitivity to colour combinations), a mechanic (with a sensitivity to materials and other materials), a writer (with a sensitivity to word combinations), and so on. But this is just one of the strange results of our being involved in joint action.

As I see it, joint action has at least the following three major features:

(1) As people intertwined their activities in with the activities of others, and 'respond' to them in what they do, what they as individuals desire and what actually results in their exchanges are often two very different things. In short, joint action produces *unintended*, and *unpredictable* outcomes. These generate a 'situation', or an 'organized practical-moral setting' existing between all the participants. As its organization cannot be traced back to the intentions of any particular individuals, it is *as if* it has a 'given', a 'natural', or an 'externally caused' nature; although, to those within it, it is 'their/our' situation.

(2) Although such a setting is unintended by any of the individuals within it, it none the less has an *intentional* quality to it: it seems both to have a 'content', as well as to 'indicate' or to be 'related to something other than or beyond itself'[22], i.e., participants find themselves both immersed 'in' an already *given* situation, but one with a *horizon* to it, that makes it 'open' to their actions. Indeed, its 'organization' is such that the practical-moral constraints (and enablements) it makes available to them influence, i.e., 'invite' and 'motivate', their next possible actions.

(3) In 'inviting' or 'motivating' the next possible actions of participants, the 'situation' comes itself to be an agency in shaping people's actions within it. Thus *joint action* involves more than people merely coordinating their actions with each other in their meetings: a whole 'world' or 'reality' is created with its own special contents and qualities, its own 'callings', along with unique interactional identities for its participants. We can call them *conversational* or *dialogical realities*. In short, as outlined above, we create many different, ephemeral, person-world relationships in our self-other relationships.

In other words, as I indicated above, to the extent that such activity is not *action* done by individuals alone, nor is it simply *behaviour* caused by external influences, it constitutes a distinct, third sphere of activity, *sui generis*, with its own distinctive features:

(1) First, in giving rise to a special kind of nonrepresentational, sensuous or embodied form of *practical-moral* (Bernstein, 1983) knowing, it is constitutive of people's social and personal identities, and is thus prior to and determinative of all the other ways of knowing available to us.

(2) Further, activities in this sphere lack specificity; they are only partially determined. They are a complex mixture of many different kinds of influences. They are just as much material as mental; they are just as much felt as thought, and thought as felt.

(3) Their intertwined, complex nature makes it very difficult for us to characterize their nature: they have neither a fully orderly nor a fully disorderly structure, neither a completely stable nor an easily changed organization, neither a fully subjective nor fully objective character.

(4) While they can exhibit progressive changes, they can also exhibit retrogressive ones too.

(5) They are also non-locatable, i.e., they are 'spread out' among all those participating in them.

(6) They are neither 'inside' people, but nor are they 'outside' them; they are located in that space where inside and outside are one.

(7) Nor is there a separate before and after (Bergson, 1922), neither an agent nor an effect, but only a meaningful, 'enduring' whole which cannot divide itself into separable parts – a whole that, in enduring, dynamically sustains itself in existence ["duration"].

(8) But, as living activities, they have a 'style' and 'point' beyond themselves toward both events in their surroundings, and what can come next in the future. Indeed, as Giddens (1984) suggests, the "unintended consequences [of such socially constructed, joint or dialogically-structured activity] may systematically feedback to provided the unacknowledged conditions for further acts" (p.8). In other words, our joint actions can provided, from within themselves, the very conditions required for their own continuation – our 'going on' within them.

Thus, the notion of joint action is, I claim, just the kind of notion we need, *through* which to see the fleeting and usually unnoticed workings of processes of social construction[23], their *detailed* workings. Indeed, it is precisely its lack of any pre-determined order, and thus its openness to being specified or determined *by those involved in it*, in practice – while usually remaining quite unaware of their doing it – that is its central defining feature. And it is precisely this that makes this sphere of activity interesting for at least the two following reasons: (1) It means that there is a need for practical investigations as to how people actually do manage to 'work things out' between them, and the need to study the role of our different ways of talking in such transactions. But also, (2) it opens up the possibility for investigations into how we might refine and elaborate such spheres of activity, and how we might extend them into novel spheres as yet unknown to us.

For instance, by its use, we can see that within the ordinary two-way flow of activity between them, people create, without a conscious realization of the fact, a changing sea[24] of moral or ethical enablements and constraints, of privileges and entitlements, and obligations and sanctions, in short, an ethos. And the changing settings created are *practical-moral* (Bernstein, 1984) settings, because the different 'places' or 'positions' they make available have to do, not only with the nurturancc or injury one can experience to one's being as a person, but also with the "involvement obligations" and "offences" (Goffman, 1967) one can experience, moment-by-moment, as to whether the interaction is unfolding appropriately or not. For individuals can only have a *sense* of 'belonging' or of being 'proper participants in' a current conversational reality if the others around them are prepared to respond to what they say and do *seriously*, i.e., respond to what they actually utter, and not ignore it by using it merely as the occasion to offer their own, already formulated, opinion. For only then, if the conversation in which they are engaged is a genuine dialogical whole, with each utterance within it linked responsively to previous utterances, will participants within it feel the reality constructed within it is as much their's as anyone else's. In other words, to the extent that we all participate in our own different ways, 'we' can be the authors not only of 'our realities' but also of our own 'selves'. This does not mean that we will unthinkingly feel a sense of total harmony with those around us. But it does mean not having a sense being an intrusive alien, of being able to realize one's 'true self' in the world around one (rather than only in one's dreams).

This view – of what it is to *belong* to a social group, to feel that one not excluded from the social activities involved in that group's construction its own reality – is very closely connected, I feel, with Harré's (1983, 1990) claim, that the primary human reality is conversation. Although many may disagree and feel that many other (more nonverbal) spheres of human interaction are more basic[25], here I shall take it as primary in the following (judgmental) sense: As human realities do not endure through the physical rigidity of their structures (indeed, it makes no sense even to talk of them in this way), to repeat the by now familiar theme, they must be sustained in existence by being continually remade in people's everyday social activities. In such processes, however, people mutually judge and correct both each other and themselves as to the 'fittingness' of their actions to what they take their reality to be. As Wittgenstein (1953, no.242) insists, "if language is to be a means of communication there must be agreement not only in definitions but also (queer as this may sound) in judgments..." Utterances are judged, then, not solely or primarily in terms of their grammatical form, but are evaluated in terms of the "countless" (Wittgenstein, 1953, no.23) uses they can have in relation to the social reality in which they occur. And conversation is the ultimate sphere in which all such judging and evaluating takes place, and in which such assessments are negotiated and shared agreements are reached. But this judging and evaluating is done against a certain background, an ethos, a common sense, and it is to the nature of that background, that "structure of feeling" (Williams, 1977) that I now want to turn – although it will be some time before we are in a position to grasp its nature comprehensively, for it is complex in the extreme.

Knowing of the third kind, Vygotsky, and sensuous ways of talking

In discussing the nature of conversational realities[26] and our 'basic' ways of talking, I want to argue for the importance within them of the third, extraordinary form of nonrepresentational, embodied or sensuous, practical-moral knowledge I introduced in chapter one, and have discussed above. As I have said before, it is a separate, special kind of knowledge, *sui generis*, which is prior to both theoretical and merely technical knowledge, for, in being linked to people's social and personal identities, it determines the available forms of these other two kinds of knowledge. It is an embodied form of practical-moral knowing in terms of which people are able to influence each other in their being rather than just in their intellects, i.e., to actually 'move' them rather than just 'giving them ideas'. Given our current 'basic' ways of talking, however, we cannot easily grasp the nature of such ways of knowing. Indeed, to the extent that we cannot "command a clear view" (Wittgenstein, 1953, no. 122) of its overall nature, we cannot rationally imagine it. Further, because it cannot be represented (or formed) as an object of knowledge within a normative or disciplined form of talk, i.e., within a discourse, its nature, for it is more of the character of an activity than a thing, it is for us *extraordinary*. Yet, I want to claim, nonetheless, that there are still ways (see below, especially Chap 5 on Wittgenstein's methods) in which we can elucidate its nature – one method, as we shall see, is to turn to detailed descriptions of its nature.

With this issue in mind, it will be relevant att this point to turn in some detail to Vygotsky's work: His project is, he says (Vygotsky, 1978), to show how "all the higher functions originate as actual relations between human individuals" (p.57). We develop from creatures functioning under the control of our surrounding (social) circumstances into persons functioning under our own control. We come to be able to plan, direct, control, and to organize our own "higher mental functions or processes" as we come to incorporate within ourselves the forms of talk that others use in controlling, directing, and organizing our behaviour for us.

Thus, at the centre of his whole approach, is the fact that besides (and prior to) their referential-representational function, words also work in a non-cognitive, formative way to 'shape' our unreflective, embodied or sensuous ways of looking and acting. In short, they work as commands, directives, or instructions to 'move' us. Indeed, without the sensory, sensuous, or affective function of words, to 'move' people to perceive and act in different ways, his whole project falls to the ground. Thus, in attempting at the outset to clarify the nature of the problem, as he sees it, we find him saying that "when we approach the problems of the interrelation between thought and language...

the first question that arises is that of intellect and affect" (Vygotsky, 1986, p.10). If they are separated, he says, then "the door is closed on the issue of the causation and origin of our thoughts...," for we are unable to understand "the motive forces that direct thought into this or that channel." Hence, the approach he adopts "shows that every idea contains a transmuted affective attitude toward the bit of reality to which it refers." In other words, the affective attitude which provides the thoughts and ideas of an individual with their dynamic, i.e., with their particular motives and valencies[27], thus linking them both to each other and to their surroundings in a particular way, is a transmuted version of a social relationship. But of what kind?

Well, quite literally, of an "instructional" or "directive" kind. We come to 'instruct' ourselves as others instruct us: They 'point things out to us' ("Look at this!"); 'change our perspective' ("Look at it like this"); 'order' our actions ("Look at the model first, then at the puzzle pieces"); 'shape' our actions ("Turn it over, then it will fit"); 'remind' us ("Think what you did last time," "What do you already know that's relevant?"); 'encourage' us ("Try again"); 'restrain' us ("Don't be too hasty"); 'evaluate' for us ("That's not right," "Don't do that, that's greedy"); 'set our goals' ("Try to put these pieces together to match that [pointing at a model]"); 'count' ("How many will it take?"); make 'measurements' ("Will that fit properly?" "Just compare"); make us 'check' our descriptions ("Is that right?" "Who else says so?" "What's the reason for your belief?"); and so on, and so on, for no doubt a countless number of functions. Indeed, we can form such instructions into sequences, to construct step-by-step programmes of perception and action: First: "survey," then "choose," then "act," then "survey again," and so on.

These are the *means* Vygotsky has in mind when he says (Vygotsky, 1986) that "the main question about the process of concept formation – or, about any goal-directed activity – is the question of the means by which the operation is accomplished... To explain the higher forms of human behavior, we must uncover the means by which man learns to organize and direct his behaviour" (p.102, my emphasis). And he continues: "Our experimental study proved that it was the functional use of the word, or any other sign, as means of focussing one's attention, selecting distinctive features and analyzing and synthesizing them, that plays a central role in concept formation" (p.106). "Learning to direct one's own mental processes with the aid of words or signs is an integral part of the process of concept formation" (p.108).

Wertsch (1991, p.27) quotes a useful illustrative example from Tharp and Gallimore (1988) which illustrates the role of other's speech (which later can become our own speech) in directing a child's process of remembering:

> "A 6-year-old child has lost a toy and asks her father for help. The father asks where she last saw the toy; and the child says 'I can't remember'. He asks a series of questions – did you have it in your room? Outside?

Next door? To each question the child answers 'no'. When he says 'in the car?', she says 'I think so' and goes to retrieve the toy" (p.14).

In such a case, as Wertsch points out, we cannot answer the question 'who did the remembering?' by pointing to one person or the other. It is a joint accomplishment, and what the child now does with the father's help, she later comes to do for herself, i.e., she learns how to 'manage' the relations between her knowledge, thought, and action herself, in terms of similar such 'instructions'.

And at a more advanced level, this is what one learns to do in thinking conceptually. In Vygotsky's terms, one learns not to compare the configuration of a supposed mental representation with the configuration of a state of affairs in reality, but something else much more complicated: one has grasped how to organize and assemble in a socially intelligible way, i.e., a way which makes sense to the others around one, bits and pieces of information dispersed in space and time in accordance with 'instructions' they (the others around one) at first provided, and which now a supposed 'concept' provides.

A rhetorically, relationally, and ethically negotiated 'inner life'

In this view, what it is to have formed a concept is to have formed for ourselves, from the words of others, a "psychological instrument" *through* which we can both perceive and act, i.e., an instrumental aid in terms of which we can both 'instruct' ourselves in a program for gathering and organizing perceptual data, as well as, for ordering and sequencing a plan of action. Thus, rather than a self-contained, simply subjective activity within an individual – dealing with merely inner, cognitive 'pictures' which may, or may not, be accurate representations of an outer reality – thinking conceptually (according to the 'instructions' of others) becomes a special kind of social practice. And furthermore, it becomes a social practice in which speech, thought, and feeling are, at least at first and for the most part, interlinked with their surrounding circumstances in "a dynamic system of meaning" (Vygotsky, 1986, pp.10-11). Only gradually, and probably as a result of the effects of becoming literate - in which, "in learning to write, the child must disengage himself from the sensory aspect of speech and replace words by images[28] of words" (Vygotsky, 1986, p.181) – can we learn to think like self-contained academics, and develop modes of formal, decontextualized rationality, i.e., to think in wholly representational[29] terms. Influenced by this 'picture' of what thinking is, traditional methods fail "to take into account the perception and the mental elaboration of the sensory material that gave birth to the concept. The sensory material and the word are both indispensable parts of concept formation" (Vygotsky, 1986, pp.96-7).

But, if this is so, what kind of account of the act of speaking do we need to describe the relation between words and their sense, to elucidate the relation of form to feeling? As Vygotsky (1986) sees it, rather than issuing mechanically, from already well-formed and orderly cognitions at the centre of our being, the expression[30] of a thought or an intention, the saying of a sentence or the doing of a deed, first originates in a person's vague and unordered *sense* of the situation they are in. Its appropriate *orderly* realization or formation (see the references to Garfinkel (2004, p.184) in the Introduction) is then 'developed' in a complex set of temporally conducted, interwoven negotiations, connecting themselves (or, their 'selves'), their feelings, their utterances, and, those to whom they must address their utterances. In other words, speakers are sensitive in their very acts of speaking, to the kind of 'links' – between themselves, their listeners, and their circumstances – that they must construct as they speak. Thus:

> "the relation of thought to word is not a thing but a process, a continual movement backward and forth from thought to word and from word to thought. In that process, the relation of thought to word undergoes changes that themselves may be regarded as developmental in the functional sense. Thought is not merely expressed in words; it comes into existence through them. Every thought tends to connect something with something else, to establish a relation between things. Every thought moves, grows and develops, fulfils a function, solves a problem" (Vygotsky, 1986, p.218).

And, at a later points in the text he adds that, "the structure of speech does not simply mirror the structure of thought; that is why words cannot be put on by thought like a ready-made garment" (p.219). "Precisely because thought does not have its automatic counterpart in words[31], the transition of thought to word leads through meaning. In our speech, there is always the hidden thought, the subtext" (1986, p.251). The unique *sense* of our words in the context of their use is 'shown', not in the form or pattern of the words we have said, but in our saying of them, in our intoning[32] of them. In our actual speaking, we 'show' more than we are ever able to 'say' (Wittgenstein); what we 'show' is there 'in the movement' of our words (see Chap.10).

Thus there is a 'subtext' to our speech, as every utterance constitutes only *an attempt* (which is hardly ever completely satisfactory) to 'develop' a sensed thought-seed into a voiced utterance-flower. What we try to say, and what we are understood as meaning, are often at odds with each other. Hence the necessity for the realization of a thought to be 'successively developed' (and checked) in a back-and-forth process, in which the transition of thought to word is through meaning. Unformulated in words, a thought-seed remains vague and provides only the possibility of having a meaning: "The relation between thought and word is a living process; thought is born through words. A word devoid of thought is a dead thing...

But thought that fails to realize itself in words remains a "Sygian shadow" [O. Mandelstam]... The connection between thought and word, however, is neither preformed nor constant. It emerges in the course of development, and itself evolves" (Vygotsky, 1986, p.255). The voiced utterance flower, which can move us and guide us in our actions, emerges in the course of a dialogic process of what Vygotsky calls "inner speech," a process which can vary in its character according to the 'others' involved the thought's 'development' – those with whom, about whom, and to whom, in one's inner speech one speaks.

In other words, even when all alone, the 'inner' process in which one's vague thoughts are formulated into clear programmes for sequencing and guiding socially intelligible and legitimate action, are similar to the 'outer' transactions between people. Thus, people's attempts to realize their thoughts, i.e., to formulate their thoughts to themselves in ways which make those thoughts socially usable, so to speak, must be negotiated in an inner back and forth process, in which they must attempt to understand and challenge their own proposed formulations as the others around them might. For one's task in developing into a morally autonomous adult in one's own society is not just that of learning to direct one's own mental processes with the aid of words or signs, but of doing so in a way that makes sense and is considered legitimate by others. In this view then, our 'inner' lives are structured by us living 'into' and 'through', so to speak, the opportunities or enablements offered us by the 'others' and 'otherness' both around us and within us. Thus our mental life is never wholly our own. We live in a way which is both responsive, and in response to, what is both 'within us' in some way, but which is also 'other than' ourselves.

Conclusions

In this communicational view of ourselves then, the current view we have of persons, as all equal, self-enclosed, (essentially indistinguishable) atomic individuals, possessing an inner sovereignty, each living their separate lives, all in isolation from each other – the supposed experience of the modern self – is an illusion, maintained by the institution between us of certain 'basic ways of talking', as I have called them above. It is an illusion which, besides misleading us about our own nature as human beings, also misleads us about the nature of thought and of language – we have come to think about both as if they are like the closed, unitary systems of signs in mathematics rather than as a heterogeneous set of means or devices for us to link ourselves to our surroundings[33]. This is precisely the assumption Vygotsky (1986) challenges at the very outset of his work:

> "The unity of consciousness and the interrelation of all psychological functions were, it is true, accepted by all; the single functions were

> assumed to operate inseparably, in an uninterrupted connection with one another. But this unity of consciousness was usually taken as a postulate, rather then a subject of study... It was taken for granted that the relation between two given functions never varied; that perception, for example, was always connected in an ideal way with attention, memory with perceptions, thought with memory" (pp.1-2).

Yet, as he goes on to say, "all that is known about psychic development indicates that its very essence lies in the change of the interfunctional nature of consciousness" (p.2).

In other words, Vygotsky opened up 'gaps' between all the different psychological functions, 'responsive gaps' that we can bridge in many different ways, at different times, in different circumstances, by the use of various, socially fashioned "mediatory devices." The bridging of the 'gap' – between, say, a first speaker's question and a second speaker's answer – by the second speaker responding 'into' the context fashioned by the first's asking of question, *is* the making of that link. And there are not just a few 'principled' or 'rule-governed' ways of making such links, but countless creative ways in which such links might be made. And it is in treating the 'links' between thoughts and words as having a 'developmental', 'formative', or 'creative' character, rather than being related in a merely systematic, mechanical, or logical manner, that leads to the introduction of an ethical and rhetorical (justificatory) note into accounts of how people organize and 'manage' their own mental activities – as well as, of course, to a much less systematic and less unified, i.e., heterogeneous, view of language itself.

Indeed, when I begin later (in chapter five) to discuss *styles* of thought, speech, and writing, I will return to these comments of Vygotsky's above. For we can begin to see that in the unfolding dynamics of a person's speech, say, that some speak slowly, stopping for thought, to bring the views of other's in, to see if there's any evidence to be considered, and so on; while others speak impulsively, in broad outlines, in terms just of their own opinions, and so on. We can thus think of s person's *style* of expression as having to with the moment by moment changing of function and direction in their activities: moments of thought, followed by moments of exposition, followed by moments of remembering, followed by moments of opinion gathering, and so on. But I will return to this issue more fully later, when discussing the special *style* of Wittgenstein's remarks, and how it is that in the very dynamics of our reading of them as its unfolds, a "movement of thought" (Wittgenstein, 1980a, p.20)[34] is generated within us, i.e., ways of 'moving around' between our own mental capacities.

What then, in this view, is the nature of our supposed 'inner' lives? It would seem that people's 'inner' lives are neither so private, nor so inner, nor so merely orderly or logical, as has been assumed. Instead, the 'movement of the mind' reflects essentially the same ethical and rhetorical considerations as those influencing the transactions between people, out in the world. This is because, as Vygotsky claims, it is only through the semiotic mediation of signs that 'the mind' as such comes into existence at all. Thus our thoughts, our self-consciously known thoughts, are not first organized at the inner centre of our being (in a nonmaterial 'soul', or a physiological 'lingua mentis'), thus later to be given outer orderly expression or not in words. They only become organized, in a moment by moment, back and forth, formative or developmental process at the boundaries of our being, involving similar 'linguistically mediated ethical negotiations' as those we conduct in our everyday dialogues with others. As Vygotsky (1966) noted, "reflection is the transfer of argumentation within..." (p.41).

In this view, then, the process of *internalization* occurring in a person's development, their supposed 'acquisition' of their culture, is not the transferral of something (some already existing 'thing') from an external to an inner plane of activity, but the actual *constitution* of a distinctly socio-ethical mode of psychological being within our conversation intertwined activities with the others around us. In learning how *to be* a responsible member of certain social groups, in learning the relevant *ontological skills* (Shotter, 1984), as I termed it above, one must learn how *to do* certain things in the right kind of way: One must, in an embodied fashion, learn how to perceive, think, talk, act, and to experience one's surroundings spontaneously and unproblematically, in ways that make sense to the others around one.

Thus, in this view, what one has in common with other members of one's social group is not so much a set of shared beliefs of values as such, but a set of shared semiotic procedures or ethnomethods (Garfinkel, 1967) for making sense of things in ways similar to others in the group. As Wittgenstein (1969) puts it: "Giving grounds, justifying the evidence, comes to an end; – but the end is not in certain propositions striking us immediately as true, i.e., it is not a kind of *seeing* on our part; it is our *acting* which lies at the bottom of the language-game" (no.204). And in different settings with their different overall aims and horizons, we shall find, differently *ordered* forms of communication, or "speech genres" (Bakhtin, 1986), spontaneously emerge. Indeed: "An essential (constitutive) marker of the utterance is its quality of being directed to someone, its *addressivity*... Both the composition and, particularly, the style of the utterance depend on those to whom the utterance is addressed, how the speaker (or writer) senses and imagines his addressees, and the force of their effect on the utterance. Each speech genre in each area of speech communication has its own typical conception of the addressee, and this defines it as a genre" (p.95).

Thus internalization is not a special geographical movement inwards, from a realm of bodily activity into nonmaterial realm of 'the mind', but a socio-practical-ethical movement, in which "children grow into the intellectual life of those around them" (Vygotsky, 1978, p.88). And the child, not only learns how "to practise with respect to himself the same forms of behavior that others formerly practiced with respect to him, " but also learns the socio-practical means to bring other people (along with *their* mental resources) within his or her own personal agency to control. Hence, in becoming an autonomous adult within a group, one learns a grasp of what might be called the 'ethical logistics' involved in the management of personal transactions within that group, the means to coordinate the different responsibilities involved in negotiating the social construction of meanings.

But yet more than this is involved in learning how properly to 'position' oneself within particular speech genres than the ways of sense-making they entail, for speech genres can be characterized by the 'topics' they embody, the sources in terms of which utterances belonging to the genre are formulated. If this is so, then the character of our 'inwardness' – the way we appear (or feel we should appear) to ourselves – will depend upon the speech genres within which we account for ourselves (Gergen, 1989). Where, as Billig (1987; Billig *et al*, 1988) argue, many of the 'topics' within a genre are dilemmatic, i.e., they are two-sided. Hence, even within a genre, quite different argumentative positions may be intelligibly formulated. If this is so, then our 'basic' ways of talking about ourselves are neither so closed or so limited as to wholly exclude alternatives. Thus, our account of internalization as an ethico-rhetorical phenomenon clearly has a number of further strands to it worth investigating. I shall study Billig's (1987, 1991; Billig *et al*, 1988), Bakthin's (1981, 1984, 1986), and Vico's (1965, 1968, 1988) contributions in more detail in the next chapter, and attempt there to make more prominent there some of the alternatives till now ignored in our current 'basic' ways of talking. Where it is important to understand our own part in their construction, for, as I have said before, it is only from within the contested social realities they sustain, that we can reach out to attempt to make contact with that which is other than ourselves.

Chapter Three

BAKHTIN:

DIALOGUE AND RHETORIC IN THE CONSTRUCTION OF SOCIAL RELATIONS

> "Artistic form, correctly understood, does not shape already prepared and found content, but rather permits content to be found and seen for the first time" (Bakhtin, 1984, p.43, my emphasis).

> "We must renounce our monological habits so that we might come to feel at home in the new artistic sphere which Dostoevsky discovered, so that we might orient ourselves in that incomparably more complex artistic model of the world which he created" (Bakhtin, 1984, p.272).

> "The actual reality of language-speech is not the abstract system of linguistic forms, not the isolated monologic utterance, and not the psychophysiological act of its implementation, but the social event of verbal interaction implemented in an utterance or utterances. Thus, verbal interaction is the basic reality of language" (Voloshinov, 1973, p.94).

In moving on further towards a grasp of how our 'basic' ways of talking are formed and transformed, it will be useful to turn to Voloshinov's, Bahktin's and to Wittgenstein's accounts of the dialogic nature of speech communication, and to explore what might be called the primary relationally-responsive function of *utterances* – for in these accounts (as in Vygotsky's), the referential-representational function of speech becomes a secondary and derived function. In particular, we shall be interested in the *method of comparisons* Wittgenstein (1953) introduced in his *Philosophical Investigations* for bringing many important features of our language and our ways of talking to our attention. Although we may not be able to accurately and correctly represent the nature of our everyday ways of talking theoretically, that does not prevent us, Wittgenstein (1953) notes, from introducing other special ways of talking, *though* which to perceive certain of their features, special ways of talking that work to draw our attention to certain characteristics that we would otherwise ignore. Certain metaphors play a central part in these special ways of talking, not only the *metaphor* of "language-games" in all their different varieties, but many others: of words as being *like* "tools" or "instruments"; of them as being *like* the other items in a "tool box" too, such as the glue and nails; but also of our language a being *like* an "ancient city;"[35] or of words as being *like* the "handles in the cab of a steam locomotive;" and so on. These all functioned as aids in guiding us toward paying attention to features of language, language-use, and our knowledge of language that we might not otherwise notice, by drawing our attention to differences between such models and our actual linguistic activities and practices.

Like Voloshinov and Bakhtin, Wittgenstein is also concerned to combat the misleading comparison of language with a system of mathematical signs operating according to strict rules, a calculus. As he saw it, the temptation to identify the use of words with games and calculi, and to say someone who is using language *must* be playing such a game, is to be resisted - you must even resist saying that it is *nearly* like it. For, "if you say that our languages only *approximate* to such calculi you are standing upon the brink of a misunderstanding. For then it may look as if we are talking about an *ideal* language," (Wittgenstein, 1953, no.81) when none such exist (at least, so he would claim). Our use of language is not as if it is *ideally* according to rules, but in practice falls short – like bodies falling under gravity are prevented by air resistance from achieving their ideal velocity; the context or conditions to which it is sensitive in its use are of a different kind entirely. Indeed, because it is in the *details* of our actual utterances that we can find their unique meaning for us, that Wittgenstein (1953) finds such idealizations completely in appropriate. "We have got on to slippery ice where there is no friction," he says, "and so in a certain sense the conditions are ideal, but also, just because of that, we are unable to walk. We want to walk: so we need friction. Back to the rough ground!" (no.107). What some would see as distracting departures from the ideal[36], others see as the facts we must confront; where some see reality as hidden *behind appearances*, others see reality as being *in appearances*.

Yet the *comparison* with ideals is useful nonetheless, for the differences it reveals: rather than rationality-as-representation we have here a rationality-achieved-through-contrasts (Edwards, 1982). Like Wittgenstein, Bakhtin and Voloshinov also are concerned to combat the notion of language-as-a-system. They also take utterances, or *words in their speaking*, rather than sentences, or *patterns of already spoken words*, as the basic unit of dialogic speech communication. This distinction is a crucial one. It opens up our inquiries into the *unfolding dynamics* of the voicing of our utterances, to the fact that we can 'pick up' information from the unfolding temporal contours of a person's speech. I will explore this issue more thoroughly in chapter ten. Here I will introduce some of the important ways in which the turn way from sentences toward utterances, as the basic analytic unit of speech communication, opens up for us the topic of the spontaneous responsiveness of our utterances to the situation of their utterance, and also to the special realm of dialogically-structured, joint activities – creative activities which cannot be attributed to the intentions of any individuals. It is to an introductory account of Bakhtin's (1986) and Voloshinov's (1986) remarks on the notion of the utterance that I will now turn.

Baktin and Voloshinov
Utterances and the dialogical

Bakhtin feels that the claim – made by such linguists as Saussure (followed, of course, by Chomsky): that the single sentence, with all its individuality and monologic creativity, can be regarded as a completely free combination of forms of language – is not true of our actual utterances in our everyday affairs. Our actual utterances must take into account the (already linguistically shaped) state of affairs to which they are a response, and into which they are directed. Thus for Bakhtin (1986):

> "Any concrete utterance is a link in the chain of speech communication of a particular sphere. The very boundaries of the utterance are determined by a change of speech subjects. Utterances are not indifferent to one another, and are not self-sufficient; they are aware of and mutually reflect one another... Every utterance must be regarded as primarily a *response* to preceding utterances of the given sphere (we understand the word 'response' here in the broadest sense). Each utterance refutes affirms, supplements, and relies upon the others, presupposes them to be known, and somehow takes them into account... Therefore, each kind of utterance is filled with various kinds of responsive reactions to other utterances of the given sphere of speech communication" (p.91).

Listening too must be responsive, in that listeners must be preparing themselves to respond to what they are hearing. Indeed,

> "...when the listener perceives and understands the meaning (the language meaning) of speech, he simultaneously takes an active, responsive attitude toward it. He either agrees or disagrees with it (completely or partially), augments it, applies it, prepares for its execution, and so on. And the listener adopts this responsive attitude for the entire duration of the process of listening and understanding, from the very beginning - sometimes literally from the speaker's first word" (p.68).

And the speaker too, instead of a passive understanding that "only duplicates his [or her] own idea in someone else's mind" (Bahktin, 1986, p.69), also talks with an active expectation of a response, an agreement, sympathy, challenge, criticism, objection, obedience, and so on.

Indeed, as we have already seen, speakers shape their speaking in terms of that "which has not yet been said but which is needed and in fact anticipated by the answering word" (Bakhtin, 1981, p.280). In other words, the relationally-responsive form of understanding at work in the practical conduct of a dialogue, is very different in kind from the referential-representational form of understanding required by the reader of a text, concerned with what the text is 'about'. Unlike readers, speakers taking their turn in a verbal exchange must be almost continuously sensitive to the utterances of other 'voices'.

It is this entry of the voice of an 'other' into the shaping of our 'own' utterances that makes our focus on *joint, dialogically-structured* events so crucial. For it means that in such events, something *unique* can occur, a *first-time* event, instead of an event occurring as an outcome, as the product, of an already existing, logical system or framework – the continual re-production of sameness.

It is this that makes the dialogical so special. As Bakhtin (1984) puts it: "Language lives only in the dialogical interaction of those who make use of it. Dialogic interaction is indeed the authentic sphere where language *lives*... Dialogic relationships are reducible neither to logical relationships nor to relationships oriented semantically toward their referential object, [they are] relationships *in and of themselves* devoid of any dialogical element. They must clothe themselves in discourse, become utterances, become positions of various subjects expressed in discourse, in order that dialogic relations might arise among them" (p.183).

Thus, in such circumstances: "An utterance is never just a reflection or an expression of something already existing and outside it that is given and final. It always creates something that never existed before, something absolutely new and unrepeatable, and, moreover, it always has some relation to value (the true, the good, the beautiful, and so forth). But something created is always created out of something given (language, an observed phenomenon of reality, an experienced feeling, the speaking subject himself, something finalized in his world view, and so forth). What is given is completely transformed in what is created" (Bakhtin, 1986, pp.119-120).

For instance (in fact, Bakhtin's example), if we take the two judgmental statements: 'Life is good', and 'Life is not good', we can say, logically, that one is the negation of the other. Coming out of one mouth, they would seem to cancel each other out. But coming out of different mouths, we can imagine the beginning of a very emotional argument or discussion indeed. Similarly, with the two seemingly identical judgments: 'Life is good', 'Life is good'. Said by one voice twice, we can, to be sure, speak here of the logical relationship of identity between two judgments, but more likely, we would focus on the speaker's 'point' in adding *emphasis* to his or her judgment. "But if this judgment is expressed in two utterances by two different subjects," says Bakhtin (1984), "then dialogic relationships arise between them (agreement, affirmation)" (p.184). In other words, something new has been created within the exchange that did not previous exist within it. And further, the first speaker is able (amongst other things) to make use of the second speaker's response in *evaluating in the course of their listening* both whether the second speaker has understood them aright, and where the second speaker thinks they now stand (i.e., are positioned).

Thus, as I noted above, unlike readers, speakers taking their turns in a verbal exchange must be almost continuously sensitive to the utterances of other 'voices', not only to grasp the ways in which other speakers have 'updated', i.e., further specified, refined, or elaborated, the 'matter being talked about', but also to assess in the course of their listening the acceptability of their own, previous utterance.

The uniquely new in the midst of the repeated: speech genres and novel utterances

With this last point in mind, I want to add another component to this 'responsive' or 'bodily reactive' account of an utterance's meaning: namely, the idea – following Billig's (1987; Billig *et al*, 1988) work upon the rhetorical, and ideological, nature of speech communication – that our utterances are not, of course, always acceptable to, or accepted by others, is. They respond to what we say or do with criticisms, with challenges to justify ourselves, and we must show how our actions 'fit in with' their's (Mills, 1940). Acceptable responses must quite often be negotiated within a context of argumentation. Hence my designation of this account of language use as not just *responsive*, as not just *relational*, but also as *rhetorical*[37]. When a person utters a word, whose word is it? For "a word is territory shared by both addresser and addressee, by speaker and his interlocutor... The immediate social situation and the broader social milieu wholly determine – and determine *from within*, so to speak – the structure of an utterance" (Voloshinov, 1973, p.86). Where here, of course, its structure does not inhere in the formal pattern of syntax it can be seen as matching (or approximating), but in its responsive voicing, the temporal unfolding of its intoning: as angry, indignant, confident, arrogant, apologetic, indifferent, as inviting or repulsing reply, and so on. Thus what matters also are the wilful efforts we put into organizing our expressive acts in the world, efforts that are manifested in what Bakhtin (1993) calls their "emotional-volitional tone." As we shall see, it is this that guides us in understanding how to *orient* or to *relate* ourselves to a persons' utterance, i.e., to get a sense of its 'point' and 'purpose', their degree of commitment to it., and why they are motivated in such an aim. Thus, the "mere fact that I have begun speaking about [an object] means that I have already assumed a particular attitude toward it... And that is why the word does not merely designate an object as a present-to-hand entity, but also expresses *by its intonation* my evaluative attitude toward the object... and, in doing so, sets it in motion toward that which is yet to-to-be determined about it... [Thus] everything that is actually experienced... as something given and as something-yet-to-be-determined, *is intonated*, has emotional-volitional tone, and enters into an effective relationship within the unity of the ongoing event encompassing us" (pp.32-33, our emphases) – I will discuss these features of our utterances, that show up in the temporal contours of our utterances, more fully in Chapters 6, 9, and 10.

Here, it is important to add in relation to the comments above, that Voloshinov and Bakhtin do not see the contexts of our speech as being often of a merely transitory, ahistorical kind. Although unfolding only moment by moment, they may often manifest in the details of their organization deeply historical influences. The claim that any concrete utterance is a link in the stream or chain of speech communication of a particular sphere, means, as they see it, that in being responsive, our utterances must not only always strike into an ongoing flow of conversational activity of one kind or another, but they must do so in a way or ways sensitive to fluctuations in the conditions of the social situation in which they are uttered. And it is this, the historically sensitive nature of the ways of talking in question, not the fact of our language belonging to a system, that influences the acceptability of our forms of talk to those to whom they are addressed. Indeed, we will often find the ease with which our utterances find acceptance is a matter of whether we are speaking in one or another of the more institutionalized centres of social life, or, on the more disorganized peripheries. We need a sense of the 'atmosphere' into which we must speak, for to gain acceptance in institutional situations is a matter of acquiring the requisite linguistic competence, while on the peripheries, 'on the street', it is a very different matter. It is a much more 'open' situation, with every dimension of one's identity being at stake.

Voloshinov (1986) and Bakhtin (1986) both characterize that atmosphere as being a matter of the *speech genres* that have currency in the situation of one's talk; it is

> "is first and foremost an atmosphere made up of multifarious speech performances that engulf and wash over all persistent forms and kinds of ideological creativity: unofficial discussions, exchanges of opinion at the theatre or concert or at various kinds of social gatherings, purely chance exchanges of words, one's manner of verbal reaction to happenings in one's life and daily existence, one's inner-word manner of identifying oneself and identifying one's position in society, and so on. Social psychology [the term they use to designate this atmosphere] exists primarily in a wide variety of forms of the 'utterance', of little *speech genres* of internal and external kinds – things left completely unstudied to the present day... All these forms of speech interchange operate in extremely close connection with the conditions of the social situation in which they occur and exhibit extraordinary sensitivity to the fluctuations in the social atmosphere" (Voloshinov, 1973, pp.19-20).

In the more institutionalized centres of social life, with a competence in the more orderly genres in place there, we will be able to speak with some sensitivity to the fluctuations in social atmosphere there, and expect (mostly) to be routinely understood – such a sensitivity is a part of what it is for us to be competent in these spheres. However, on the more disorderly margins of social life, we cannot expect such routine understanding; a more negotiated, back-and-forth, precarious process is to be expected. But even here, on the margins – as is only too predictable – life is not without its foreseeable characteristics; one's cultural history is still of use to one.

To sum up: The importance of the above account of *utterances* lies in the way in which it opens up to study those *dialogical or interactive moments* when, and where, there is a 'gap' in the stream of communication between two (or more) speaking subjects. And no matter how *systematic* the speech of each may be whilst speaking[38], when one has finished speaking and the other has to respond, the bridging of that 'gap' is an opportunity for a completely unique, unrepeatable response, one that is 'created' or 'crafted' to fit the unique circumstances of its utterance. It is in this way that all *dialogically-structured* events inevitably bring into a situation something novel and unpredictable, something that goes beyond all pre-existing schematisms. Indeed, it is on the boundary between two consciousnesses, two subjects, that the *life* – whatever it is that is 'living' in the communicative act – is manifested (Bakhtin, 1986, p.106). Thus we can appreciate, as Voloshinov (1986) says, that:

> "What the speaker values is not that aspect of the form which is invariably identical in all instances of its usage, despite the nature of those instances, but that aspect of the linguistic form because of which it can figure in the given, concrete context, because of which it becomes a sign adequate to the conditions of the given, concrete situation. We can express it this way: *what is important for the speaker about the linguistic form is not that it is a stable and always self-equivalent signal, but that it is an always changeable and adaptable sign"* (p.68).

It is this that affords speakers the opportunity to express what is unique about themselves or their circumstances. In their responsive voicing of words at this, that, or some other particular moment, in this, that, or some other particular way, speakers can express their own unique (intended) meanings at *that* point in time, in relation to *that* situation. It is in the particular *difference* their words make, in *that* situation, that they can exert their effect.

Voloshinov thus emphasizes how supportive, so to speak, the speech context is to the life of linguistic signs. Thus, just as the effect produced by poking a stick into a stream of water depends upon the whole character of the flow of water at the time – with different effects depending upon the power (or lack of it) already in the stream's flow – so for us, the effect of our words depends upon whereabouts in the stream of communication they occur. "The organizing centre of any utterance, of any experience," says Voloshinov (1986), "is not within [the individual] but outside – in the social milieu surrounding the individual being" (p.93).

It is in their 'rooting' in the stream of communication, both in their responsive connection to the other voices in that stream, and to events occurring in their surroundings, that our words have their 'life' – by their use, we continually live out our connections with the others and othernesses around us. Indeed, in both Billig's and Bakhtin's views, even within the speech of a single individual or the writing of a single author, as an event in the stream, in a living text or utterance, many 'voices', many influences can be at work, and as such, 'gaps' can be found in what they say or write that prompt us to react affectively to what they have to say, that arouse a responsive understanding in us of their expressions.

Thus, with Vygotsky's notion of 'instructional' forms of speech in mind, along with the Bakhtin's relationally-responsive of speech communication, and Billig's rhetorical account, it will be useful to return to the problem of our 'basic', embodied forms of talk to examine their nature further. For, if the 'gaps' in our forms of talk are not bridged systematically and automatically, how are they bridged in our everyday talk? Here we shall find Vico's account of a culture's common sense, and the working of rhetorical forms of communication important.

The importance of the 'sensus communis', rhetoric, and metaphor

Elsewhere (Shotter, 1984, 1986, 1991a, 1993b), I have discussed Vico's account of the origin's of a culture's 'common sense' (*sensus communis*). Briefly: The social processes involved, he claims, are based not upon anything pre-established either in people or their surroundings, but in socially shared *identities of feeling* they themselves create in the flow of activity between them. These, he calls "sensory topics" – "topics" (Gr: *topos* = "place") because they give rise to "commonplaces," i.e., to shared moments in a flow of social activity which afford common reference, and "sensory" because they are moments in which shared *feelings* for already shared circumstances are created. A paradigm situation here, is everyone running to take shelter from thunder, everyone's responsive reaction to the fear expressed in the character of people's bodily activities, gives a shared *sense* to an *already shared* circumstance. It is at this point that he introduced the idea of an "imaginative universal:" In the case of thunder, this is Jove, the image of a giant being speaking giant words, but one can easily imagine other such shared circumstances in which shared feeling, expressed in the same responsive, bodily reactions might occur - the birth of a child, the death of a group member, and so on.

Thus these first anchor points are to do, not with 'seeing' in common, but with 'feeling' in common, with the 'giving' or 'lending' of a shared *significance* to shared *feelings* in an *already shared* circumstance. In other words, the first mute language is the immediate responsive representation in gesture of a moment or place of common reference, where the gesture functions *metaphorically*, not to refer to something already known about, but to indicate an 'is', to *establish* a 'something' with common significance.

What Vico outlines above then, is a poetic image, a metaphor, in terms of which one might understand the *mute*, extraordinary, common sense basis for an articulate language – where such a basis constitutes the unsystematized, primordial contents of the human mind, its basic paradigms or prototypes. These are the feelings or intuitions – the sensory topics or commonplaces that make up the basis of a community's *sensus communis* – in terms of which our first words can have their sense, and against which, much later, the adequacy of our concepts may be judged.

Vico was particularly interested in what might be called "civic rhetoric" and the problem of what constituted good government (Mooney, 1985; Schaeffer, 1990), but he developed his views against a background within which the tradition of rhetoric was under attack by the new "geometric method" of reasoning promoted by the Cartesians. And to an extent, his arguments constitute a counter-attack upon it, for he saw it as completely inimical to his concerns. In his *On the Study Methods of Our Time* (first pub, 1709), he defends rhetoric on many grounds, but particularly upon the necessity for eloquence in one's speech: For, says Vico, quoting Cardinal Ludvico Madruzzi: "'Rulers should see to it not only that their actions are true and in conformity with justice, but that they *seem* to be so [to everyone]" (Vico, 1965, p.36). In other words, those who are satisfied with abstract truth alone, and do not bother to find out whether their opinion is shared by the generality of people, cause political calamities. Thus, not only should politicians judge human actions as they actually *are*, rather than in terms of what they think they *ought* to be, they should also – in terms of the *sensus communis* – be able eloquently to persuade the people of their judgment's correctness. But how might such persuading be done? What is involved in us accepting (if not the absolute truth) the truth of a claim relative to our current circumstances?

Here we are back again at our original problem – the understanding of that speech which, rather than simply influencing us in our intellects, 'moves' us to accept its claims in our very being – but we are now in a somewhat stronger position to confront its nature: The problem arises when we give *reasons* for any claims we may make; for why should these reasons be accepted as a *proof* of the claim?

They are accepted, suggests Vico, not because we as speakers supply a demonstrable proof, a full syllogistic structure which our listeners are passively compelled (logically) to accept. But because in their incomplete, enthymemic structure, we offer initially unconnected premises that (most of) our audience will be able to connect up for us – and feel that it is they who have 'seen' the point! They themselves make the connection by drawing upon the (perhaps in themselves inarticulable) *topoi* in the *sensus communis* already existing between them and us as speakers. Hence, for Vico, the importance in rhetoric, of what he calls the "art of topics" [*ars topica*]. Where 'argument' in this art

> "...is not 'the arrangement of a proof', as commonly assumed, what in Latin is known as *argumentatio*; rather, it is that third idea which is found to tie together the two in the issue being debated – what in the Schools is called the 'middle term' – such that topics is the art of finding the middle term. But I claim more: Topics is the art of apprehending the true, for it is the art of seeing all the aspects or *loci* of a thing that enable us to distinguish it well and gain an adequate concept of it. For judgments turn out to be false when their concepts are either greater or lesser than the things they propose to signify..." (Vico, 1988, p.178... although I have preferred Mooney's, 1985, p.134 translation here).

So, the special nature of the speech that we use here, works to create the 'space', in which a 'proof' can come into existence as such. Grassi (1980, p.20), a Vico scholar, characterizes this kind of speech as

> "... immediately a 'showing'– and for this reason 'figurative' or 'imaginative', and thus in the original sense 'theoretical' [*theorein* - i.e., to see]. It is metaphorical, i.e., it shows something which has a sense, and this means that to the figure, to that which is shown, the speech transfers [metapherein] a signification[39]; in this way the speech which realizes this showing 'leads before the eyes' [phainesthai] a significance."

This, says Grassi, is *true rhetorical speech*; it is non-conceptual, moving and indicative; it does not just function persuasively, but practically: the metaphor is central to it. In transferring[40] significance from the *sensus communis* to what is said, a metaphor makes 'visible', or 'shows', listeners a common quality that is not rationally deducible. As such, it cannot be 'explained' in any way (either from within an academic discourse, or in any other way); indeed, it is the speech which is the basis of all rational thought. Thus, it is with such a way of talking that we must begin all our investigations[41].

After explanatory theory: a critical descriptive approach

Until recently (until these so-called 'Postmodern' times), we in the West, in our attempts to make sense of our social lives, seem to have been entrapped in what might be called a modernist "way of theory"[42] – a procedure that has worked very effectively in aiding our 'mastery' of the 'natural' world, but which gives us nothing but trouble when applied to our social lives. As with the natural world, so with our social lives, we have felt motivated by a desire to be able, contemplatively, as an external observer of it, to survey a whole *order*. Indeed, associated with the modern way of theory is a strong (in fact) embodied compulsion to search for such a form of knowledge, for without it, without an inner mental picture, an orderly, mentally surveyable image of a "subject matter's" structure, we feel that our knowledge is of a quite inadequate kind. Without such a compulsion, much of our present academic activity would make little sense to us. Thus, in our studies we have attempted to treat sets of essentially historical, often still temporally developing events, retrospectively and reflectively – as if they are a set of 'already-made' events in which we are not involved – with the overarching aim of bringing them all under a unitary, orderly, conceptual scheme. Thus, in following the way of theory, the project of individual researchers becomes that of formulating, monologically, a single framework to function as a 'structured container' for all such events, thus to create a stable, coherent and intelligible order amongst them, one that can be intellectually grasped in a detached, uninvolved way, by individual readers of the theoretical (textual) formulations they write.

In discussing the source of this compulsion, we could argue, of course, that such a project manifests a dream that has come down to us, through the Enlightenment, from the ancient Greeks. Indeed, we might articulate the dream thus: If there is an already determined but 'hidden' inner *order* to be discerned in things, then it might be possible to 'see' into their inner workings and interconnections so well (as if with a God's eye view) as to be able to 'play' through possibly important sequences of events, ahead of time, thus to be ready for them in some way when they occur. And thus, we could *rationally* justify it as such. But that would be to misdescribe its character entirely. For, as Wittgenstein (1969) points out, this is not a form of knowledge amenable to doubt or justification; it is "an absolutely solid part of our *method* of doubt and enquiry" (no.151); our enquiries must come to an end somewhere, "but the end is not an ungrounded presupposition: it is an ungrounded way of acting" (no.109). In other words, just as for the Dinka or the Hopi – who literally do not know how to doubt that, for them, the influences we speak of as in our heads, are in their surroundings – so for us. We find the idea that our thought goes on in our heads, and that it consists in inner representations of outer states of affairs, so basic to our way of being in the world, that we (almost) do not know how to doubt it. It is *basically* what we 'are' to ourselves, and what our world 'is' for us. Yet doubt it we must, if we want to grasp the nature of our third, sensuous, involved kind of knowing. But how might we provoke such a doubt within ourselves, let alone the task of giving it intelligible expression?

Here, we must turn to Wittgenstein's (1953, 1969, 1980) account of our language use: First, we must note (as is well known) that the meaning of our words shows up, he claims, in their use. In other words, if we think of words as being reflexively like the tools of the carpenter, in that they can be used both (1) for the doing of many things to do with shaping and joining, and making a difference to things, but also(2) as reminders for the general kinds of functions they can serve, then we can perhaps appreciate one of his most basic claims: that "grammar tells us what kind of object anything is" (1953, no.373). For it is a person's choice of words as they shape and formulate their utterances – sensing the adequacy of what they are saying to what they feel is the subject matter of their talk – that reveals the *essence* (for them) of what they are talking about. Thus, for Wittgenstein, a wrong description of a usage is *not* one "that does not accord with established usage," but "one which does not accord with the practice of the person giving the description" (1980, I, no.548).

In other words, the crucial event to focus upon, is not speaking in general, but upon this or that particular act of speaking; and the task is to describe (critically) the influences at work in its shaping, i.e., not to say theoretically what *must* be the case in general, in principle, on the basis of evidence, etc., but to be able to say in particular, according to an utterance's particular circumstances, what the influences are at work in it – "*in spite of* an urge to misunderstand them [i.e., those workings]" (1953, no.109). This is why the kind of description we need is a *critical description*: for we must overcome the compulsions and urges we feel as to what a supposed proper understanding here is like (i.e., those I have identified as belong to the way of theory), and we must search for a new kind of understanding. But how can we investigate the nature of something that lacks specificity, whose very openness to being specified or determined by those involved in it, is its central defining feature?

This is where Wittgenstein's notion of "perspicuous representations" play their part: In breaking away from the way of theory, he set up the metaphor of language-games, not to serve as an idealization (as a usual first move, prior to the production of a rigorous theory), but for another reason altogether:

> "Our clear and simple language-games are not preparatory studies for a future regularization of language – as it were approximations, ignoring friction and air resistance. The language-games are rather set up as *objects of comparison* which are meant to throw light on the facts of our language by way not only of similarities, but also of dissimilarities" (no.130)[43].

We must not begin with a preconceived idea to which the reality of our language *must* correspond (if our idea of it is to be correct); what we want is something with which to contrast it, some measuring rod or instrument which, by its very existence, serves to create a dimension (or dimensions) of comparison, a way of talking about the character of what it is we want to study, where each 'instrument' reveals interconnections between aspects and characteristics otherwise unnoticed. Thus all the metaphors used by Wittgenstein (many of them already mentioned above), bring to our attention aspects of language, and of our knowledge of language, that were previously rationally-invisible to us, e.g., its 'rule-like' features, the characteristics of its 'boundaries', its 'archeology', and so on. They serve the function of creating

> "an order in our knowledge of the use of language: an order with a particular end in view; one out of many possible orders; not *the* order. To this end we shall constantly be giving prominence to distinctions which our ordinary forms of language easily make us overlook..." (no.132).

Such metaphors cannot *represent* any already fixed orders in our use of language, for, by their very nature in being open to determination in the context of their occurrence, they do not belong to any such orders. But what they do do for us, in artificially creating an order where none before existed, is to make an aspect of our use of language 'pictureable', i.e., both (1) to make that aspect of our language use "rationally-visible" (in Garfinkel's terms) and thus publicly discussable and debateable; and also, (2) to make it into a "psychological instrument" (in Vygotsky's terms) and thus into a practical resource or instrument, *through* which, and *with* which, we can think, act, and perceive.

Practical-descriptive theory: 'accounts' or 'portrayals' as guides to perception

In this view, then, the task of characterizing the nature of conversational realities is not, if Wittgenstein is correct, a task for explanatory theory – concerned as it is with trying to present a finally 'correct or true view' of the nature of our human being as linguistic creatures. Indeed, along with Wittgenstein and Rorty, I think we are deceiving ourselves in pursuing that as a still possible goal. The dream of such a 'view' is an impossible dream. But a project of a much more partial and particular kind *is* possible: by the use of *objects of comparison*, we can throw light on the facts of our use of language in our conversation-intertwined-activities, not only by way of similarities but also of differences. And by attending to features of our language use *through*, or guided by, certain general concepts – functioning, in Vygotsky's (1978, 1986) terms, as psychological tools or instruments – we can become both *sensitized* to paying attention to features of our own activities that we would not otherwise notice, as well as *motivated* into 'making or creating possible connections' between of that have not occurred to us before.

This is the power and the worth of certain crucial terms (words) expressed in philosophical writing (particularly in Wittgenstein's and Bakhtin's writings): as psychological instruments they can 'instruct' us in new ways of "learning to direct [our] own mental processes" (Vygotsky, 1986, p.108), and function as "means of focussing one's attention, selecting distinctive features and analyzing and synthesizing them" (p.106), thus to bring otherwise unarticulated aspects of our own activities into rational-visibility, and thus render them amenable to critical discussion and further collaborative investigation. In this, the power of words, of certain particular words – our own words as well as those of others – to call out from us, spontaneously, precise responses of some kind or other, to *motivate* particular consequential actions of some kind, is crucial. In other words, in opposition to the generalities of explanatory theory, the answers to our most general questions are, seemingly paradoxically, to be found in the fine details of our lived lives, especially in the particular words we use.

To this end, as aids in noticing such details, I have, among others, introduced the following notions (some from Wittgenstein, others from Bakhtin and Voloshinov, also from Vygotsky, along with others of my own): Besides those of *perspicuous representations* and *psychological instruments*, I have also introduced those of *joint action*, Bakhtin's notions of the *utterance*, of *responsive understanding*, and *speech genres*; Billig's extension of responsive understanding into a *rhetorical* contexts; Vico's notions of *sensory topics*, *imaginative universals,* and his concern with "ars topica," i.e., with rhetorical enthymemes in which an argumentative structure, unavailable to an individual speaker, is completed by the speakers audience as an aspect of joint action. In previous chapters, I have also introduced the concepts of "knowing from within," "rational-invisibility," "traditions of argumentation," the "negotiated nature of social phenomena," and other such notions.

All these are examples of what elsewhere (Shotter, 1984, p.40) I have called practical-theory, but should have called practical-descriptive theory[44]: for these ways of speaking, terms of art, metaphors, or images, can all function as "objects of comparison," as "measuring-rods," as probes or prostheses *through* which, like blind person's sticks or like telescopes or microscopes in other sciences, to 'see' influences at work which would remain otherwise rationally-invisible to us. They are 'tools' for use by us in *accounting* for our claims as what is actually occurring in the disorderly zones of uncertainty in which we conduct the politically negotiable aspects of our everyday social lives – where an account can be distinguished from an explanatory theory in this sense: "an account of an action or activity is concerned with talking about the action or activity as the activity it *is* ... In other words, an account is an aid to perception, functioning to constitute an otherwise indeterminate flow of activity as a sequence of recognizable events, i.e. events of a kind already known about within a society's ways of making sense of things" (Shotter, 1984, p.3).

Someone who has explicitly adopted this Wittgensteinian approach is Clifford Geertz[45]. He talks of what I have called above, following Vygotsky, "psychological instruments," as falling into two distinct classes: "experience-near" and "experience-distant" concepts:

> "An experience-near concept is, roughly, one that someone – a patient, a subject, in our case an informant – might himself naturally and effortlessly use to define what he or his fellows see, feel, think, imagine, and so on, and

> which he would readily understand when similarly applied by others. An experience-distant concept is one that specialists of one sort or another – an analyst, an experimenter, an ethnographer, even a priest or an ideologist – employ to forward their scientific, philosophical, or practical aims. "Love" is an experience-near concept, "object cathexis" is an experience-distant one. "Social stratification" and perhaps for most peoples in the world even "religion" (and certainly "religious system") are experience-distant; "caste" and "nirvana" are experience-near, at least for Hindus and Buddhists" (p.57).

While we cannot perceive precisely what others perceive, what we can perceive is they perceive 'with', 'by means of', or 'through'[46]. And we can get a "sense we have of how things stand with someone else's inner life... through their expressions, not through some magical intrusion into their consciousness" (Geertz, 1986, p.373) – we can gain a sense of the depths in their lives from a close attention to what is visible *on the surface*. Thus as Geertzian investigators into the 'inner lives' of others, the idea is to make sense of *their* ways of life, *their* experience-near concepts, 'through' *our* experience-distant concepts: Where we "grasp concepts that, for another people, are experience-near... [by placing] them in *illuminating connection with* experience-distant concepts theorists have fashioned to capture the general features of social life" (Geertz, 1983, p.58, my emphasis)[47].

But how can they be used to do this, how can that produce the kind of illumination we require? Well, a part of the task is the familiar hermeneutical one, that of "hopping back and forth between the whole *conceived through the parts that actualize it* and the parts *conceived through the whole that motivates them*" (1983, p.69, my emphases).

As presented here, this 'circular', back-and-forth, hermeneutical process might seem a simple alternative to our usual attempts to make sense of something by fitting it into an already existing theoretical schematism of some kind. In practice, however, it is not that simple, nor is it that systematic. Indeed, it is quite different.

While an *explanation* is something we can *have* 'in a flash', so to speak, by fitting an event into theory, the gaining of an illuminating account, the fashioning of an appropriate portrayal, is something we must *do*, but not only step-by-step, but also after the taking of each step, we mus 'make room', so to speak, for a dailogically-structured moment to occur. In other words, the fashioning of an adequate portrayal requires far more *orientational* work on our part, i.e., the *inter-relating* of ourselves to the events occurring in our surroundings, than the fashioning of an explanation. For, as I outlined in the previous chapter, if our accounts or portrayals are to be illuminating ones, they must in their telling 'move' us over the details of the 'terrain' of the topic in question (all the relevant details) in a way sufficient for us to gain a conceptual grasp of their interconnections, and thus of their nature *as a meaningful whole*, even though we lack a vantage point from which to view it. But to gain this 'inside view', we must, to repeat, 'live' in it, just as we must in getting to 'know our way around' inside our own town or city. Thus rather than being able to see it all at once from a single external standpoint (in terms of a single, logical order of connectedness), it is a grasp that allows us to 'see' all the different aspects of the topic in question as if it were arrayed before us as a 'landscape', each detail of which we can only see *by our choosing to focus on it.*

This is where our more academic knowledge of experience-distant concepts can come to play a crucial role. If I can become familiar, say, with the nature and character of *joint action* – if I can come, so to speak, to know 'my way around' inside it as a concept – I may not be able to predict exactly what will happen in an actual meeting between two of more people (as in predicting the Newtonian trajectory of the docking of a space shuttle with a space station). But my knowledge of *joint action* can, nevertheless, play a real part in my practical understanding of the events occurring in such a meeting: it will set me up with, sensitize me to, various expectations and anticipations which, if they are fulfilled, will, in appropriate circumstances, enable me to say: "Yes, that is just like what I expect of joint action; these people are truly acting jointly" or, if they are not fulfilled: "No, that is not at all what one would expect of joint action in this situation; there is something missing from the picture; one is not reciprocally responding to the other." Thus, with my knowledge of what joint action *is*, I can learn both to attend knowledgeably, and to interact meaningfully, with an event of joint action even though I cannot mechanically predict the details of its actual unfolding.

What this means, I think, is that, instead of speaking *monologically*, instead of voicing a stream of speech in which each fragment of utterance is logically or systematically connected to the next in terms of an already existing single order of connectedness, we can teach ourselves to think and speak *dialogically*: That is, as we utter each fragment, we can teach ourselves to pause, and then to produce a response to it from within ourselves in terms of a 'reminder' drawn from the lexicon of experience-distant concepts we have accumulated from our more academic inquiries into relevant events. In other words, instead of one's inner mental activities having the form of geometric deductions, they can begin to take on the form of multi-voiced conversations, with the voices of Wittgensgtein, Bakhtin, Voloshinov, Vico, etc., etc., all having a part to play.

Explanatory theory and its dreams

The search for explanation, typically, is driven by our search for causes – precise, unambiguous, absolutely determining causes. We want to be able to say, "Ideally, X causes Y – all other things being equal." We gain our precision by quantifying these causes and effects, by ignoring or allowing for 'side-effects', and putting them into the form of ideal mathematical laws. Unfortunately, all other things never are in fact equal. Not only do we need friction, and other inconvenient, detailed features in and of our surroundings to survive as the beings we are, but we cannot treat our surrounding, as Descartes (1968) hoped, as merely composed of different parts of matter, "agitate[d] diversely and confusedly" according to God's "established laws" (p.62). Things all seem to be interconnected. Thus every strict, mathematical formulation of a law, principle, or rule said to be governing our living behaviour, indeed, the behaviour of any living process, inevitably leaves out something of what is happening in the larger scheme of things. Indeed, as we have already seen, if what we are after is only the most exact mathematical prediction possible, it is as if we want only to walk on ice; we resolutely ignore the friction we need to walk in the real world: "Back to the rough ground" (Wittgenstein, 1953, no.107). And to find the kind of ground most suitable to our walking, we must examine the ground itself: "The difficult thing here is not, to dig down to the ground; no, it is to recognize that the ground that lies before us as the ground" (Wittgenstein, 1978, p.333).

But the task, though, of gaining a familiarity with the general characteristics of the groundings that become available to us in our meetings with each other, is not an easy task. It involves the continual inter-relating – the *chiasmic* intertwining (Merleau-Ponty, 1968), as I will later call it – of the myriad details that become available to us as we *survey*, or hermeneutically 'look over' (in Geertz's sense), the landscape of activities in which people engage, in living out their lives together. At stake in our doing this, our aim in surveying this landscape, is to arrive at, as Wittgenstein (1953) has put it, "just that understanding which consists in 'seeing connections" (no.122). Indeed, just as in looking out of the window at the landscape before us, we can as we range over it pick out a detail here or a detail there, first to focus on, and then to explore the possible connections between them, so in our hermeneutical 'looking over' here: rather than to the single, logical order of connectedness of a systematic, explanatory theory, it can give rise to an unending multiplicity of "relational dimensions" – and in this sense, of course, just as our surveying of a visual scene, we arrive a 'view' that has a certain "depth" to it, in the sense of things only coming into focus as we fixate on them (I will treat these complex issues at much greater length in Chapter 4).

Although (metaphorically) possessing depth, unlike a visual scenes arrayed only in space, the hermeneutical landscapes we can arrive at in our hermeneutical explorations have their being in time as well as space. Indeed, they are open-ended in the sense of not only being open to further specification – albeit, of an already specified kind – but also able to exert "calls" upon us *motivating* us (in terms of arousing expectations and anticipations with us) to seek such further articulations – thus providing us with, in the jargon of the day, "actionable knowledge."

Because it is open-ended, and thus in relation to explanatory theory not well defined, it does not lack rigour. The rigour required to range over the depths it makes available to us, to bring into focus the different particular relational dimensions among the multiplicity it makes available to us, is at least as great as the rigour demanded of the mathematicians. As Goethe (1995), who in outlining what was involved in seeing a growing, developing whole in this indivisible way (he was interested in what we might call the dynamic portrayal of plant forms, so that he could 'think' though, both forward and back, a plant's growth), noted that all the details must align with each other and constitute a demonstrated unity in the same compelling way as the steps in a mathematical proof: "From the mathematician we must learn the meticulous care required to connect things in unbroken succession, or rather, to derive things step by step. Even where we do not venture to apply mathematics we must always work as though we had to satisfy the strictest of geometricians," he said (p.16).

The difficulty of doing this, though, must not be ignored. While the quantitative preoccupations of explainers allow them to focus on a one-dimensional focus on measurable *things*, and on the construction of a single, logical order of connectedness, portrayers, by contrast, have a much more taxing task. They must attend to many differently detailed facts, which they must somehow inter-related in a dynamic, developing whole[48]; as such, they must attend, not so much *to things* as to *the relations between* them.

Although it is perfectly legitimately view human expressive events in their fixed and measurable aspects, if we do, then we tend to ignore the larger whole, the background of ongoing, living movement within which they have their being as the expressive events they are. But if we are truly to do such events justice, as the *expressive* events they are, we cannot legitimately ask the question: *How much?* We can only ask: *What is it like?*

The urge to explain events in terms of their causes leads the 'natural' scientist into a single-minded analysis of things into separate parts. And it is the *external* relations between these parts that are then construed as *explaining* the behaviour of the things. Such explanations work in a bottom-up fashion, with a thing's behaviour depending on the individual properties just of its parts – so that a society's social order, for instance, depends on the beliefs and values of the individuals of which it is composed. In a portrayal, by contrast – as Geertz (1983) makes clear – the attempt is to grasp a whole that *in-forms* its parts through their *internal* relations to it, for they owe their character (their so-called 'properties') and their very being, to their participation within it.

Indeed, the (chiasmic) interweaving of parts into a unified, living whole is necessarily qualitative, i.e., non-quantitative. Quantitative entities, if they are to be countable, must be entirely self-contained and have all their properties within themselves, so to speak. They cannot owe any aspects of their character to their placement within a larger whole. On the other hand, qualitatively characterized events can interpenetrate, or become dynamically entangled with each other, with one playing into, altering, and becoming inseparable from, i.e., qualifying, another. Without such mutual entanglement, we can have parts existing side by side, but no unity of the whole. In every case, say, of sexual reproduction, we see in the offspring an intertwining of the qualities of the parents so as to create a new unity. There is no mere side-by-side aggregation of separate parental traits here; rather, each parent qualifies the whole. Such is also the case in joint action: it is *qualified* by all who participate in it.

Conclusions: dialogical versus monological practices

Above, then we have been exploring a form of rationality-achieved-through-contrasts, rather than rationality-as-representation. In it, we bring out the nature of what *we* do, *our* practices by comparison with what others (actual and invented) do, or don't do. So, for example, we make use of the notion of language games, or of joint action, not to *explain* our use of language, but simply to note what in certain situations of language use we seem to be actually doing; and often, if the portrayal we offer brings out unnoticed connections between aspects of that situation, that is sufficient to give us the kind of understanding we need to conduct our practical affairs more effectively – for some things we just do spontaneously understand in practice without the need of any analysis or explanation. If we had always to understand a person's reply to our questions by use, say, of a logical or scientific analysis to *explain* them, then the ordinary play of questions and answers in everyday life (as well as the understanding of the logical or scientific analysis) would be impossible.

But clearly, this form of relationally-responsive understanding – that consists in seeing connections – depends upon the use of that special form of true rhetorical speech that, as Vico and Grassi suggest, relies upon its dialogical and metaphorical nature. It is not a form of reasoning that can be conducted by individuals alone, nor can it be mechanized. Thus, in the current atmosphere, in which such forms are valued, we cannot expect the transition to such dialogical and metaphorical ways of reasoning to be to an easy one. We can expect a struggle: with current *monological* forms of reasoning at the centre attempting to repel or expel *dialogical* forms out onto the margins. For, "monologism, at its extreme, denies the existence outside itself of another consciousness with equal rights and equal responsibilities, another *I* with equal rights (thou). With a monologic approach (in its extreme or pure form) *another person* remains wholly and merely an *object* of consciousness. Monologue is finalized and deaf to the other's response, does not expect it and does not acknowledge in it any *decisive* force" (Bakhtin,1984, pp.292-3).

And this is, of course, is exactly the implicit power exerted over us by the traditional scientific view of things: it leads us to treat what we are studying as an object of thought in order to form theories to guide our further, deliberate actions in relation to it. Our representations of things suggest to us ways in which they can be manipulated and give us power over them. Lacking such 'inner' pictures, we feel an uncertainty, a lack of confidence in an our knowledge; we don't quite know were we stand. If our traditional approaches cannot give it us, we tend to seek it in our ne approaches.

But this urge for certainty cannot be satisfied by a turn to dialogic approaches either! For traditions of argumentation, the multivoiced polyphony of a world in dialogic discussion with itself cannot ever be accurately 'pictured'. Its open, unfinished, still developing nature intrinsically precludes that possibility.

However, instead of certainty (as accuracy of representation), we can concern ourselves with *adequacy*, with doing justice to the being of what we are studying (Shotter, 1991, 1992). Where, according to Bakhtin (1984), "the single adequate form for *verbally expressing* authentic human life is the *open-ended* dialogue. Life by its very nature is dialogic. To live means to participate in dialogue: to ask questions, to heed, to respond, to agree, and so forth. In this dialogue a person participates wholly and throughout his whole life: with his eyes, lips, hands, soul, spirit, with his whole body and deeds" (p.293).

For too long in our social sciences, we have hidden these essentially political struggles – between a natural scientific approach in terms of explanatory theories and a more dialogical approaches in terms of practical-descriptive theories – from publicly debatable investigation by simply assuming that social life just *is* a 'natural' phenomenon, awaiting our discovery of its 'laws' in the same way that we discover those governing the movements of fundamental particles in physics. Thus, as social scientists, we have treated our *topics of inquiry*, as if they all already exist as ready-made entities out in our 'external' world – rather than as still developing socio-historical constructions, constitutive of our own being as the individuals we currently experience ourselves as being. We have not realized that what we experience ourselves as being, and what we experience as the being[49] of our world, are both determined by us, and for us, in all the self-other relationships in which we are involved. Nor have we realized the degree to which current social scientific traditions of investigation and debate have come to permeate our ordinary everyday forms of thought and talk, and to constitute the 'standards' or 'norms' for what its considered to be a 'proper' discussion.

For us in the West, enthralled by the power of theory, it has long seemed as if we can *individually* investigate the character of the 'world' around us. We now must begin to face the fact that such an activity is only possible if what we study is already ordered. In the movement to a nonmodernist science of mental life, the assumption that we all live within the same (socially) ordered world can no longer be sustained; we have to accept that there is no single, already-made meaningful order to be found in our social lives. But if that is the case, if there is no *a priori* social order, if our practical, everyday activities take place in, and deal with, a pluralistic, only fragmentarily known, and only partially shared social world, then we must turn away from the project of attempting to understand our social lives through the imposition of monologic, theoretical systems of order, and turn to a study of the more dialogic forms of practical-moral knowledge in terms of which they are lived. For the task now is to invent appropriate practical-theoretical devices, i.e., the apposite perspicuous representations, that work to render rationally-visible the influences at work upon us, thus to fashion them as topics of public discussion and debate.

Thus, within a research tradition organized around dialogical, rather than monological practices, instead of the simple Darwinian struggle for the survival of the supposedly fittest theory (representing an already existing order), we can expect to see a whole host of other and new kinds of struggle. Especially, we can expect struggles to do with claims of an ethical kind, to do with what is involved in treating others (and otherness) with due respect - to replace the struggles we have had in the past over how they (and it) might best be manipulated. Thus, we can expect a concern with fashioning new orders of relationship (out of chaos). Consequently, we can expect contests between different perspicuous representations, i.e., between different metaphorical accounts which 'give form' to our circumstances in ways which have not been 'seen' before, providing novel understandings 'making new connections'[50]. We can also expect to see such representations, and claims for their worth, issuing from many different 'positions' in the tradition other than from within the mainstream (center). Further, such claims will not just critical of the mainstream, but of each other also. There will be struggles too between different genres of writing, and the form-producing ideologies, i.e., the 'imaginary worlds', they embody. Indeed, the study of writers's practices, rather than their content, can be expected to extent to a study of the *tone* in which they write, for the different dialogical opportunities for relationship (and being) offered to readers by authors, will become important[51]. Finally, there will be political struggles over which representations of a 'worldview' should be 'literalized' (Rorty, 1980) into an 'world-order'. For, in what is now becoming an almost world-wide phenomenon, those who are concerned with finding a 'history' or a 'tradition' of their own, have begun to object to the monological, ahistorical systems of 'central-planning and administration' which exclude them.

Indeed, as we move out of a political world of supposed equals, of people existing as indistinguishable atoms, psychologically, all in competition with one another for *power*, and move into a political world of people possessing psychological characteristics according to their 'positions' in relation to each other, we begin to see a whole different dynamic at work. Instead of a 'politics of power', a new 'politics of identity' is beginning, a politics of access to or exclusion from a political economy of ontological opportunities for different ways of being. If one is to participate in this political economy with equal opportunity, then 'membership' of the community of struggle, the tradition of argumentation, cannot be conditional: one must feel one has a right, unconditionally, to 'belong'. And these claims to 'belong' are now being posed by a whole host of groups previously marginalized by professional academics: not only women, black and other ethnic movements, ecologists, and so on, but also many others without 'expert' or 'professional' credentials. We are moving into a new world of problems posed by a genuine recognition of the importance of differences rather than similarities, and, the importance of that world in influencing the character of the questions we now feel it crucial to pursue.

Chapter Four

THE CHIASMIC NATURE OF THE DIALOGICAL: A NEW REALM OF INQUIRY

"The propositions describing this world-picture might be part of a kind of mythology. And their role is like that of rules of a game; and the game can be learned purely practically, without learning any explicit rules. It might be imagined that some propositions, of the form of empirical propositions, were hardened and functioned as channels for such empirical propositions as were not hardened but fluid... But I distinguish between the movement of the waters on the river-bed and the shift of the bed itself; though there is not a sharp division of the one from the other" (Wittgenstein, 1969, nos.95, 96, 97).

"The way in which the word conceives its object is complicated by a dialogic interaction within the object between various aspects of its socio-verbal intelligibility... If we imagine the *intention* of such a word, that is, its *directionality toward the object*, in the form of a ray of light, then the living and unrepeatable play of colors and light on the facets of the image that it constructs can be explained as the spectral dispersion of the ray word, not within the object itself (as would be the case in the play of an image-as-trope, in poetic speech taken in the narrow sense, in an 'autotelic word'), but rather its spectral dispersion in an atmosphere filled with the alien words, value judgments and accents through which the ray passes on its way toward the object; the social atmosphere of the word, the atmosphere that surrounds the object, makes the facets of the image sparkle" (Bakhtin, 1981, p.277).

Traditionally, as we have seen, language has been thought of as an already established, self-contained system of linguistic communication, working in terms of a set of rules or social conventions that people make use of in expressing themselves. In this account – that we can call an *intellectualist*, Cartesian account of language – people are thought of as understanding the linguistic representations contained each other's sentences by mentally decoding the *forms* of words to arrive at their *content*. However, in another account, a *dialogical* account articulated by Bakhtin, Wittgenstein, Garfinkel, and Merleau-Ponty, among many others, is of a much more dynamic, participatory, relational kind. In it, language and the world are intertwined in a *chiasmic* relation with each other, in which we are shaped just as much, if not more, by events in the world around us, as the world by us. Thus, to switch to this very different view of language is also to switch to a very different view of the world in which we live: it is to see it as a living, dynamic, indivisible world of events that is also still coming into being. In this view, we primarily understand another person's *utterances* in terms of the bodily responses, the felt tendencies, they spontaneously arouse in us, responses that *relate* or *orient* us both toward them *and* toward events occurring in our shared surroundings. In other words, language is not a system for use by individuals to give shared expression to *already* clearly conceived significations, but is a way of *organizing* shared or sharable significations between us for always *another first time* – with each utterance being a *once-occurrent event of being* (Bakhtin, 1993).

In suggesting this, Bakhtin goes way beyond the Cartesian account of knowledge as an intellectual achievement between a subjective knower and objectively known events. For, in arguing for the importance of an utterance's *tone*, he is arguing that our knowledge as an intellectual achievement is dependent on a more fundamental, spontaneously occurring, nonintellectual, sensuous attunement to the events occurring in our surroundings. I want to explore the consequences of this very radically changed view of our language-world relations for its implications in our more practical inquires into our conduct of our daily lives in what follows below.

Six themes

In particular in this chapter, in line with the overall theme of this book – that everything in our daily affairs continually happens to us for yet another first time – I want to explore how we can, from rare, unrepeatable, unique, fleeting, and utterly particular experiences, learn something general, something that we can carry across to other circumstances. Let me open my exploration by introducing six themes: (1) As was perhaps already apparent in the Preface to this book, along with the focus on *first-time* events, another central theme in this book is to do with how we might come to know a unique other or otherness *as unique*, as who or what they are *in themselves*. How can we 'enter into' *their* world in a way which acknowledges and respects their otherness, and allows them to express themselves to *us* in *their own* terms? Or, to put it another way: How is it possible for a person (or patient in psychotherapy, a business situation, a company, or whatever) to express their (or its) own unique individuality within a language made up, seemingly, of only a limited number of repeatable forms... or, for that matter, for a work of art, to teach us a new way of looking at, or listening to, the world around us, a new *way* or *style* of looking or listening, a new sensibility?

(2) This question is connected with a second theme, to do with how we might understand *change*, changes within ourselves or others, changes in our social lives together, deep changes of the *river-bed* (see Wittgenstein, 1969,

no.97, quoted among the epigraphs above): We are very used to talking of change as something that can be explained in terms of principles, rules, or conventions, of changes taking place *within* a reality already well-known to us, changes that we might call *ordinary* changes – one's occurring within the routine background (river) flow of our daily activities. But here, I want to talk about surprising changes, changes that happen unexpectedly, changes that strike us with amazement or wonder, *extraordinary* changes, changes in the very (river-bed) character of what we take our reality to be – changes that Bakhtin (1993) calls "once-occurrent events of being." In short, instead of changes of a quantitative and repeatable kind, I want to talk about first-time, unique, irreversible changes, novelties, changes of a *qualitative* kind.

(3) A third theme of importance in all that follows is one which (strangely) focuses on something quite novel in our study of our own human affairs, a topic that, although it is quite well-known and familiar to us in an everyday sense, has not yet aroused in us any distinctive acknowledgment of its very special nature. This new topic is simply "life" or "livingness," the properties, characteristics, or *aspects* of living, growing bodies, of organic forms as enduring, self-maintaining, self-reproducing, *structurizing structures*. Thus, in all living activities, there is always a kind of *developmental continuity* involved in their unfolding, such that earlier phases of the activity are indicative of at least the *style,* the *physiognomy*, i.e., the unique living identity, of what is to come later. Thus, just as acorns only grow into oak trees and not rose bushes, and eggs only produce chickens and not rabbits, so all living activities, it seems, give rise to what we might call *identity preserving* changes or deformations – their possible ends are already 'there' in their beginnings.

(4) A fourth consideration – arising out of the special nature of living things – is that everything of importance to us in this realm of spontaneous, living activity, occurs in *meetings* of one kind or another. Something very special occurs when two or more living beings meet and begin to *respond* to each other (more happens than them merely having an *impact* on one another). As Wittgenstein (1953) puts it: "our attitude to what is alive and to what is dead, is not the same. All our reactions are different" (no.284). But more than this, there is the creation in such meetings of qualitatively new, quite novel and distinct forms of life, forms of life which are more than merely averaged or mixed versions of those already existing (see comments in the Preface), but which express quite unique, never-before-realized, *chiasmicly* structured forms of dynamic unfolding.

Given these all these themes so far, let me try to sum up their influence by saying that, running through everything I have to say below, is a focus on *spontaneous, living, bodily, expressive and responsive activity*:

— *spontaneous*, because it is immediate and not pre-mediated;
— *living*, in that it has its existence only in a continuous responsive and

adjustive relation with events occurring in its surroundings;
— *bodily*, in that it is not hidden inside individual people's heads;
— *expressive*, in that it is a kind of activity that moves others to respond to it;
— and *responsive*, in that it occurs spontaneously in response to events having their source in the activities of the others and othernesses in its surroundings.

The power of living expression is that a person, in their living activity, can 'call out' a response from those around them, and in so doing, inaugurate a meeting, inaugurate the beginning of a new language-game: "The origin and primitive form of the language-game," says Wittgenstein (1980a), "is a reaction; only from this can more complicated forms develop. Language – I want to say – is a refinement, 'in the beginning was the deed' [quoting Goethe]" (p.31). "The primitive reaction may have been a glance or a gesture, but it may also have been a word," he notes (Wittgenstein, 1953, p.218). "But what is the word 'primitive' meant to say here?" he asks. "Presumably that this sort of behavior is *pre-linguistic*: that a language-game is based *on it*, that it is the prototype of a way of thinking and not the result of thought" (Wittgenstein, 1981, no.541).

(5) Now all these new foci of concern – understanding the unique otherness of the other; the power of extraordinary changes; the special nature of the "livingness" of some entities; the chiasmic structuring of living meetings; and the power of our living expressions – raise for me a fifth concern, a concern that seems to me to be of the utmost importance. It is to do with our taking into account what must be 'already there' in the dynamics of the background to our meetings, making it possible for us to 'go on' with each other, to 'follow'[52] each other without being misled, becoming disoriented or confused. It is this concern with the very present "background" that determines what it is possible for us to want and do, that takes us to the very edge of current versions of social constructionism. It is the nature is this background that I will turn to in just a moment as the central topic of this chapter. But first, let me mention a final theme: the importance of what in traditional parlance is called the *will* as distinct from the *intellect* – but which I will discuss as to do with the importance of the different *living relations* that we can and do have to our circumstances[53].

(6) This, then, is my sixth theme: Having focused on the importance of events occurring in our *meetings*, it is also necessary to focus on the nature of people's *initial stance or initial attitude* as they *approach* each other in such meetings. For these 'set the scene', so to speak, the 'relational dimensions', the 'style', the 'way of going on' for how participants will react to everything occurring within *the event of their meeting*. It clearly makes an enormous difference if we approach another person on meeting them with a clenched fist ready to strike, or with an open hand ready to shake their's. And this initial approach is up to us, a matter of our choice, of

our will. Indeed, as the interaction unfolds, if we use our judgment and allow ourselves to be appropriately responsive to their expressive movements, then we can 'go on' with them in an unconfused, straightforward manner.

What we are concerned with here, then, is with a whole set of issues that we touched on earlier, namely, those to do with our *orientation* toward events occurring in our surroundings, the *relations* we have or adopt toward them. With this said, we can thus distinguish between *two* kinds of difficulties that we might face in not knowing quite what to do in relation to the circumstances we face: (1) those that we call *problems* because we can arrive at a *solution* to them by the application of a method or process of reasoning (often conducted within a theoretical framework or schematism of some kind); and those (2) I will here call *difficulties of orientation* or *relational difficulties*, difficulties in which we need to *resolve* a *line of action*, a *style* or *way* of approach.

Our ways of proceeding, our methods, or the steps we must take in relation to these two quite different kinds of difficulty are themselves quite different: For the difficulty to be called a *problem*, it must be possible to describe the initial state of affairs in terms relevant to an already well-known process of reasoning, and to 'work out' a clear link between the known and the unknown but desired states of affairs. But a relational or orientational difficulty presents itself as almost the reverse of this situation – for it is only *after* we discover a way of *relating* ourselves to our surroundings, a way of organizing or orienting *ourselves* to attend to certain aspects of our surroundings rather than others, that the data relevant to our achieving our goal can be brought to light (and then, and only then, can our problem solving reasoning be, if still necessary, applied).

This where a portrayal – as distinct from an explanation – can be of help. As was made clear in the previous chapter, a portrayal can give one a sense of the larger whole to which the particular events confronting one are related, and which thus *in-forms* their character, their being what they *are*. Without know quite 'what' something is – a living or a dead thing, a human or an animal, an intelligent or stupid person, something with 'a life of it own' – we are at a loss as to how appropriately to interact with it.

As we have already seen, with respect to these kinds of *orientational difficulties*, Wittgenstein (1953) talks of them in terms of: "I don't know my way about" (no.123). He then notes that one's real need in such a situation is not to be able to say, "Now I see it" (i.e., the solution to the problem), but to be able to declare to others, "Now I know how to go on" (no.154). For 'to see' something is to be able to assimilate it to an already existing and known category, which in most practical situations is to ignore its unique and often important deviations from the already well known. Whilst being able to 'go on' is to be able to do something *for a first time*. In other words, the resolution of an orientational difficulty is achieved, not at an intellectual level, as something one can talk about to others, but at a practical level, as something that is manifested or shown in one's unique way of being *responsive* to the unique details of a situation by one's actions within it[54].

In other words, the task we face in our relations with the others around us is different from that we face in science: While scientific objectivity requires us to talk of things in our surroundings as having a life of their own *independent of* us, I aim here only to explore what it is for them to have a life of their own *in relation to* us. But how can we relate ourselves to them, how we can make the appropriate choices and judgments that makes such a relation possible? It this question bewilders us – and it is just at the dispelling of this bewilderment that the account of withness-thinking outlined below is aimed. But how might we begin to get a grasp if such a kind of thinking?

The background: chiasmic interweavings

A first step is to try to understand the kinds of things our individual bodies automatically *do for us*, so to speak, without our having to exert much choice or intellection in the matter. Consider first just the simple activity of looking over, visually, the scene before us – with the aim in mind of readying ourselves to move about within it. As our eyes 'flick' from one fixation point to the next, looking at a distant point to the right, next at a near point to the left, with our two eyes working like the autofocus in an automatic camera – giving us a sense of 'depth' as they automatically find for us, at each moment, both a common point of fixation *and* a clear focus. Thus as our eyes dart about, we nonetheless get the sense of a seamless whole, an indivisible 'something' that is not just 'there' before us as a picture, but which is there before us as a set of 'invitations' and 'resistances', as a set of openings and barriers to our actions – in relation to our present 'position' within 'it'. And furthermore, in such involvements as these, we can *all* – more or less – see the same whole, the same landscape, the same face, etc. So that, although I might look from the door on the left to see the window on the right, and you might look from the window on the right to see the door on the left, from within the overall time-space we both share, everything is similarly ordered. Thus if there are some disagreements over exactly what it is before us, we can make use of what we do agree on, to discuss the features we see differently. For we all must see, ultimately, in *accord with* (Merleau-Ponty, 1964)[55] what the visual scene before us *affords* (Gibson, 1979).

And perhaps it is worth adding here, for future reference – as it will not have escaped notice that so far I am talking only of individual activities – that I can see the man over there looking over the same room or landscape as me. I can see the direction in which his head is pointing, I can see him turn it this way and that, I can see his concentration in his tense stance, I can see that he has seen me as he waves his hand toward me. That is, his spontaneously responsive activities are in large part expressive for me. His seeing expresses something of his interest in the room or landscape to me. I approach him: "Beautiful, isn't it?" I say. "What captured your attention?" "Oh, this is where I used to live," he says, "I was looking at the changes!" Clearly, he can see 'more' than me. Perhaps he can tell me what he sees that I cannot. As I shall say later, he is looking *with* a certain living experience in mind to *guide* him in his *style* of looking, to guide him in how he 'orchestrates' his looking as a subtle and complexly unfolding activity in time, with its own developmental trajectory.

What, then, is special in many of our individual bodily activities (but not in all), is that their responsive sequencing is expressive – not so much of how *we* order them – but of how a 'something out there' *requires* us to order them. If the separate elements we encounter in responsively relating ourselves to our surroundings unfold, not just haphazardly, but according to their own *character* or *style*, then they can give rise in all who encounter them, i.e., prior to any thought or deliberation on their part, a *shared* (or at least *shareable)* background sense in terms of which our individual actions can, in such circumstances, have meanings intelligible to others.

This claim, that *the sequencing* of our individual human activities is not just formless, that not just anything can follow or be connected with anything, is clearly connected with Wittgenstein's (1953, 1974) claim, that most of our activities on investigation seem to have a "grammar" to them. It is this – our creative seeing in accord with what is 'out there', not the constraints passively imposed on us externally by a physical reality – that makes an 'anything goes' relativism impossible for us. We cannot just to talk as we please and still do justice to the world around us: "Grammar is not accountable to any reality," he claims, "it is grammatical rules that determine meaning (constitute it) and so they are not answerable to any meaning and to that extent are arbitrary" (Wittgenstein, 1974, no.133, p.184).

In other words, because it is to an extent a matter of our *will* as to how we look over and choose to inter-relate and to respond to certain features of the scene before us, on the one hand, while on the other, we can only look *according to* the opportunities for looking afforded us by our surroundings, there must always be *a grammar* in our looking[56]. Due to the needs of our two eyes as we scan over a scene – the achievement of common points of fixation and focus – we cannot just look as we please. Yet we can adopt – as, for instance, with the well known faces-vase ambiguous figure – different *ways* or *strategies* of looking, so that as we scan from one point to another, we look with different sequences of anticipation and expectation in mind, e.g., we look down from what seems like a 'nose' region with the expectation of next seeing a 'chin', or, we look down from a seeming 'stem' region to an expected 'base' region of a vase. And to the extent that our expectations are satisfied, we see what is before us *as* a face, or *as* a vase. In other words, the grammar is 'there' in our living relations to our surroundings prior to any linguistic expressions we might apply there, yet due to our choice and judgment in the matter, the grammar in question is still, as Wittgenstein notes above, to an extent arbitrary.

Now to many, this may seem as outrageous a claim as the claim that there is no prior, already fixed and categorized physical reality to which to appeal in adjudicating the worth of our claims to truth. But it has at least the implication that, prior to any of the claims as to the nature of things and events in our surrounding that we might as individuals address to those around us, all such claims must be couched in a certain *shared style*. If they are not, then they will not be properly understood by those to whom they are addressed; they will be confusing or misleading. In other words, although there may be no prior criteria to which to appeal in judging *the truth* of a person's claims – for their truth must be investigated in terms of their entailments – there are criteria immediately available as to *their intelligibility* in the context of their utterance. These criteria arise out of the fact that all the elements involved are mutually determining, interwoven, or inter-related with each other in a certain way, according to a certain style or grammar.

But why should we call this kind of 'mutual determination' chiasmic? In choosing this term, I am following Merleau-Ponty (1968), who called the second to last chapter of his book, *The Visible and Invisible*: *The Intertwining – The Chiasm*. And then I want to add to that, the fact that both he (Merleau-Ponty, 1962, 1968) and Gregory Bateson (1979) take binocular vision as paradigmatic of the special nature of our living relations to our surroundings. To quote Bateson (1979):

> "The binocular image, which appears to be undivided, is in fact a complex synthesis of information from the left front in the right brain and a corresponding synthesis of material from the right front in the left brain... From this elaborate arrangement, two sorts of advantage accrue. The seer is able to improve resolution at edges and contrasts; and better able to read when the print is small or the illumination poor. More important, information about depth is created... In principle, extra "depth" in some metaphoric sense is to be expected whenever the information for the two descriptions is differently collected or differently coded" (pp.68-70).

In other words, much much more is happening here than the mere blending or interweaving of separate constituents which remain identifiably separate even when complexly interwoven. In our looking over a visual scene, in accord with the demands of the scene, *something utterly new and novel is being created* – what earlier I called the 'seeing' of new "relational dimensions," which we can signify by our metaphorical talk of depth.

Indeed, something quite radical is entailed, as we shall see, in the recognition of the fact that our relations to our surroundings are not just simply relations of a causal kind, nor of a systematic, logical or rational kind either, but are *living*, dynamic relations. In fact, although it may perhaps seem surprising to say it, I don't think that we have made a proper attempt at all – in either our ways of thinking and talking, or in our institutional ways of relating ourselves practically to the others and othernesses in our surroundings – to acknowledge the fact of our *livingness*, and the fact that we live in surroundings that are *also living*. We still simply pre-suppose a non-living world of earth and rocks, of oceans and gases, to which we must simply adapt or die, a world which is just 'there' independently of our living participation within it, and to which we relate, officially, in only a dead, mechanical way.

The nearest we have got to taking life and living being seriously, is in our concern with "cognitive psychology" and a "philosophy of mind." But even here, as you now all well know, we have assimilated our "mental lives" to the activity of digital computers, of dead mechanisms. While extremely clever and ingenious, however, this work is far from convincing. Most of us, despite the vehemence of the arguments presented to us, still feel far from spontaneously compelled, on entering our places of work in the morning, to greet our computers as we greet our colleagues – certain *responsive and expressive qualities* still seem to be lacking *in the movements* of their 'bodies'. It makes no sense at all to talk in this responsive and expressive way of computers as having bodies at all.

Living expression: a new vocabulary of terms

As I noted in chapter 3, in discussing the use of intellectually fashioned, experience-distant, practical-descriptive theoretical talk to illuminate spontaneously occurring, experience near talk, I listed a whole 'tool-box' of such possible useful terms. Here, I want to continue that process.

In everything that I have to say here I want, either explicitly or implicitly, to assume the *spontaneous, living, expressive-responsiveness of our bodies*, i.e., our ability to immediately and directly affect or 'move' the others around us, bodily in a meaningful fashion, and to be affected by them in the same fashion. And we can immediately note here, the *chiasmicly organized nature* of the expressive-responsiveness of our bodies: for example, as I speak, you can see my body moving in synchrony with my voicing of my utterances, my hands in synchrony with my intoning of my words, my eye movements with my pauses, and my facial expressions with certain of my linguistic emphases – I shall use the word 'orchestration' to denote the unfolding structuring of these intricately timed, creative intertwinings and inweavings of the many inter-related participant parts or 'bodily strands' of our responsive-expressions.

1. Orchestration: But this term 'orchestration' – the attempt to capture in a form of words the whole notion of the chiasmicly organized, *expressive-*

responsiveness of our bodily movements – is just one of the new expressions we will find we need as we begin, seriously, to focus on life and on the activities of living beings. Indeed, I shall want to introduce to you a whole raft of radically new expressions to do with the nature of living responsive expressiveness.

2. Physionomic expressive: Straightaway, let me add another: Instead of the kind of movements or changes we are used to – in which a set of separate elements of reality take up a sequence of different instantaneous configurations or positions in pace at different instants or moments of time – we must recognize the existence of self-sustaining, living unities, enduring through time. Such unities, rather than undergoing changes of place or position in space, exhibit expressive or *physiognomic* changes, dynamic changes within the boundaries of their growing and developing, self-sustaining bodies, short-term changes (as in facial expressions and bodily gestures) as well as long-term one's in overall *style* which, as we will discover, are *expressive* in some way of events of importance their life. Indeed, although such physiognomic events are bodily events occurring out in the world observable to all, it is events of this *physiognomic expressive* kind that we take as indicative of a living being's 'inner' or 'mental' life.

3. Chiasmicly-organized meetings: But, to return once again to what seems to me to be the most unusual concern I want to introduce here: the importance of what occurs in the meetings between two of more individual forms of life, and the chiasmic organization of such meetings. For the complex, dynamically intertwined character of the living unities to which they give rise, cannot (as we shall see) be wholly captured in subjective nor in objective terms; neither are they wholly orderly nor wholly disorderly; nor need they in fact be constituted wholly from living components but may incorporate dead and inert parts in certain regions too.

Indeed, as Merleau-Ponty (1968) notes with respect to the nature of our chiasmicly organized perception of our surroundings, that: "Since the same body sees and touches, visible and tangible belong to the same world. It is a marvel too little noticed that every movement of my eyes – even more, every displacement of my body – has its place in the same visible universe that I itemize and explore with them, as, conversely, every vision takes place somewhere in the tactile space. There is double and crossed situating of the visible in the tangible and of the tangible in the visible; the two maps are complete, and yet they do not merge into one. The two parts are total parts and yet are not superposable" (p.134). Their relations to each other must be played out dynamically, over time.

In other words, to repeat the point made above, that the complex dynamic realities which here we are calling chiasmicly organized, are not constituted from causally related parts, nor from any rationally related parts either, nor are they formed by an kind of mixing or blending or averaging we can imagine. The concept of chiasmic relations thus introduces a uniquely novel quality into our thinking of a previously unencountered kind.

Indeed, in this vein, Merleau-Ponty (1968) draws our attention to what he calls *reversibility*, the fact that, as we noted above, that we can only 'see' what the scene before us *affords* us; thus we must look over it *in accord with* what *it requires of us* if we are to focus on it clearly and to 'look over' all its details. Thus we must note "that he who sees cannot possess the visible unless he is possessed by it, unless he *is of it*, unless, by principle, according to what is required by the articulation of the look with the things, he is one of the vesicles, capable, by a singular reversal, of seeing them – he who is one of them" (Merleau-Ponty, 1968, p.135). Thus it is, that a new *style* of painting, say, can teach us a new way of looking, a new way of orienting, toward paintings.

Later (in Chapter 9), I will outline the full-blown distinction that can be drawn between what we might call *withness*-thinking, *withness*-looking, *withness*-talking, *withness*-valuing, and so on – in which one is "possessed" by an otherness in one's actions – and with *aboutness*-thinking, in which one assimilates all othernesses to already possessed schematisms or frameworks.

4. Primordial unities: For these reasons, such living unities are best called *primordial*, not in the sense of being old or being located in the distant past, far from it, but in the sense of being the more richly intertwined origins or sources from out of which we can differentiate our more focal concerns (our concerns with language and speech, for instance) – while at the same time also attending to the developing web or network of chiasmically intertwined relations, usually ignored in the background, within which our focal concerns actually have their being.

5. New starting points or points of departure: We can also call such meetings *primordial* in the sense that they are the basic units, the starting points, the living contexts within which we can situate everything that we take to be of importance to us in our inquiries below.

This claim has resonances for me with Wittgenstein's (1980) claim, already mentioned above, that "the origin and primitive form of the language game is a reaction" (p.31). Where, as we already noted, what he means by the word "primitive" here, he notes elsewhere, is that "this sort of behavior is *pre-linguistic*: that a language-game is based *on it*, that it is the prototype of a way of thinking and not the result of thought" (Wittgenstein, 1981, no.541).

But this also has resonances also with Merleau-Ponty's (1968) search for a new, non-metaphysical starting point for philosophical inquiry: "If it is true," he says, "that as soon as philosophy declares itself to be reflection or coincidence it prejudges what it will find, then once again it must recommence everything, reject the instruments reflection and intuition had provided themselves, and install itself in a locus where they have not yet been distinguished, in experiences that have not yet been 'worked over', that offer us all at once, pell-mell, both 'subject' and 'object', both existence and essence, and hence give philosophy resources to redefine them" (p.131). Indeed, as we continue, we shall find that many of our central, taken-for-granted concepts – especially those of space, time, matter, and motion (Capek, 1961) – will need re-consideration. All these issues and more are relevant to the discussion of the new realm of inquiry – to do with life and living beings – being introduced here.

The 'move' to an orchestrated, indivisible world of 'invisible presences'

As we saw earlier, in the currently taken-for-granted world we have inherited from Descartes, we assume everything of importance to us arises out of the orderly motions of a *limited* set of particles of matter moving according to (God's) pre-established laws. Such a world is both lifeless place(as matter cannot be created *ex nihilo*), and, because it is possible for such a limited amount of matter to reappear in the same configuration – to repeat itself, so to speak – it is also a timeless place. Indeed, in such a world, as Laplace (1886) realized, an intellect that was vast enough, could, by knowing the position and velocities of all these basic particles, "embrace in the same formula the motions of the greatest bodies in the universe and those of the slightest atoms; [and as result] nothing would be uncertain for it, and the future, like the past, would be present to its eyes." In such a world as this, all change would only be of a quantitative nature, changes of configuration; there can be no qualitative changes, no creation of novelty, no unique, first-time occurrences, no events which could, like works of art, have their unique meaning *in themselves* (see Wittgenstein, 1980, p.58, quoted above)

Here, then, we have a basic set of concepts – of space and time, and of matter and motion – in terms of which we in fact conduct almost all our daily enterprises. This the *picture* currently holding us captive, for this is what lies in our language and what we repeat to ourselves inexorably, in our ordinary daily activities, in our institutional and administrative practices, and in our intellectual inquiries. Indeed, it is a picture of the world *as a picture* (a 'pointillist' picture, in fact) – "we are indicating by the very choice of the word its most significant feature: its *pictorial* character" (Capek, 1961)[57].

Indeed, we can now see why those versions of social constructionism which either still leave this Cartesian picture unquestioned in place, or in fact still make use of it maintaining that things can be totally re-constructed as one pleases, raise so much anxiety over their deconstruction of everything that seems fixed and solid within it. For a background that has been decomposed into "a chaos as disordered as the poets could ever imagine" (see quotation from Descartes in the New Preface) cannot exert any structured or guiding influence of a shared kind on those immersed in it.

But notice its origins, note Descartes's relation to his surroundings from within which he fashions this 'view': he fashions it as a thinker, as an observer, and as a deliberate, self-conscious actor. He is not *a participant* in any ongoing practical action, concerned to engage with and make himself understood in the action, to the others around him; he never acts spontaneously, in responsive reaction to events occurring around him; he is acting alone, deliberately concerned with being the master and possessor of nature.

Indeed, whatever the movements of those he observed "crossing the square," he is unmoved or untouched by them. Should one of them turn to catch sight of him at his window, how would he react, how would he respond? For, the meeting of people's eyes, our eyes with those of animals... the spontaneous "interplay of gaze and expression" (Sacks, 1985, p.8)... is something very basic in our lives. Spontaneously, we sense ourselves as in contact with more than just a dead body in motion; we have become involved with a being that has a soul, an 'inner life'; and we know straightaway if they have that same attitude toward us. As Goffman (1967) points out, our's and other people's sense of offence is direct and immediate if we feel those around us are not properly honoring their "involvement obligations." "My attitude towards him," says Wittgenstein (1953), "is an attitude towards a soul. I am not of the *opinion* that he has a soul" (p.178).

If we attend, then, to the kind of meeting occurring between Descartes and his surroundings, the relations between them, we find them somewhat distant. The surroundings that concern him are 'over there'; it is an 'external world'; he is not himself *a participant* within it – he is merely thinking of himself as 'viewing' it. Thus in this 'thought-view'[58], space is holds a privileged place, and it is treated as an immutable, unchanging, homogeneous, causally inert, empty 'container', a place in which separate 'particles' of matter may occupy different 'positions'. Time is secondary to space, and often thought of as a fourth, 'spatial' dimension. As such, it too is an empty, neutral, unchanging 'container'. While instants *of* time are differentiated by their succession, time is prior to change: changes occur *in* time. As unchanging containers, both space and time are there for things to happen in them. The only changeable stuff is matter, not within itself, but in its location; it may change its position in space – hence our feeling that what is of central importance for us, are static *structures* – or our linguistic *representations* or our ways of *picturing* such structures in language – in making sense between us of what counts for us as our world.

But let us note again, that this kind of world is not the world that contains us as active *participants* within it, the world in which we, along with the others and othernesses around us, have our being within a dynamic interplay involving us all. It is, to repeat, the world of an individual who has withdrawn himself from such shared participatory involvements, and who has turned himself instead only toward the aims of mastery and possession. Thus for such an individual, this is an 'external world', a world in which time has been 'spatialized' as merely another spatial dimension, i.e. as an already existing dimension of reality in which the future positions of the particles making up a configurations 'await', so to speak, occupation. It is thus 'natural' in such a reality, to think of motion as following a path in space, a space which 'there' both before and after the motion.

But in the dynamic time of life and living, in irreversible time in which things grow and develop, internally articulate and refine themselves, flower, blossom, and reproduce themselves in others of their kind, and then die, in this kind of time, movement and motion cannot simply be a change in position in a pre-existing space. Motion is to do with the creation of novelty; it is *physiognomic*, in that it is an "organic deformation" (Whitehead, 1975, p.160), or "coherent deformation" (Merleau-Ponty, 1964, p.91), i.e., a qualitative change *within* a living whole. And what is special about such living wholes – even such entities as paintings, pieces of music, or written texts – is that just like the other persons around us, they can have *agency*, that is, they can exert an influence on us through their *expressions*; not the direct impact of a physical force, but the kind of influence another can exert on us by, for instance, calling our name, the kind of influence that plays upon our inescapable responsiveness as living beings to events of concern to us occurring in our surroundings. It is in this kind of world in which we live and participate.

The 'agency' of real but invisible presences

But how shall we talk of it, how shall we – not *picture it or view it*, for that again will lead us back into all the difficulties of timelessness we must avoid – but, *express a sense of it* in some way? And what does it mean to say that such a world is populated with *agencies* over an above the individual agencies of the individual people around us? How can something like a text – that seems to be a dead thing in itself – exert an invisible influence upon us? What does it mean to talk of the *real but invisible presences* influencing the *style* of our lives at the moment, to talk, say, of the current 'grammar' of our language, or of what it is like to have to live, currently, in what we might call 'the age of money'?

Well, strangely, there is no shortage of familiar, everyday activities, *which only take place over time*, to which we can refer as paradigms in orienting ourselves as to what is entailed in identifying the nature of *felt understandings*, what it is to have a *shaped and vectored sense* of a circumstance without in fact having a visual or pictorial image of it. But before I turn to an exploration of them, let me influence your orientation toward them by reminding you that they are all instances of the unfolding of a living processes. Thus we should view them with the expectation that they all will exhibit both a *developmental continuity* in their unfolding – such that their earlier phases are indicative of at least the style of what is to come later, and they will also all exhibit what we might call *identity preserving* changes or deformations, such indications of the unitary whole to which they *will ultimately give rise* are already 'there' in their beginnings.

Consider, for instance, the simply activities (1) of listening to a piece of music, (2) of beginning to recite a poem or tell a story, or (3) of another asking a question of us:

(1) To consider first a simple melody unfolding in time: The first point to make, is about its *successive* nature, and the sharp distinction between the *internal relations* involved in the unfolding of a temporal succession and the *external relations* constituting a structure formed by juxtaposing a set of parts in space. As long as its 'movement' continues, the musical expression remains incomplete, yet due to the properties of living expression mentioned above, at each moment we already have an anticipation of what might come next. And as, at each particular moment, a new tone is 'added' (we are tempted to say) to the previous ones, each new moment is in fact constituted – or better, re-constituted – by the *creation* of a new musical *quality*. This is a truly strange process that cannot be represented, cannot be pictured – as Wittgenstein (1980a) remarks, "the work of art does not aim to convey *something else*, just itself" (p.58). While a picture, a spatial array contemplated at any given instant is complete, it is a *static* structure with all its parts are given *at once*, simultaneously. Our experience in listening to a piece of music is very different. In spite of the irreducible individuality of each new tone, its *quality* is 'tinged' or 'colored' by the whole preceding musical context into which its 'strikes', and which in turn, its retroactively changes by contributing to the emergence of a new musical quality, which in turn arouses tensions and expectations which... ? ... and so on.

The 'building' or 'construction' of a musical phrase over time is thus very different from the construction of a structure in space. Even the most complex of 'man-made' systems, machines for instance, are constructed piece by piece from objective parts; that is, from parts which retain their character unchanged irrespective of whether they are parts of the system or not – this is what is meant by saying that they are *static* structures constructed from *externally* related parts. Such structures only have their character when they are complete: we put in the last engine part, switch on, and drive away; any attempt to drive a car before all its parts have been installed is the court disaster. But in something like a piece of music, all its 'participant parts' all have a *living* relation with each other; that is, as we noted above, they constitute a *dynamically* emerging or *growing* structure, a *structurizing structure* one might say. As such, they develop from simple, already living individuals, into richly structured ones – they do not have to wait until they are complete before they can express themselves. They develop in such a way that their 'parts' (if we are still justified in using such a term?) at any one moment in time, owe not just their character but their very existence both to one another *and* to their relations with the 'parts' of the whole at some earlier point in time. In other words, their *history* – i.e., where they have come from and where they have been headed – is just as important as the instantaneous logic, in their growth.

So, in considering again a piece of music, we find that while the individual tones are not externally related units from which the melody is additively built, their individuality is not simply absorbed or dissolved in the undifferentiated unity of the musical whole. Each individual tone matters, makes a difference while being related to the whole. Thus, the musical phrase is a *successively differentiated whole* which, remains a whole in spite of its successive character, and which remains differentiated in spite of its dynamic wholeness. In other words, as a dynamic whole, it resists description in terms of any one *single order of connectedness* – hence my comment above, that we might designate such living wholes as *primordial*, in the sense of being the richly intertwined origins or sources from out of which we can differentiate our more ordered concerns – while at the same time being able to attend to the web of chiasmically intertwined relations within which they have their being.

(2) As we noted earlier, with regard to our utterances, Bakhtin (1981) remarked that: "The word in living conversation is directly, blatantly, oriented toward a future answer-word; it provokes an answer, anticipates it and structures itself in the answer's direction" (p.280). William James (1890) also remarks: "Suppose three successive people say to us: 'Wait!' 'Hark!' 'Look!' Our consciousness is thrown into three quite different attitudes of expectancy, although no definite object is before it in any one of the three cases... The truth is that large tracts of human speech are nothing but *signs of direction* in thought, of which direction we nevertheless have an acutely discriminative sense, though no definite sensorial image plays any part in it whatsoever... [these *signs of direction* in thought] must be described as in large measure constituted of *feelings of tendency*, often so vague that we are unable to name them at all" (pp.250-254). It is, again as Bakhtin (1986) points out, in our actual uttering of our words – in their intoning, pacing, pausing, emphasizing, in the way in which they *responsively gesture* their temporal contouring toward features in the situation of their use – that we can gain a sense of a speaker's *relations* or *positioning* within the circumstances of their talk. With these comments in mind, we can try a little experiment:

(1) With a matter of fact, flat intonation, we can utter the following statement: "The cat sat on the mat. The mat was red, the cat was black" – the expected reaction from listeners: "I get the picture... so what?"

(2) But now, if we intone it with very pregnant pauses and appropriate strong emphases, as follows: "The cat... sat... on the mat... the mat.. was *red*... the cat... was *black*..." – the expected reaction will be very different: the beginning of a ghost story, perhaps, or a detective story?

Clearly, it is in arousing anticipations of the not-yet-said – at first vague and undifferentiated ones, and later, more well differentiated ones – that the two very different ways of intoning these words can arouse two very different transitory understandings of them, two very different ways of 'going on' from them. The first arouses us to say: "OK, I get the picture, but... so what?" – but then an interpretation is needed as to why it has been said at all. While the second is, or can be, directly understood; but it tantalizes us into a suspenseful waiting for what next will come.

A second little experiment: Let us take a few lines from "Little Gidding" in T.S. Eliot's (1944) *Four Quartets*: "What we call the beginning is often the end/ And to make an end is to make a beginning. /The end is where we start from...," (p.47), and try the following three intonings on friends:

> (1) Quick, flat, matter of fact, monotonic intonation: "What we call the beginning is often the end, and to make an end is to make a beginning. The end is where we start from..." [an objectivist/logical positivist reading].... likely to provoke the reaction: "What!? That's garbled nonsense; and surely it's not logical!"
>
> (2) With pregnant pauses and appropriate emphases: "What *we* call the *beginning... is* often the end, and to make an *end... is* to make a beginning. The end *is* where *we* start from..." [a more realist reading].
>
> (3) Again with pregnant pauses but with different emphases: "What we *call* the beginning... is often the *end...*, and to *make* an end... *is to make* a beginning... The end is where we start from..." [a more social constructionist reading].

If I now ask: How can we account for the effects of these different reading on those listening to them? We will very easily experience the temptation to try to *explain* the phenomenon. But that impulse, that felt tendency – to form *theoretical pictures* as in science – leads us to forget the essential difference between the juxtaposition of parts in space, and the unfolding succession of qualities in time, and to reduce the differences between the past, present, and future to simple *differences of position*: with 'past' events being symbolized by positions lying to the left of the point representing the 'present moment' on an already existing 'time line' drawn in space, while 'future' events lie to the right of it. The inadequacy of thinking of time as a fourth dimension of space, at least in relation to the growth and development of living processes, should not be very apparent.

(3) Turning now to a final example, consider now the possible (somewhat over complicated) exam question: "What are the differences between Gergen's and Shotter's versions of social constructionism, considering that Gergen developed his version in an American background in objection to experimental *social* psychology, while Shotter developed his in a British context, not only in objection to the experimental approach in *developmental*

psychology, but also in objection to the whole idea that human behavior could ever be likened to computation and understood in *formal*[59] terms?"

Before attempting to articulate what is involved in our answering such a question, let me introduce a piece of orienting material: George Mead's (1934) claim that: "The mechanism of meaning is present in the social act before the emergence of consciousness or awareness of meaning occurs. The act or adjustive response of the second organism gives to the gesture of the first organism the meaning it has" (pp 77-78). I quote this to make the point, already made by Wittgenstein above, that meaning begins with our spontaneous responsive reactions. Such reactions can be thought of as beginning a sequential process of differentiation, of specification, of making something within a still undifferentiated array of possibilities clear and distinct – while still, of course, embedded within that same array. We can now turn toward what might be involved in our attempts to 'answer' the question.

While we hold the question 'in mind', so to speak, as 'point of orientation' as we try mentally to assemble the landscape within which we are going to attempt to answer it. While not being able to articulate its influence, we keep 'hearing its voice' and 'answering to' its calls. It works as both a provocation and a guide. In the jargon I have been using currently, it provides us with a shaped and vectored sense of the landscape in which we must make our 'moves' if we are to respond to the questioner as he or she already anticipates and expects. For there is in the very asking of the question in those terms a veritable grammar determining what will count as an acceptable answer or not. In other words, prior to us having any clear conscious awareness of events our surroundings exerting specific, describable influences on our conduct, such influences are there (as Mead puts it) "before the emergence of consciousness or awareness of meaning occurs," and we crucially need to take note of this.

This, as we shall see later, is reiterated by Merleau-Ponty (1962) who, in discussing the bodily aspects of our understanding another's expressions, remarks: "There is... a taking up of others' thought through speech, a reflection in others, an ability to think *according to others* which enriches our own thoughts. Here the meaning of words must be finally be induced by the words themselves, or more exactly, their conceptual meaning must be formed by a kind of deduction from a *gestural meaning*, which is immanent in speech. And as, in a foreign country, I begin to understand the meaning of words through their place in the context of action, and by taking part in a communal life – in the same way an as yet imperfectly understood piece of philosophical writing discloses to me at least a certain 'style'... which is the first draft of its meaning. I begin to understand a philosophy by feeling my way into its existential manner, by reproducing the tone and accent of the philosopher... There is thus, either in the man who listens or reads, or in the one who speaks or writes, a *thought in speech* the existence of which is unsuspected by intellectualism" (p.179).

Conclusions

What I have been arguing above, then, is that we need to replace the inert world of separate particles in motion that we inherited from Descartes' philosophy, with a vision of the world around us, one in which the thins and events within are more intrinsically related to each other. I have also been arguing that many previous versions of social constructionism have been nowhere near radical enough. Embedded in the background against which many of the arguments in their support are formulated, unexamined, is this same Cartesianism, to do with: a world of separately existing element (as opposed to a world of intrinsically interrelated 'parts'); a world of difficulties posed as problems (as opposed to difficulties of orientation); a world in which we seek explanations (as opposed to portrayals); and a world in which time is spatialized as space-time (as opposed to being dyanamized as a time-space). As a consequence, although many social constructionists have directed our attention away from supposed events occurring in people's heads and toward events occurring out in the world between them, they have not overcome the idea of our social realities being composed of a limited set of separate "elements of reality." As a result, in many of what I will call *merely linguistic* versions of social constructionism, which fail to emphasize the role of our sponatenously expressed bodily responses to events occurring around us, it seems as if there are no prior connections or relations between the elements that might go into a construction. Hence the relativistic claim that 'anything goes'.

However, if what I have argued above is the case, then there are there shared, foundational, "forms of life" to be found *within the dynamics of our meetings*: Although we can agree that there are no prior justifications to which to appeal for one's claims to worth, to agree that there is no prior shared background structure of feelings of anticipation and tendency – even if that background is one without a long history, but is only created at that moment of meeting when one living being acknowledges the presence of another – would be to agree that there is no shared basis in judgements in terms of which to form agreements at all. And this is clearly not the case.

But, what exactly is the reality in which we live? Like St Augustine, when asked about time, we know perfectly well in our everyday practices what it is, most of the time – else we would spend even more of our time in chaos and confusion than we do – is only when we try to formulate its nature that we run into trouble. From what we have discovered above, we know that it cannot be pictured, i.e., it cannot made up of patterns of static forms that can be visibly put down on a page. But now, due to the recent new understandings of the nature of language provided us by Wittgenstein, Vygotsky, Voloshinov, Bakhtin, Merleau-Ponty, etc, we are coming to grasp the nature of our own, self-generated confusion here. We are now coming to realize, for instance, that as soon as we shift our attention in our study of language from our actual experience of "words in their speaking" to the *patterns* of "already spoken words," i.e., to the static shapes and forms we put down on a page – that is, from the living movement of a temporally developing whole to its static, *pictorial representation* – such self-generated confusion is inevitable. Disciplined to think logically, in terms of static forms and patterns, to think that geometry and arithmetic and other forms of calculation are the only properly disciplined modes of thought, we have given ourselves over to the authority of single, hierarchically structured forms of disengaged thought. And it is this that has disconnected us from the activities that give our words their life.

Here, however, I have begun to explore what is involved in re-disciplining ourselves to think in a different, engaged, fashion – in a way which follows the contours, so to speak, of the shaped and vectored sense one has of the particular situations in which one might find oneself embedded *in one's meetings with others*. So I would like to end this chapter with summary accounts of three issues of importance:

Dynamic chiasmically-organized wholes: Like any dynamic whole, the *reality* created within such meetings will exhibit a synthesis of unity and multiplicity, of continuity and discontinuity; but it cannot be the unity of an undifferentiated, instantaneous spatial whole, nor can it be a plurality of merely juxtaposed units. Further, although is has continuity, it lacks continuity in the mathematical sense of infinite divisibility (for many of the phenomena important to us are only realized over a certain period of time), but it certainly doesn't have the discontinuity of self-contained, rigid, atomic particles. Its continuity is of a chronotopic kind, of a time-space kind, but quite what that *is* remains, perhaps, open to further articulation – in other words, I cannot claim here by any means to have given a definitive account of chaismically organized realities.

Languaged realities: The positive significance of our "turn to language" in social constructionism, is not just in the way in which it has released us from the need to give prior (foundational) justifications for all our claims, but for the ways in which it has begun to orient us toward our experience of *word use*, and in particular, toward our detailed sensing of the temporally unfolding experience of the *chiasmic* interweaving of our voicing of our words in with the events occurring at the moment of their voicing. This has led some of us to completely distance ourselves from abstract theorizing, and to turn to the task of trying to sense and to portray (metaphorically) in words, the *nonvisual dynamical patterns* actually occurring with us as we speak and listen. Thus, rather than merely gaining a sense of that reality over there from a set of pictures that we might view in an art galley without ever going out into the actual world at large, the *nonvisual dynamical patterns* that we can come to embody, in following Wittgenstein's methods (see the next chapter), can help us in actual fact to come to be more 'at home' in our own human world.

Living, embodied, expressive-responsiveness: we must not ignore the *spontaneous, living, expressive-responsiveness of our bodies*, i.e., our ability to immediately and directly affect or 'move' the others around us, bodily in a meaningful fashion, and to be affected by them in the same fashion. Our living, bodily embedding in this previously unnoticed background, and the ways in which it both 'calls out' expressive-responses from us while utterly 'disallowing' or 'repulsing' others, has been too much ignored in all our approaches in Social Theory, social constructionism included. As I noted above, it is the *chiasmicly organized nature* of the spontaneous, expressive-responsiveness of our living bodies that is the 'background glue' holding us together in all our relationships. And it is the 'orchestration' of these intricately timed, creative intertwinings and inweavings of the many inter-related 'strands' of our responsive-expressions that we must study – for its 'in' their interweavings that we can find the new openings, the new possibilities we need to discover, if we are the develop our relational abilities further.

Chapter Five

LIVING IN A WITTGENSTEINIAN WORLD: BEYOND THEORY TO A POETICS OF PRACTICES[60]

> "Only in the stream of thought and life do words have meaning" (1981, no.173)[61].

> "You really could call it [i.e., a work of art], not exactly the expression of a feeling, but at least the expression of feeling, or felt expression. And you could say too that in so far as people understand it, they resonate in harmony with it, respond to it. You might say: the work of art does not aim to convey *something else*, just itself" (Wittgenstein, 1980a, p.58).

> "Our disease is one of wanting to explain" (Wittgenstein, 1978, p.333).

> "... all categories and methods of traditional stylistics remain incapable of dealing effectively with the artistic uniqueness of discourse in the novel, or with the specific life that discourse leads in the novel... This dilemma, however, is by no means universally recognized. Most scholars are not inclined to undertake a radical revision of the fundamental philosophical conception of poetic discourse" (Bakhtin, 1981, p.267).

> "... philosophy ought only to be written as a *poetic composition*" (1980, p.24).

In this chapter, in line with the theme that everything in our practical, everyday, social activities is always being done for yet another first time, I want to explore a number of new methods for coming to an understanding of how we conduct our practical activities, methods that are displayed in Wittgenstein's later works (1953, 1966, 1969, 1980a, 1980b, 1981) but not always made completely explicit, for many of his methods simply reside in his *style* of writing[62].

For us as modern, professional, social theorists, used to taking people's *experiences* (in the form of inner, mental representations in the heads of individuals) as our touchstone, these methods will seem very unusual, for rather than our experiences they have our *practices* as their central focus. As ordinary people, however, primarily concerned with getting on with the practicalities of our lives, they should not be at all strange. Indeed, many of them have their provenance in our everyday, mundane ways of making sense to each other. For instance, as Wittgenstein says in one of his earlier works, "one thing we [i.e., LW] always do when discussing a word is to ask how we were taught it" (1966, p.1), a move that leads us to focus "on the enormously complicated situation in which [an] expression has a place" (1966, p.2) – and to realize that the influence of the situation is so great that "the expression itself has an almost negligible place" (1966, p.2). In our intellectual talk about ourselves, we are unused to paying much attention to the moment by moment changing circumstances surrounding our talk; usually, they pass us by unremarked. Thus his methods offer us individualistic, scientistic, and mechanistically inclined theorists – obsessed with static, objective, systems of knowledge, and factual information, fixed patterns and regularities – something radically different: ways of grasping our continuously changing sense of living relatedness, both to each other, and to the larger world around us.

Our modern, intellectualistic and individualistic notions of understanding leave these unique relations-in-motion, occurring always for *another first time*, unnoticed in the background to our activities. And currently, we lack the conceptual resources required to acknowledge not only their fleeting, changeable nature and enormous complexity, but also their strange *dialogical* nature: which ensures that everything we do in practice, in being a response to an other or otherness in our surroundings, inevitably relates us to them in some way. It is our embodied embedding in this whole flow of temporally irreversible relational activity, that we must in some way in social theory now characterize[63].

Wittgenstein's works can, I think, provide us with some of the new intellectual resources we require to gain a grasp of the meaning of these fleeting, changeable relations. But how can we open ourselves up to them? How might we come to a grasp of *their* meaning, their meaning for us in our practices[64]? For they are not easy to read or to understand. They are written as a sequence of numbered remarks, not always apparently connected with each other. They point or gesture toward ends that are somewhat alien to our current preoccupations. Unlike our current academic texts, they do not seem to consist in a coherent narrative or argument; neither do they seem to be 'about' anything, nor to be concerned with discovering anything hidden; nor do they offer us any theories or other claims amenable to evaluation in terms of truth or falsity, or error or correctness. Indeed, he often ridicules 'official' forms of philosophical talk. For instance in *On Certainty* (1969) he imagines the following little vignette: "I am sitting with a philosopher in the garden; he says again and again 'I know that that's a tree', pointing to a tree that is near us. Someone else arrives and hears this, and I tell him: 'This fellow isn't insane. We are only doing philosophy'" (no.467).

To counter what he saw as a misuse of language – in which we do not use our talk to any practical purpose, but puzzle in a reflective, disengaged way over our *experience* of a word's meaning, in itself[65], while unrelated to any particular context of use – he turned to more everyday forms of talk, which, although seemingly much more vague, are not in themselves an abuse of language. He turned to what we might call directive, instructive, and specificatory forms of talk, as well as to more poetic forms, to what we might call a more practical, *gestural* use of words: to the use of striking similes, to utterances that call out particular responses from us, to expressions that produce in us what might be called 'arresting moments'. Where the point of his words, is to direct our attention to something as yet unnoticed, to *point* toward something actually present in our surroundings at the moment of their use. In effect they say: "Look at *this*," "Look at *that*," "Notice those *details* or these *differences*," "Notice these *relations* or *connections* between these details."

Methodically, their function is, as he says, to give "prominence to distinctions which our ordinary forms of language easily make us overlook" (1953, no.132), and to change our "*way of looking at things*" (1953, no.144) – to influence of *styles* of looking and thinking, speaking and listening, reading, touching, remembering, and so on, and the ways in which we inter-sequence them. Thus, in his use of these methods, he is not concerned "to hunt out new facts; it is, rather, of the essence of our investigation that... we want to *understand* something that is already in plain view. For *this* is what we seem in some sense not to understand" (1953, no.89). And, although his aim in his investigations is to leave "everything as it is" (1953, no.124), they are not directed simply toward the articulation of the existing *status quo*; they are directed, "not towards phenomena, but, as one might say, towards the '*possibilities*' of phenomena" (1953, no.90). That is, he wants to see what else there is at work, or can be at work, within our talk entwined activities, that we have so far failed to see – because often, our picture of meaning as a mechanical or logical sequence of inner experiences has stood in the way of us seeing how we actually do use our words in practice (cf. 1953, no.305).

While his aim in all of this, is to produce in us "just that understanding which consists in 'seeing connections'" (1953, no.122), that is, to enable us to notice the links and relations between our talk and the rest of our activities (and their surroundings) that so far, in our practices, we have failed to notice, this is not to say that nothing new can come of his investigations. Indeed, as we have seen, it is in the very dialogical nature of our everyday communications that something new is always created, and it is the aim of his investigations to bring thta to light.

But, as we have already seen, the function of his expressions is not epistemological but ontological; they seek to change us not in our intellects but in our wills, in how we relate ourselves both to events occurring around us, as well as to those occurring within us. He is not interested in changing our theories, or in providing us with any new knowledge, but in changing our sensibilities and sensitivities, in changing us in our very being[66]. Indeed, as I see it (though I'm sure that here he would disagree), it is the politics of our identities as social theorists that is at the very heart of his (and our) "struggl[es] with language" (1980, p.11) – for as the communal thing it is, it makes it very difficult for individuals to express as yet unnoticed, unique details. Yet, if Wittgenstein is right, we cannot change ourselves simply by 'putting a general theory into practice', for all our general theories must draw for their intelligibility upon already agreed categories and typifications. It is only by a re-ordering our practical relations to the others and othernesses around us, i.e., by developing new practices, that we can change ourselves – and this is not often easy to do.

Thus Wittgenstein's philosophy has, I think, radical implications for the part social theorists might play in changing both their own social practices, and in helping to develop new practices in our culture at large – and I shall return to this issue toward the end of this essay. Let me now turn, however, to the task of trying to understand how his writings might originate new forms of life, new practices in us professional academics.

The origin of new language-games in our spontaneously responsive gestures and reactions

If we are to be changed by Wittgenstein's writings, in what way should we be sensitive to his striking phrases and arresting moments, to his poetic ways of talking? For he talks about language as a 'game', as an 'ancient city', as a 'toolbox', of words as being like the levers in 'the cabin of a locomotive', and so on, without any specificity as to which game, city, toolbox, or locomotive cab he means. How can such vague, confusing talk, 'coming out of the blue', outside the confines of any obvious language game, without any clear understanding of what it represents or to what it refers, making no use of any particular paradigms, or rules, or other schemes or frameworks, be of any help to us at all? What is the character of such talk and writing? And what is, or should be, the nature of our responses to it?

It will be useful at this point to remind ourselves of the practical nature of some of Wittgenstein's central themes, the nature, that is, of his world: He is not primarily concerned with anything mysterious going on inside our heads, but simply with us being able to 'go on' with each other in practice, with us being able (we say) to sensibly 'follow' each other – although, as we have seen, it is more a matter of our being able to 'anticipate' each other, if we are to intertwine our activities in with those of others. And in doing this, we act spontaneously, bodily; our being able to do it is not a matter of thought or calculation, it is something that we need to be "trained" in (Wittgenstein, 1953, no.5).

As he sees it, "language did not emerge from some kind of ratiocination" (1969, no.475). "The origin and primitive form of the language game is a reaction; only from this can more complicated forms develop. Language – I want to say – is a refinement, 'in the beginning was the deed'[57]" he says (1980, p.31). Thus, new language-games can begin anytime, anywhere. For example: "'At these words *he* occurred to me'. – What is the primitive reaction with which the language-game begins – which can then be translated into these words?," he asks. "The primitive reaction may have been a glance or a gesture, but it may also have been a word" (1953, p.218). On some occasions, the mere flicker of an eyebrow at an appropriate moment is all that is needed to 'speak volumes'.

It is in this connection that we can, perhaps, appreciate the point of his striking phrases, similes, analogies, and so on. For, as he remarks: "Not only rules, but also examples are needed for establishing a practice. Our rules leave loop-holes open, and the practice has to speak for itself" (1969, no.139). And it is a new practice of image guided thinking – of thinking *with*, or *through*, or *oriented by* the expectations and anticipations aroused in us through thinking, looking, and acting *with* certain quite particular dynamic images in mind (I will discuss the special nature of what I will call 'withness'-thinking, to distinguish it from the 'aboutness'-thinking with which we are much more familiar, in Chapter 9 below).

Here, with respect to the situated nature of meaning in practice, it is worth noting at this point, the resonance of Wittgenstein's notions with those of George Herbert Mead. After commenting on the power of a gesture on the part of one organism always to call out related responses in the other organisms around it, Mead (1934) goes on to remark: "The mechanism of meaning is... present in the social act before the emergence of consciousness or awareness of meaning occurs. The act or adjustive response of the second organism gives to the gesture of the first organism the meaning it has" (pp.77-78). That is, the gestural aspect of a person's deeds is important in that, given their emergent nature, others can always to an extent anticipate how someone will go on in relation to what they have already done, and react and respond accordingly. So, although it is necessary to refer to certain pre-established standards of rightness and wrongness in judging one's own actions as one performs them, it is unnecessary to refer to any pre-established standards of appropriateness to the immediate circumstance – criteria of appropriateness emerge in and through our practices themselves as we perform them. It is in terms of the anticipations and expectations that our actions spontaneously generate in the others around us, and the way that they point beyond, or outside, themselves to connect with our surroundings, that our gestures have their appropriateness to our practical lives[68].

People's gestures, however, are open and vague; their use requires further working out if we are to follow their meaning precisely. Some – like us pointing a finger – carry with them immediate commitments. We expect those to whom we point out something, to respond by looking in the appropriate direction, while they expect us to go on to say or do something with respect to it. We don't expect them just look at the end of our finger expectantly. Such a practice is a normative practice, a custom into which we have been trained. Other gestures and gestural meanings, however, are much less conventional and much more momentary and vague, and can thus at first be easily misunderstood. Their meaning will depend both on their precise momentary placement in a flow of activity, and on what one says or does subsequently. For example: "If you say 'As I heard this word, it meant... for me' you refer *to a point in time* and *to an employment of the word.* – The remarkable thing about it of course is the relation to the point in time... And if you say 'I was wanting to go on...' – you refer to a *point of time* and to *an action*" (1980a, I, nos 175, 176). And such momentary, spontaneous meanings are worked out, in terms of one's subsequent doings and sayings, as one goes along. Indeed, as all teachers at the blackboard know, one writes up a concept at the beginning of a class, and continually interweaves gestures toward it as one develops its meaning in one's further talk – even after having rubbed it out and written something else in its place!

It is this emphasis on the gestural aspect of our social practices, and upon the poetic nature of utterances that can 'strike' or 'arrest' us, and can thus create momentary spaces of possibility for their change, that makes Wittgenstein's stance toward our understanding of our own behavior (and our talk of things) so distinctive... strange even! For he is not so much concerned with us seeing the supposedly true nature of what something *is*, contemplatively, as with attempting to articulate how in fact, moment by moment, we conduct our practical, everyday affairs. Their strangeness arises out of the simple fact that, in responding to the gestures of others, one's replies are never wholly one's own; they are always, to an extent, 'shaped' by being spontaneous, situated 'answers' to *their* 'calls'. Thus what any one individual is doing is a part of what of what a 'we' is doing. Such joint activities have a dialogical or mixed character to them. In such circumstances, outcomes cannot be attributed to the desires or plans of any of the individuals involved, neither can they be attributed to any outside agencies. It is as if the particular situation itself were a third agency in the exchange with 'its' own unique requirements, a *superaddressee* in Bakhtin's (1986, p.126) sense (see Shotter, 1980, 1993a and b, 1995, for further discussions of the strange nature of joint action).

Thus, there is an aspect of the emerging *relations* between ourselves and our surroundings, that is an entirely unique, novel, unforeseeable, and spontaneous creation; and in the movement of these changing relations, we *show* our relations to our individual circumstances – that is, we point or gesture toward them. At the same time, however, there ought to be another dimension to our activities, one in which, if others look back on our activities when complete and challenge us to account them, we should be able to show how their relation to the form of life in which we are currently involved. We might call these, the *essential* references of an utterance. Where, says Wittgenstein (1980a, I): "If I speak of the essential *references* of the utterance, that is because this pushes the inessential special expressions of our language into the background" (no.177), when it is just these inessential special expressions that he wants to bring to our attention[69].

Wittgenstein's world: 'Now I can go on'

In his pursuit of his interest in the more practical aspects of our daily activities, then, Wittgenstein is focally interested in our words in their speaking, and in the many different (practical) roles such voicings might play at different moments in these activities as we live out of our lives. He wants to be able to 'see' the whole range of possible relations and connections they might in fact have (or 'point toward') with all the other events occurring around them, as they occur. Aware that we "tend to predicate of the thing what lies in the method of representing it" (1953, no.104) – that we tend to see the world just as much through our words as through our eyes – he wants divert us from describing our practical activities as we *think* they *must* be, when we look back on them in reflective thought. Patterns of already spoken words, what is said, is quite different from what is shown in our speakings. And this is what he wants to show us through his 'poetic' remarks; he wants to draw our attention to "observations which no one has doubted, but which have escaped remark only because they are always before our eyes" (1953, no.415). He wants to move us as social theorists, not simply into a new position to get a new perspective on the everyday activities of our lives, but to 'seeing' them from within a new form of life, a new way of living. One that will enable us to see what our talk entwined practices look like in the ongoing flow of their practice, rather than retrospectively, in theory.

This, I think, is the reality that we are failing to see, the reality right in front of our eyes, everyday: the details of what is involved in us living out our daily lives *in practice*. It is *this* that we do not know how to see for what it is, without continually distorting it, without continually telling ourselves that it *must* have this of that kind of special nature to it, a nature that we feel must be captured reflectively, within an orderly, explanatory theory. Thus a part of Wittgenstein's philosophy, is to do with trying to help us overcome this urge to theorize, to turn to the way of theory, whenever we find ourselves faced with questions as to why we act as we do. To this end, he tries to re-describe the *detailed* practicalities of many topics and events, that *we* might be tempted to put into theoretical terms, i.e., to *mis*-describe in *general* terms.

For instance, he attempts to draw our attention to the practical nature of even philosophical problems, to repeat: "A philosophical problem has the form," he says, "I don't know my way about" (1953, no.154). Or, concerning the *understanding* of mathematical formulae, he suggests, "try not to think of understanding as a 'mental process' at all... But ask yourself: in what sort of case, in what kind of circumstances, do we say, 'Now I know how to go on'..." (1953, no.154). Indeed, in practice, "understanding is like knowing how to go on, and so is an ability: but 'I understand', like 'I can go on' is an *utterance*, a *signal*" (1980, I, no.875); for, in practice, such utterances indicate to those to whom I address them, something of my changed relation to both my own circumstances, and to them. In other words, as he sees it, our talk of 'understanding' is not simply, if at all, related to events occurring inside a person's head; but for us, "it is the *circumstances* under which he had such an experience that justify him in saying... that he understands, that he knows how to go on" (1953, no.155).

Thus, in his much more practical view of our everyday world and our activities within it – although it may seem very strange to say it – he is not necessarily concerned with us 'understanding' each other in the sense of us sharing any 'ideas', nor with us 'communicating' in the sense of sending each other any clear messages, nor with us discovering the 'true' nature of our surrounding circumstances, nor with us necessarily doing anything in particular, let alone any single thing or principle that is basic to us being human[70]. His primary concern, is with us being able to 'go on' with each other (1953, nos.146-155), with us being able merely to make 'followable', 'responsible', or 'answerable' sense to each other – simply reacting or responding in ways that makes it possible for us to continue our relationships in accountable ways is sufficient for him.

To send messages; to fully understand each other; to routinely and skillfully discourse upon a subject matter; to be able to 'reach out', so to speak, from within a form of life and talk about the 'contacts' one has made, and to formulate 'theories' as to the nature of what is 'out there'; all these abilities are, or can be, later developments in one's communicative activities. Indeed, as we saw in the Introduction, it is in terms of the each speaker's anticipations of each listener's responses that they will find each other's responses satisfactory, or not, and to the extent that they do, they are able to develop *their* meaning of *their* exchange amongst themselves in their own terms (see Garfinkel, 2004, p.134, quoted in the Introduction to this book). Being able to 'go on' with someone in this way is thus not trivial; it means that the terms in which are an exchange is being conducted *belong* to all concerned, and that the meanings of others, outsiders to the exchange, are being imposed on them[71]. (In Chapter 9 I discuss Roger Lowe's and Jaakko Seikkula's accounts of why, in psychotherapy, it seems to be better to 'go on' in this way, than to impose outside frameworks in therapeutic exchnages.)

Thus, as I see it, Wittgenstein's prime concern is to explore the nature of these liminal, interhuman 'worlds', these 'primordial', pre-ordinary, pre-intellectual, gestural responses and reactions that make it possible for us simply to 'follow' or to 'grasp' the sensible 'tendencies' in each other's conduct; to study the circumstances in which we can 'go on' with each other *in practice*, thus to socially construct our new forms of life[72]. Indeed, as he sees it, our ways of 'going on' with each other in a sensibly 'followable', i.e., anticipatory, way are foundational because, it is in doing so that we can achieve all the other things we think of as being important to us – including, to repeat, the constructing of *theories* in terms of which we claim to be able to *explain* the nature of the things around us. But, if we are to follow Wittgenstein, upon what should we 'focus' in our studies? 'Where' might we view such 'spaces of possibility'? What should be the *site* of our investigations?' And what *methods* might be available to us, in such investigations? I will explore these two questions in the next two sections respectively.

From within our forms of life

Instead of turning immediately, as we have in the past, to a study of how individuals come to know the objects and entities in the world around them, we must begin in a quite different way: we must study how, by interweaving our talk in with our other actions and activities, we can first develop and sustain between us, different, particular *ways* of relating ourselves to each other. That is, that we should first study how we construct what Wittgenstein calls our different shared *forms of life* with their associated *language-games* – where "the term 'language-*game*'," he says, "is meant to bring into prominence the fact that the *speaking* of language is part of an activity, or a form of life" (1953, no.23). And then, once we have a grasp of the general character of our (normative) relations both with each other and to our surroundings – a grasp of their logical grammar, i.e., a grasp of the inevitably, spontaneous expectations generated in us by the use, the utterance, of the words in question – should we turn to a study of how, as distinct individuals, we can 'reach out' *from within* these forms of life, so to speak, to make the myriad different kinds of contact with our surroundings *through* the various ways of making sense of such contacts, our forms of life provide. Where some of the contacts we make, perhaps, can elicit new or previously unnoticed reactions and responses from us, to function as the origins of entirely new language games[73]. And it is these fleeting, often unremarked responses that occur in the momentary gaps between people as they react to each other – from within an established form of life – that must become the primary focus for our studies here, for it is in these reactions that people reveal to each other, what *their world* (their 'inner life') is like for them; and can also, perhaps, initiate a new practice.

In centering our studies in such moments, however, we must note a couple of simple but crucial points: (1) The first is, that although all our talk of ourselves and our language – that we have 'minds', that we 'think in our heads', that 'words stand for things', that we can 'explain' occurrences 'in the world' in terms of 'theories', and so on – can only make clear and intelligible sense, routinely, *from within* the confines of a language-game. This does not mean that language itself is unusable outside of a language game. Far from it. It simply means that all such talk is, by its very nature, initially, of indeterminate meaning, open to determination only in the context of its use; its meaning must be developed in relation to the person's subsequent doings and sayings. (2) The second is, as we have already noted, our speakings are only a part (sometimes almost an almost negligible part) of a larger activity; that is, "our talk gets its meaning from the rest of our proceedings" (1969, no.229). Thus, in our practical usage of words, they often draw their influence very little from our saying of the words, in themselves, so to speak, but from our use of them at *crucial moments*, to make crucial differences, in the larger flow of activity within which we are involved. Both these points will be important below in appreciating the nontheoretical, practical nature of Wittgenstein's methods.

Why do I say nontheoretical? Because, as we have already seen, for him, theories are both *beside the point* and *after the fact*: beside the point, because, in orienting us toward regularities, they divert our attention away from those fleeting moments in which we have the chance of noting new reactions in ourselves, previously unnoticed; and after the fact, in that if our aim is to understand what has not as yet happened, what is being anticipated, we cannot find it in what has already happened. The general nature of a theoretical picture "stands in the way of us seeing the use of [a] word as it is" (1953, no.305). Indeed, as he sees it, it is the very insistence on the classical search for an order hidden behind or beyond appearances, and our belief that we ought to *convince* others of the *truth* of our claims by systematic argument, that deflects or precludes us coming to a grasp of what is utterly unique and novel *in* the moment by moment emergence of appearances (our voicings) as they unfold before our very eyes (or, better, in our ears) in particular practical circumstances.

But what, exactly, is his problem with these particular moment by moment 'movements' of thought and language? What can he tell us about them that we do not already know? For although we are seeking a better understanding our everyday activities, in one sense – a spontaneous practical sense – this does not seem to be our problem at all: for we already seem to understand them perfectly well -- we have no trouble, for instance, in following the moment by moment changes in people's tones of voice and sensing whether in those changes, they are being unfriendly, imperious, hesitant, or inviting; or in recognizing the moments of struggle and uncertainty both in ourselves (and others) before we reply. Indeed, such delays almost always indicate to us people's reluctance to tell us of something. Yet, for all our everyday, social discretion, prudence, and judgment, we have a nagging feeling that something still eludes us.

So, what kind of understanding are we seeking here? In this connection, it will be useful to remind ourselves again: (1) of the 'gestural' nature of our practical, embodied understandings; (2) of our concern with the tensions, the struggles, and the ambiguities at work in such gaps; (3) of the possibility of constructing other than already existing relations from the resources available in such 'gaps'; and (4) of our concern with how, in the making of such new connections and relations, we are projecting various, possibly new, forms of life. Where, what Wittgenstein draws to our attention in his remarks, strangely, is that to gain *this* practical kind of understanding, we can make use of the very same methods we use in gaining that practical kind of understanding in the first place – that is, he can use the self-same methods for drawing *our* attention to how people draw each other's attention to things, as they themselves (we all?) in fact use!

This, then, gives us a first clue to Wittgenstein's methods. For, although they are as many and as various as those we use in life itself, they are all related in that they work in just the same way as our 'directive', 'instructive', and 'organizational' forms of talk in everyday life work[74]. For example, we 'give commands' ("Do this," "Don't do that"); we 'point things out' to people ("Look at this!"); 'remind' them ("Think what happened last time"); 'change their perspective' ("Look at it like this"); 'place' or 'give order' to their experience ("You were very cool... you acted like a madman); 'organize' their behavior ("First, take a right, then... ask again..."); and so on. All these *instructive* forms of talk 'move' us, in practice, to do something we would not otherwise do: in 'gesturing' or 'pointing' toward something in our circumstances, they cause us to relate ourselves to our circumstances in a different way – as if we are continually being 'educated' into new ways. Indeed, as we have already seen, as one of his methods, he asks how we were first taught our words. For, among other things, such a consideration brings to our attention the original circumstances of the teaching, where "one thing that is immensely important in teaching is exaggerated gestures and facial expressions" (1966, p.2), that emphasize the "characteristic part [they play in].. a large group of activities... the occasions on which they are said..." (1966, p.2). It is the gestural function of these instructive forms of talk that is their key feature, that gives them their life: for they 'point beyond' themselves to features in the momentary context of their utterance. It is the way in which we do this, i.e., 'show' our possible connections to our circumstances in their voicing, that makes such talk revealing of our individual 'inner lives'[75].

Wittgenstein's methods

Wittgenstein uses these 'gestural', these 'educative' forms, then, in drawing our attention to what is there, in the circumstances of our talk, before our eyes, that we fail to see. Where the forms of talk, the remarks he uses to draw our attention to what is, in fact, already known to us, he calls "reminders:" For, "something that we know when no one asks us, but no longer know when we are supposed to give an account of it [cf. Augustine, below], is something we need to *remind* ourselves of" (1953, no.89).

This then gives us some further clues as to his methods. They work, first: (1) To *arrest* or *interrupt* (or 'deconstruct') the spontaneous, unself-conscious flow of our ongoing activity, and to give "prominence to distinctions which our ordinary forms of language easily make us overlook" (1953, no.132)[76]. Thus his talk is full of such expressions as "Think of...," "Imagine...," "It is like...," "So one might say...," "Suppose...," and so on, in which he confronts us with a concrete scene or vignette featuring a particular aspect of human conduct, and to 'take us inside' the unfolding details of its conduct. Where all these vignette's (portrayals) are designed "to draw someone's attention to the fact that he [or she] is capable of imagining [something]... and his *acceptance* of the [new] picture consists in his now being inclined to regard a given case differently: that is, to compare it with *this* rather than *that* set of pictures. I have changed his *way of looking at thing*" (1953, no.144). That is, in provoking us to bring new responses to our words and actions into play, he shows us further possibilities in a circumstance that previously we had overlooked. Alone, however, such a move could be more confusing than clarifying; it is his close attention to our use of language that is so crucial, especially in his concern with how we formulate questions to ourselves.

(2) *Questions:* Wittgenstein uses questions (in response to what he sees as bewildering 'philosophical questions', i.e., decontextualized questions of a general kind, such as: 'What is the mind?') to help us bring our into the light of day the 'grammar' at work in use of words in our coming to an understanding of each other in particular everyday life settings. Or, to put it in other words: to call to mind the detailed inter-relationships between our use of words and the influential concrete features in their surroundings at the moment of their use. His questions redirect our inquiries away from the abstract and general to the concrete and particular, and challenge us to resolve our questions – the events that trouble us – in the original context in which they were first experienced. In so doing, he not only directs our attention toward unnoticed details in our surroundings, but he also redirects our expectations regarding the kind of answers we anticipate receiving from our inquiries. Often, he does this simply by showing us that we can *rephrase* the question in other words, thus to arouse other expectations. For example, we are less perplexed by the question: 'What's the *use* of a word?' than by 'What's the meaning of a word?' – because the first formulation orients us toward looking at both our words *and the actions into which they are interwoven*, and is thus less likely to lead us to look for a mysterious entity or process (within the brain?) that we might call 'meaning'. I will return to a fuller account of his 'grammatical investigations' into the misleading questions we ask ourselves below.

This suggests to us a third aspect of his methodology that is sometimes important: (3) By the careful use of selected *images*, *similes*, *analogies*, *metaphors*, or '*pictures*'[77], he also suggests new ways of talking that not only orient us toward sensing otherwise unnoticed distinctions and relations for the first time, but which also suggest new connections and relations with the rest of our proceedings. Here, his notion of a "perspicuous representation (Ger: übersichlichte Darstellung)" is central: "A main source of our failure to understand is that we do not *command a clear view* of our use of words – Our grammar is lacking in this sort of perspicuity. A perspicuous representation produces just that understanding which consists in 'seeing connections'. Hence the importance of finding and inventing *intermediate cases*" (1953, no.122). If we are 'to find our way about' inside our own linguistically shaped forms of life, we need to grasp their inner 'landscape', or their 'grammatical geographies', so to speak.

Such images can have the effect of arousing in us just the kind of spontaneous reactions that can give rise to the beginning of new language-games (see Wittgenstein's (1969, no.139) remark above, on the importance of examples in establishing and teaching a new practice).

This brings us to a fourth and important method: (4) By the use of various kinds of *objects of comparison*, e.g., other possible ways of talking, other "language games" both actual and invented, etc., he tries "to throw light on the facts of our language by way of not only similarities, but also dissimilarities" (1953, no.130). For, by noticing how what occurs differs in a distinctive way from what we otherwise would expect, such comparisons can work, he notes, to establish "an order in our knowledge of the use of language: an order with a particular end in view; one of many possible orders; not *the* order" (1953, no.132). The importance of the use of comparisons – often the comparison, or the bringing into living contact, of different *scenes* (see note 15) – cannot be overemphasized. Such dialogical juxtapositions work in a living way to create a circumstance in which differences are realized and articulated: *here*, we use our words like *this*; *there*, we use them like *that*. That is, in providing new occasions for the realizing of new differences, they create a new 'movement' of thought, a new 'gesture'[78].

Indeed, if we turn to some remarks of his on how we understand the theme in a piece of music, we find him likening the music's movement to human speech and other gestural movements" "... the theme... is a new part of our language; it becomes incorporated into it; we learn a new gesture" (1980b, p.52). But: "Doesn't the theme point outside itself?," he asks. "Yes, it does! But that means: – it makes an impression on me which is connected with things in its surroundings – e.g., with our language and its intonations; and hence with the whole field of our language-games" (1981, no.175).

In other words, such dialogical juxtapositions bring to life new gestures, new ways of pointing beyond our immediate circumstances to bring to light new connections and relations between and within them. And indeed, there is no end to such an investigatory practice as this. Unlike our attempts to place something within a closed framework or system, such a method is open to extension, as long as we can find or create new metaphors and images through which to discover yet further contrasts and distinctions. Thus, as we cross boundaries and 'move' from functioning within one language game to an other, we can experience the changed commitments, urges, wants, desires, and temptations, as well as the ways of handling, looking, and evaluating, associated with each.

In particular, as we move from the 'inside' to the 'outside' of a *disciplinary system*, it becomes possible to sense how – from within the system – its (metaphorical) ways of talking seemingly *entraps* those within it in 'its' reality. For, in these disciplinary circumstances, in which we use our words in a wholly lifeless, monological, decontextualized manner, and seek only a passive, representational kind of understanding, there is a built-in exclusion of more active, responsive understandings: we must bridge all the gaps in our talk in terms of a certain theoretical order. Thus, in our disciplinary forms of talk, as we have seen, "a *picture* [holds] us captive. And we [can] not get outside it, for it [lies] in our language and language [seems] to repeat it to us inexorably" (1953, no.115). Thus: "When philosophers use a word – 'knowledge', 'being', 'object', 'I', 'proposition', 'name' – and try to grasp the *essence* of the thing, one must always ask oneself: is the word ever actually used in this way in the language-game which is its original home? – What *we* do is to bring words back from their metaphysical to their everyday use" (1953, no.116).

It is at this point that it will be useful to say more about Wittgenstein's (1965) concern with how we formulate the questions we pose ourselves[79]. He begins his investigations in *The Blue and the Brown Books*, by posing the question: "What is the meaning of a word?"

The questions that philosophers have racked their brains over have, as Wittgenstein sees it, two characteristics: First, they involve things and issues with which we are very familiar; but second, they appear to require answers that are impossible to obtain. Typically, St. Augustine's question: 'What is time?' is just such a question: 'What then is time? If no one asks me, I know: if I wish to explain it to one who asketh, I know not...' is of this kind. Perplexity concerning 'meaning', 'thinking', 'wishing', etc., is similar to St. Augustine's perplexity concerning time:

> "The questions 'What is length?', 'What is meaning?', 'What is the number one?' etc., produce in us a mental cramp. We feel that we can't point to anything in reply to them and yet ought to point to something. (We are up against one of the greatest sources of philosophical bewilderment: a substantive makes us look for a thing that corresponds to it.)" (1965, p1).

Yet why are we so perplexed when we ask: 'What is ...X...?' Everything of interest and importance concerning our use of the words: 'thinking', 'length', 'meaning', 'the number one', is already known to us in some sense, for we are the ones who invented these words and their uses in the first place. Thus our bewilderment must be to do with, Wittgenstein suggests, our phrasing of the questions: they lead to a quite wrong set of anticipations regarding the kind of answers we expect. More often that not, they lead us to expect a difficulty that can be solved as a problem rather than to see it as an orientational difficulty.

In bringing these issues to a head, he suggests a discussion of the question: 'How can one think what is not the case?': "This is a beautiful example of a philosophical question. It asks 'How can one...?' and while this puzzles us we must admit that nothing is easier than to think what is not the case. I mean, this shows us agin the difficulty which we are in does not arise through our inability to imagine how thinking something is done; just as the philosophical difficulty about the measurement of time did not arise through our inability to imagine how time was actually measured. I say this because sometimes it almost seems as though our difficulty were one of remembering exactly what happened when we thought something, a difficulty of introspection, or something of the sort; whereas in fact it arises when we look at the fact through the medium of a misleading form of question" (1965, pp.30-31). Our difficulties can often be resolved, not by seeking new and unknown empirical facts, but by realizing that we have disoriented ourselves – bewitched or mystified ourselves – by the very form in which we have posed the question. The answer to our difficulties is to be found by re-situating the question within a, or the, practical context within which it made sense to ask it in the first place:

> "We must do away with all explanation, and description alone must take its place. And this description gets its light, that is to say its purpose, from the philosophical problems. These are, of course, not empirical problems; they are solved, rather, by looking into the workings of our language, and that in such a way as to make us recognize those workings: in despite of an urge to misunderstand them. The problems are solved, not by giving new information, but by arranging what we have always known. Philosophy is a battle against the bewitchment of our intelligence by means of language" (1953, no.109).

Indeed, in social theory generally, it is only too easy to talk of such things as 'society', 'the individual', 'the person', 'identity', 'social class', 'social structure', 'power', 'agency', and so on, as if we all already know perfectly well what these things are, and to plan empirical research projects into their features, characteristics, and relations to each other. And in psychology too, we find it difficult to accept that sense impressions, for instance, are not the basis of our talk of objects, but the reverse: that is, talk of supposed events or processes 'within' us, individually, is a refinement of the talk between us of material objects. For we do not react to an object in any single uniform way. We respond and relate ourselves to them in different ways in different circumstances, and sometimes we make mistakes. What we call our inner states of mind are shown in the complexity of our responses. "So how does doubt [for example] get expressed? That is: in a language-game, and not merely in certain *phrases*. Maybe in looking more closely; and so in a fairly complicated activity... One simply tends to forget that even doubting belongs to a language-game," (1980a II, no.342) – and that a term (like doubt) only has a *clear* meaning within a form of life. Although this does not mean that it cannot be used meaningfully at all, poetically.

A poetics of practices

Thus in applying his methods, our task as social theorists is no longer that of searching for the final Archimedean standpoint from which to understand everything, but a task of a much more mundane and fragmentary kind. As Wittgenstein has already put it: "A philosophical problem has the form: 'I don't know my way about'" (1953, no.123), and our task is to find our way about inside the diversity of our own everyday ways of knowing and speaking a little better – thus to render the character of our own and other people's practices, publicly discussable and teachable. Currently, we tend to take all our talk *of* objects as being *about* objects, as if they all must already 'out there' in some naturalistic sense, else we would not be able to refer to them meaningfully in our talk. But this is to take our talk as having only a single, fixed relation to its circumstances, a representational relation. But language is not just for the deliberate and self-conscious representation of facts. Instead, there are "countless different kinds of use of what we call 'symbols', 'words', 'sentences'" (1953, no.23). And our direct and unplanned responses to other peoples' smiles, their facial expressions, and other spontaneous bodily gestures and movements, are all to do with us first finding "our feet with them" (1953, p.223), with us beginning 'to go on' with them. The representing of facts to each other, can only occur as a refinement of such a beginning.

If we are as social theorists to attend to these 'gestural' forms of talk, we must 'cure' ourselves of this tendency to see our language as having only a single, representational function, and of our urge always to theorize, always to look for something hidden behind appearances. We must attend to what our 'spontaneous' reactions and responses are, to what seems 'real' for us in the circumstances of our talk with the others around us, to how we actually do act and respond to our circumstances, in practice. Our ignoring of these aspects of our own functioning, and our obsession with replacing them with nonexistent, mythical entities of our own devising, are, as Wittgenstein sees it, matters of the *will* rather than the *intellect* (see Chapter 4). Hence his claim that "we may not advance any kind of theory... We must do away with all *explanation*, and description alone must take its place" (1953, no.109) – for our task here is not to understand what they are in themselves, i.e., how they should be categorized, but simply to recognize their role in, or relations to, the rest of our affairs.

Thus, as we have seen, his methods do not provide us with any new *theories* as the nature of our words, but with a new *practice*: instead of helping us 'find' something already existing but supposedly hidden *behind* appearances, they help us grasp something new, as yet unseen, *in* the emerging articulation of our speech entwined activities as they unfold in our very ears (if not before our very eyes!). He uses his similes, his "perspicuous representations," etc., to draw to our attention possible aspects of our own activities with which we are already in fact conversant, but for which they act as ‘reminders’. And they ‘move’ us toward a new way of ‘looking over’ the ‘play’ of appearances unfolding before us, such that, instead of seeing the events concerned in terms of *theories* as to what they supposedly ‘represent’, we see them ‘relationally’ – that is, we see them practically, as being embedded in a network of possible connections and relations with their surroundings, ‘pointing toward’ the roles they might actually play in our lives.

We can call his concern here, a concern with a “poetics of practices.” Where again, it is worth reminding ourselves that such a poetics would not be concerned with discovering what something *is*, but different possible ways in which we might relate ourselves to our surroundings – how we can make sense of people’s different inner worlds.

This, I think, is what is radically new in Wittgenstein’s whole approach: In being concerned with how people interconnect and make sense of their experiences in practice, with what they feel they *must* do or seek, i.e., with their *will*, their *sensibilities*, or ‘way of being in the world’, his methods of inquiry seem to entail something very like a western form of Zen. They seem aimed at something that is simple to see once seen, but that is immensely difficult to grasp if one is already trained in, i.e., ‘bewitched by’ (he would say), various well-established ways of dealing with the world. As he puts it: “The way to solve the problem you see in life is to live in a way that will make what is problematic disappear. The fact that life is problematic shows that the shape of your life does not fit into life’s mould. So you must change the way you live and, once your life does fit into the mould, what is problematic will disappear” (1980, p.27). Thus, “the clarity we are aiming at is indeed *complete* clarity. But this simply means that the philosophical problems should *completely* disappear” (1953, no.133).

His methods are somewhat Zen-like in their application also. For although people cannot use them to say explicitly what the nature of their sensibility actually ‘is’, they can nonetheless use them in to ‘show’ others what it is like to be them, i.e., they can ‘instruct’ *others* in how *they* experience their surroundings. Thus, just as we can be ‘instructed’ at school in what it is like, say, to live ‘in’ the alien and strange world of mathematics, through the activity of doing *proofs*, so we can also be ‘instructed’ in other alien forms of life in the same way. But what is this way? What is special about it?

Elsewhere, my colleague Arlene Katz and I (Katz and Shotter, 1996) have explored the meaning of a Haitian woman patient, in a medical diagnostic interview in a North-eastern American hospital, suddenly saying in the course of the interview, “Its [i.e. medicine in the U.S.] not like it is back home.” Where it was as if, so to speak, this utterance came ‘from somewhere else’ than the situation of the interview. We show how such first-person, ‘out of the blue’ utterances can, if the medical interviewer responds to them rather than ignoring them as irrelevant, be the beginning of an exchange revealing of a patient's "world of pain"[80]. These are the kinds of primitive reactions with which a new language-game can begin (see also Shotter, 1998; Shotter and Katz, 1996, 1999).

Similarly with Wittgenstein's own work, our grasp of the new and unique possibilities it suggests to us, occur only 'in a moment', and can easily be lost if we feel, yet again, that (like doctors in medical interviews) we must apply our usual methods of analysis and forms of argumentation to what he has to say: that is, if we ask for the *hidden reality* his words supposedly represent, or, for an *explanation* of the circumstance he claims is revealing of new possibilities, then we shall miss the point they gesture toward entirely. Indeed, perhaps that is why he remarked to himself that "I still find my own way of philosophizing new, and it keeps striking me so afresh; that is why I need to repeat myself so often" (1980, p.1). For the fact is, strangely, nothing can justify the (essentially first-person) claims he makes – nothing in ours or his previous employment of the words he uses; nothing in his or our experience; nor anything in his or our circumstances. His new usages are spontaneous and unforeseeable adaptations of past usages, utterances that are responsive in some way to his circumstances. And all that matters, is that we are (possibly) 'moved' by them too; that is, they *can* – if we also respond to them appropriately – re-relate us, or reorient us, afresh toward our circumstances as they reorient him. This is why we are justified in calling such utterances *poetic* utterances.

Bachelard (1992) discusses how such a "singular, short-lived event constituted by the appearance of an unusual poetic image, [can] react on other minds, and in other hearts, despite all the barriers of common sense, all the disciplined schools of thought, content in their immobility" (pp.xiv-xv). "The sudden image, a flare-up of being in the imagination" (p.xiv), is inaccessible, he says, to any intellectual methods of investigation. For such fleeting changes in our being are utterly unforeseeable and quite extraordinary; they come "*before* thought" (p.xvi), "do not pass through the circuits of knowledge" (p.xvii), and are also "a little above the language of signification" (p.xxiii). Indeed, it is just because they offer "breaks in signification" (p.xxv), that they also offer us "a new being in our language, expressing us by making us what [they] express; in other words, [they are] at once a becoming of expression, and a becoming of our being. Here expression creates being" (p.xix). "By its novelty, a poetic image *sets in motion* the entire linguistic mechanism. The poetic image places us at the origin of the speaking being" (p.xix, my emphasis). "It takes root in us. It has been given us by another, but we have the impression that we could have created it, that we should have created it" (p.xix).

If we now turn to some remarks of Wittgenstein's (1980) on how a work of art (or a poem) conveys a 'feeling'; he suggests that, "in so far as people understand it, they 'resonate' in harmony with it, respond to it" (p.58). Indeed, in such singular circumstances, he likens the 'movement' of people's thought to the 'movement' in a piece of music, and the music's 'movement' to speech and other human gestural movements: "... the theme... is a new part of our language; it becomes incorporated into it; we learn a new gesture" 1980, p.52). But: "Doesn't the theme point to anything outside itself?" he asks. "Yes, it does! But that means: – it makes an impression on me which is connected with things in its surroundings – e.g. with our language and its intonations; and hence with the whole field of our language-games" (1981, no.175). In other words, a new gesture brings to life, new ways of 'pointing beyond' our immediate circumstances, to make new connections and relations with our surroundings. Hence his feeling that "a new word is like a fresh seed sown on the ground of discussion" (1980, p.2), or, that "a good simile refreshes the intellect" (1980, p.1). For such new words do not just 'invite' new ways of looking, new responses, new gestures, new connections and relations, as if we had a choice in the matter; they come to possess us, and we them.

Conclusions

This, then, I think, is the radical nature of Wittgenstein's philosophy for us. Only recently, however, has this recognition – "both of the revolutionary break his later methods descry in philosophy, and of their relation to methodology in aesthetics and ethics," expressed many years ago by Cavell (1969, p.73) – begun to gain general acceptance (Edwards, 1982; Staten, 1984; Monk, 1990; Johnston, 1993; Shields, 1994; Malcolm, 1994). It suggests to us, not some new *theories* as to what is 'out there' in our surroundings, as self-oriented, scientifically inclined, self-contained individuals, but a new way for us 'to be': that is, as relationally-oriented, poetically inclined, dialogical individuals. As such, we can come to a more direct understanding of how to participate in human practices, *in practice* – rather than as at present, indirectly, by first attempting to understand them in terms of *theories*, as we feel we *must*. This is the power of the 'poetic': "... in its expression, it is youthful language" (Bachelard, 1992, p.xv); it can change us in our being by gesturing toward new possibilities; it can provide the 'seeds', spontaneously, for re-connecting ourselves with our surroundings in utterly new and unique ways, independently of any pre-existing systems of knowledge. Hence Wittgenstein's claim – with which I began – that "... philosophy ought only to be written as a *poetic composition*" (1980, p.24). For it is only first-person utterances of this kind, 'out of the blue', that can seize us and make us aware of another distinct consciousness, that can also break the strangle-hold on us of the supposed essential references (see again, Wittgenstein, 1980a, I, no.177) of our words. This is the power of our poetic forms of talk.

Chapter Six

LINGUISTIC RELATIVITY IN A WORLD OF EVENTS: LIFE WITHIN 'THE PRESENT MOMENT'

> "The present moment does not whizz by and become observable only after it has gone. Rather, it crosses the mental stage more slowly, taking several seconds to unfold. And during this crossing, the present moment plays out a lived emotional drama. As the drama unfolds it traces a temporal shape like a passing musical phrase" (Stern, 2004, p.4).

> "... existents do not "become later and later" all in the same way; but some do so by growing like plants, some by diffusing and vanishing, some by a procession of metamorphoses, some by enduring in one shape till affected by violent forces" (Whorf, 1956, pp.147-148).

> "We know nothing about the time of *things*" (Stern, 2004, p.5).

> "The mathematical sciences require exact measurement, but what linguistics requires is, rather, exact "patternment" – an exactness of relation irrespective of dimensions" (Whorf, 1956, p.231).

In this chapter, I want to explore further some issues already explored in the previous chapter – to do with styles of talk and writing appropriate to describing the only partially formed features of first-time events, to describing still developing social realities occurring in a world of events and activities, rather than in world of thoughts, things, and substances. For, as we have seen, our styles of talk are important in that they can direct our attention toward aspects of the unfolding processes at work in the interplay occurring between participants, as they develop understandings between them in their meeting, that we might not otherwise notice. With the appropriate forms of talk to guide, we have a chance of 'getting inside' the detailed, moment-by-moment unfolding 'steps' within that interplay, to understand the function of each step. So far, in attempting to set out an appropriate lexicon of terms, I have mostly made use of Wittgenstein's, Vygotsky's, and Bakhtin's and Voloshinov's work. But here, I want to turn to a rather different writer, an anthropologist of Native-American thought and talk, who has explored contrastively, the different formative powers of their and our very different ways of speaking: namely, Benjamin Lee Whorf (1956).

In his thesis of *linguistic relativity*, he has contrasted[81] our Standard Average European (SAE) ways of speaking with, mainly, Hopi ways of talking. His point in making this contrast is to introduce to us "a new principle of linguistic relativity, which holds that all observers are not led by the same physical evidence to the same picture of the universe, unless their linguistic backgrounds are similar, or can be calibrated. This rather startling conclusion is not so apparent if we compare only our modern European languages... [But] when Semitic, Chinese, Tibetan, or African languages are contrasted with our own... and, when we bring in native languages of the Americas, where speech communities for many millenniums have gone their own ways independently of each other and of the old World, the fact that languages dissect nature in many different ways becomes patent " (p.214)[82].

Nowhere is this contrast more apparent than in how we represent the nature of time, and thus the nature of "passing moments," to ourselves. While we spatialize or objectify time in a three-tense system of past, present, and future that can be drawn out as a line, Hopi use only a two-tense system of subjectively earlier and later events, a system which, as he suggests, seems to correspond better with the feeling of duration[83] as it is experienced. As a result, as Whorf (1956) puts it, in SAE (Standard Average European) "concepts of time lose contact with the subjective experience of 'becoming later' and are objectified as counted QUANTITIES[84], especially as lengths, made up of units as a length... [Thus] a 'length of time' is envisioned as a row of similar units, like a row of bottles" (p.140). We thus report our experience to ourselves as living in a time made up of 'instant *nows*' – with no inter-linking (or *internal* relations) occurring between each instant, so that they stand, as he puts it, like bottles in a row; or, if they are joined, it is like beads on a thread (connected only *externally* to each other by the thread) – with no *now*-instant being long enough for us to have an experience of something unfolding within it. In a two-tense system of earlier and later events, however, it *is* possible not only to give expression to the feeling of duration, of things taking their time and developing in a step-by-step manner, but also, as we shall see, to talk of *existents* developing, or of becoming later and later, *in different ways*.

Our lack of ability to express such experienced differences is important, for, as we saw in Chapter 4, William James (1890) noted that "large tracts of human speech are nothing but *signs of direction* in thought, of which direction we nevertheless have an acutely discriminative sense... [and these *signs of direction* in thought] must be described as in large measure constituted of *feelings of tendency*, often so vague that we are unable to name them at all" (pp.250-254). And it is this *discriminative sense* that is important in providing us with the ever changing expectations and anticipations that can guide us in our actions, moment by moment, as we interact with those around us.

Thus, in what follows, I want to explore how the many terms of art introduced by Whorf in illuminating the dimensions of contrast (or the relational-dimensions) between SAE and Hopi, can be useful to us in grasping the nature of, i.e., the unfolding temporal contours of, the fleeting events occurring in our meetings with the others and othernesses around us. They can contribute to our concern in this book with building an vocabulary of terms appropriate to thinking and talking *from within* the interactive moment. Here, then, as in previous chapters, I want to explore the implications of an account of language in which language is *not* primarily a device for 'picturing,' 'depicting,' or 'mirroring' (truthfully or otherwise) an already existing language-independent reality, but is primarily a formative device for *use* by people in both coordinating their individual actions (Mills, 1940; Wittgenstein, 1953), but also in creating between them new conversational realities, ones in which the language used *is* the language of the participants, i.e., they converse with each other in *their own terms*, not in terms imposed on them by others. Thus, rather than simply representing 'reality,' speaking and writing should here again be 'seen as' (talked of as)[85] 'giving shape to', or as 'forming' a state of affairs, a situation, or a circumstance appropriate to it having currency, so to speak, within the way of life in which the language is used.

In other words, something which is only partially specified and thus open to further specification, is given further specification linguistically, *but only according to legitimate communicative requirements*, i.e., only in ways that promote, in Wittgenstein's (1953) terms, people "going on" in the living of a certain "form of life." Thus our ways of speaking and writing work *practically* to articulate the topics of our discourse, and to give them a structure appropriate to our forms of life that they would in themselves otherwise lack.

My purpose, also, in introducing someone so seemingly removed form the mainstream of social constructionism as Benjamin Lee Whorf, is to show up the resonances between his work from so long along (on how people are 'pointed' by their different grammars toward reporting on their experiences in different ways), and that of Daniel Stern (2004) in his book *The Present Moment in Psychotherapy and Everyday Life*. In that book, in contradistinction to a view of time as *chronos*, i.e., as the clock-time whose 'lengths' can be measured, he introduces time as *kairos*, as "the passing moment in which something happens as the time unfolds. It is the coming into being of a new state of things, and it happens in a moment of awareness... [It] is a moment of opportunity, when events demand action or are propitious for action" (p.7). Thus he is, like Whorf, concerned to set out the "temporal architecture" (p.41), the "temporal contours" (p.62) of such moments. Before turning to these resonances, however, I would like to bring out some of the connections between Whorf's and Wittgenstein's work.

Grammar in Whorf and Wittgenstein

Whorf (1956) in suggesting in his linguistic relativity hypothesis that we are 'pointed' by the 'grammars' implicit in our language toward seeing and judging events occurring in our surroundings, is suggesting, like Wittgenstein (1953), that "grammar tells us what kind of object anything is" (no.373). In other words, they are both suggesting that our ways of speaking and writing work *practically*, to formulate the topics of our talk and to give them a structure, not that they have in themselves, but one appropriate to our forms of life.

This emphasis by Whorf (like Wittgenstein) on the *grammar* of a language, seems to me, to have been misunderstood in the past in at least the following two ways: (1) as being to do only with what linguists would call syntax, rather than with what Wittgensteinians would call "logical grammar;" and, (2) as being to do with *patterns* of already spoken words, with their *content*, rather than to do with the 'moving' or 'shaping' power of words in their speaking – a distinction I introduced in earlier chapters in this book. Indeed, this misreading of Whorf, is (it seems to me) itself a case in point of the very principle of linguistic relativity at work to which he wants to introduce us. For it is only too easy to read him as if he is talking to us *from within* a world of thoughts, things, and substances. We can (perhaps) see this, if we examine how he himself introduced its nature to a lay audience. He began by mentioning the revolutionary changes that have occurred in the world of science and the new ways of thinking they have introduced – in "relativity, quantum theory, electronics, catalysis, colloid chemistry, theory of the gene, Gestalt psychology, pyschoanalysis, unbiases cultural anthropology, and so on" (p.220) – and then he went on to say:

> "I say new ways of THINKING about facts, but a more nearly accurate statement would say new ways of TALKING about facts. It is this USE OF LANGUAGE UPON DATA that is central to scientific progress. Of course, we have to free ourselves from that vague innuendo of inferiority which clings to the word 'talk', as in the phrase 'just talk'; that false opposition which the English-speaking world likes to fancy between talk and action" (Whorf, 1956, p.220, his emphases)[86].

In fact, as is clear, just as for Wittgenstein (1953), so also for Whorf: it is our *use* of words that matters. It is this that seems to have been missed in past readings of Whorf. And it will be through an account of the formative function of talk that I shall elaborate below, that we will be able to 'see' (to use an inappropriate metaphor) Whorf's work in a new light.

Covert and overt grammar: cryptotypes and phenotypes

Such a view of linguistic functioning – of speaking and writing, not as working by the use of already fixed codes simply to represent "reality," but of them as being continuously creative or formative processes in which we construct the situation or context of our communication *as we communicate* – is, for us, to repeat, utterly revolutionary. As Harris (1980, 1981) points out, it calls in question one of the great myths of our time, a myth which since antiquity has been a part in one form or another of the Western tradition. In that myth, it is supposed that words stand for things either 'out there' in the world external to the language-user (in what Harris calls the "reocentric" version of "surrogationalism"), or (in its "psychocentric" version) for things to be located internally, "in the mind" of the language-user.

Whorf's (1956) work calls these *language myths* into question. He shows us in his work on the languages of the American-Indians, what it is like *not* to think, or talk, in this way about ourselves, amongst ourselves. Instead, he demonstrates – works out in detail on the page – how a very different way of talking, in terms of *events* and '*eventing*', instead of things and substances, could lead to us experiencing ourselves in quite a different way.

As a preliminary to this task, I want to make five points: (1) The first is to attempt to make clear that, when Whorf speaks of grammatical categories, he did not always mean what linguists now talk of as syntax, i.e., recognizable patterns of already spoken words – like Wittgenstein (1953), he often meant something quite different. He meant influences that show up only in the dynamics of speaking, not in the forms or patterns of words retrospectively visible in recorded forms of speech, once the event of speaking is over. To this end, Whorf distinguished between what he called overt and covert grammatical categories – what he also called PHENOTYPES and CRYPTOTYPES. He outlined this distinction as follows: Overt grammatical categories, or phenotypes, are syntactically marked in some explicit, formal way within the sentence in which they appear, where their formal nature is determined their place in the formal patterning of that sentence. The marking of gender is just such an over category. Covert categories, or cryptotypes, are quite different. The term, cryptotype, "calls attention to the rather hidden, cryptic nature of such word-groups, especially when they are not strongly contrasted in idea, nor marked by frequently occurring *reactances* such as pronouns. They easily escape notice and may be hard to define, and yet may have profound influence on linguistic behavior" (p.92, my emphasis). Indeed, it is only *in the use* of such words that we find they require some sort of distinctive treatment – it is this distinctive treatment that Whorf (1956) calls "the REACTANCE of the category" (p.89).

For instance: "For example, the English particle UP meaning 'completely, to a finish', as in 'break it up, cover it up, eat it up, twist it up, open it up' can

be applied to any verb of one or two syllables initially accented, EXCEPTING verbs belonging to four special cryptotypes. One is the cryptotype of dispersion without boundary; hence one does not say 'spread it up, waste it up, spend it up, scatter it up, drain it up, or filter it up'. Another is the cryptotype of oscillation without agitation of parts; we don't say 'rock up a cradle, wave up a flag, wiggle up a finger, nod up one's head', etc.
Similarly, the "names of countries and cities in English form a cryptotype with the reactance that they are not referred to by personal pronouns as object of the prepositions 'in, at, to, from'. We can say 'I live in Boston' but not 'That's Boston - I live in it'. A word of this cryptotype is referred to by 'there' or 'here' in place of 'in it, at it, to it', and by 'from there (here)' in place of 'from it'." (p.92).

As I see it, this is what Wittgenstein (1953) would called an aspect of "logical" grammar. And when he says "grammar tells us what kind of object anything is" (no.373), it is by examining the *reactance* related to our talk of 'it', that we are able to make clear to ourselves what that 'it' *is* for us. That is a part (see Chapter 5) of Wittgenstein's method of doing philosophy. And this is the reason for my claim above: that to interpret Whorf's talk of grammar in a merely syntactic sense is an utterly inadequate interpretation. The *reactance* occasioned by the use of a word only shows up in the context of its use, in our words in their speaking.

(2) Following on from this, the account of language I have given thus far in this book represents our 'basic' ways of speaking as working 'instructively' – in our voicing of our words, in the anticipations and expectations they spontaneously arouse in us – to invoke or provoke in us, as responsible and autonomous members of a certain society, a creative process in which we continually determine amongst ourselves what, officially, is 'rationally-visible' to us (Garfinkel, 1967). Their *reactance*, which we experience in their use, suggests to us that it is *this* (rather than *that*) kind of thing that we are talking about. In other words, our 'accounting practices' work to 'instruct' us in how to 'see' an otherwise indeterminate flow of activity as having this, rather than that, kind of form to it (a form which otherwise it would not in itself have). Our 'seeing' is thus 'in-formed' by the terms in the dominant discourse of the day (Rorty, 1980). But it is worth mentioning before we go any further, that by the same token, those self-same, official accounting practices will also work to render other aspects of what occurs 'rationally-*in*visible' to us.

Indeed, as both Whorf (1956) and Wittgenstein (1953) make clear to us, we fail to take account of the fact that, to its own speakers, the 'shaping' and 'moving' influences spontaneously exerted on them by their use of their language, remain in the background, outside of their critical consciousness and thus outside of their control. It is thus only too easy to think that one is expounding on the very nature of one's surrounding reality, when one is only in fact "marching in step with purely grammatical facts that have somewhat of a background character in his own language or family of languages but are by no means universal in all languages and in no sense a common substratum of reason" (p.211).

Also, as we have seen in relation to the phenomenon in *joint action*, or in *dialogically-structured* activities – in which participants are unable to separate out their own contributions from the overall intertwined activities involved – it is quite usual for participants to have no conscious grasp of the unfolding details of the interplay involved. As Whorf (1956) notes: "Two fluent speakers, of English let us say, quickly reach a point of assent about the subject matter of their speech... One of them, A, can give directions that will be carried out by the other, B, to A's complete satisfaction. Because they thus understand each other so perfectly, A and B, as natural logicians, suppose they must of course know how it is all done. They think, e.g., that it is simply a matter of choosing words to express thoughts. If you ask A to explain how he got B's agreement so readily, he will simply repeat to you, with more or less elaboration or abbreviation, what he said to B. He has no notion of the process involved. The amazingly complex system of linguistic patterns and classifications, which A and B must have in common before they can adjust to each other at all, is all background to A and B" (p.211). The task of waking ourselves up to the importance of these background details, thus to appreciate the points at which they could be in fact very different from what they at present are, is not easy to do. And it is not made easier by the pressures that others place on us (along with all the other more moral pressures, to be responsible citizens) to speak in ways they find intelligible – or else suffer the sanctions placed on those 'not understood'. Although sometimes, one feels bound to speak against the official discourse of the day.

Rational-invisibility, and illusions of discourse

(3) To elaborate on the point above further: In our everyday lives we are, as I have already said, embedded within a social order which, morally, we must continually reproduce in all the mundane activities we perform from our 'place', 'position', or status within it. Thus we must account for all our experiences in terms both intelligible and legitimate within it, and currently, we live in a social order that, officially, is both individualistic and scientistic. Everything which occurs must be made sense of in its terms. It is because of this that we have concentrated far too much attention upon the isolated individual studied from the point of view of an uninvolved observer. And ironically, what has been rendered 'rationally-invisible' to us in us making sense of our world in this way, are the sense-making procedures made available to us in the social orders into which we have been socialized. These are procedures which, as I have said, have their provenance in the history of our culture, and in terms of which, as Garfinkel (1967) and the ethnomethodologists have shown, we perceive the flow of activity around us

as 'visibly-rational'. We do not, however, see them as procedures which we ourselves perform – as the quotation from Whorf (1956, p.211) above, illustrates – they are seen in other terms: as the operation of cognitive mechanisms 'in' individual people; as structures with their own dynamic which causally determine people's observed behaviour. It is in these terms too, that language appears *not* as a formative activity in itself, but as a means for expressing the results obtained by some kind of logical calculus, or information processing mechanism, at work within the heads of individuals.

When viewed through this mechanistic language, it is impossible to 'see' our *use* of language as a creative or formative process in its own right. In this view, communication *is* simply a matter of A telling [transferring information] something to B in his or her talk. Indeed, another aspect of the rational blindness induced in us by our current individualistic modes of accountability, is our failure to attribute sufficient significance to the 2nd-person standpoint in life, to the role of 'you's' in our spontaneously responsive relations with each other. As Bakhtin (1986) notes: "The fact is that when the listener perceives and understands the meaning (the language meaning) of speech, he simultaneously takes an active, responsive attitude toward it. He either agrees or disagrees with it (completely or partially), augments it, applies it, prepares for its execution, and so on. And the listener adopts this responsive attitude for the entire duration of the process of listening and understanding... Thus, the listener who understands passively, who is depicted as the speaker's partner in the schematic diagrams of general linguistics, does not correspond to the real participant in speech communication. What is represented by the diagram is only an abstract aspect of the real total act of actively responsive understanding, the sort of understanding that evokes a response, and one that the speaker anticipates" (pp.68-69). Indeed, in this sense, listeners are co-speakers and speakers co-listeners, within the course of a single speaker's utterance. Turn-taking in speech is not a matter of completely active speakers and completely passive listeners; they activities, like so many others in the sphere of communication, are (chiasmicly) intertwined.

Second-person you's are 'participating in' the meeting, and 'involved in' the situation, *from within* which 'I's' *meanings* are perceived and understood as such, the situation which 3rd-person external observers are 'outside' of. Thus it is that only 2nd-person listeners, as 2nd-person 'insiders', who have the right to expect 1st-person speakers to be as they present themselves as being (Goffman, 1959)[87]. Thus, unlike 3rd-person outsiders, *they* can present speakers with a context of enabling-constraints, of invitations and obligations, of callings and rejections, that they *must act into*, and can thus to motivate speakers to continue with their speech. But as we shall see in the next two chapters – to do with what can be heard in the unfolding dynamics of people's speech – only if listeners undertake the duty of fully attending to the *temporal contours* present in a person's speech, is a fully dialogical relation possible. Otherwise, although people might be coordinating their individual actions perfectly well, they will not be creating between a conversational reality of their own, one in which participants converse with each other in *their own terms*, not in terms imposed on them by others.

(4) Another important phenomenon, and perhaps a more bewildering one, as we have already seen to an extent, is the imaginary or fictitious entities our ways of speaking can convince us exist[88]. These are illusions which arise from *projecting* back into the phenomena of our concern, our methods of representing it – so that it appears to us as if we *are* simply 'mirroring' in the structure of our representations the structure of reality. This tendency leads us, as Goodman (1972, p.24) says, to "mistake features of discourse for features of the subject of discourse." I have already discussed aspects of this problem in Chapter 5, but here I would like to take that discussion further.

Consider the following examples: (i) We speak of understanding as a 'mental process' and wonder what goes on in our heads which enables us to do it, and we set out to attempt to discover its nature. "But," says Wittgenstein (1981), "don't think of understanding as a 'mental process' at all. – For *that* is the way of speaking that is confusing you. Rather ask yourself: in what kind of case, under what circumstances do we say 'Now I can go on'... That way of speaking [in terms of 'mental processes'] is what prevents us from seeing the facts without prejudice...*That* is how it can come about that the means of representation produces something *imaginary*. So let us not think we *must* find a specific mental process, because the verb 'to understand' is there and because one says: Understanding is an activity of the mind" (no.446). The idea that there *must* be a distinctive and discoverable process occurring in our head when we think arises, not from what we know about our own inner mental processes, but from the influences of our own ways of talking upon us. But what if there is no such single inner process to which the word "thinking" refers? What if it has an uncountable range of different uses?

(ii) Another obvious illusion is the feeling that every 'thing' must possess a fundamental, underlying, systematic structure, amenable to a single logical description – the true description of what the thing 'is'. But *is* there always such a structure there to be described? Goodman (1972) again in discussing "the way the world is", argues not: "There are very many different equally true descriptions of the world...no one of these different descriptions is *exclusively* true, since the others are also true. None of them tells us *the* way the world is, but each of them tells us *a* way the world is" (pp.30-31). For, not everything is a fully completed, objective thing; many 'things' are incomplete, and on the way to becoming something other than what they were when they were last observed – the world included.

And what Goodman says of the world, Wittgenstein (1980, I) also says of things in general: "Mere description is so difficult because one believes that one needs to fill out the facts in order to understand them. It is as if one saw a screen with scattered colour-patches, and said: the way they are here, they are unintelligible; they only make sense when one completes them into a shape. – Whereas I want to say: Here *is* the whole. (If you complete it, you falsify it.)" (no.257).

Thus, as I have suggested before, it is in the very nature of our surrounding circumstances, that they can only ever be partially specified and lack a final specification as to their actual structure.

(5) However, as an incomplete process, practical activity is still open to, or able to take on further specification. As such, it seems to 'invite' one or another kind of completion, and this *is* exactly what, as Goodman and Wittgenstein suggest, often happens in our attempts to describe it: We describe an incomplete process by its supposed final product. William James (1890) describes this tendency as "the psychologist's fallacy": "The *great* snare of the psychologist is the *confusion of his own standpoint with that of the mental fact* about which he is making his report... Both it itself and its object are objects for him. Now when it is a *cognitive* state..., he ordinarily has no other way of naming it than as the thought, percept, etc., *of that object*. He himself, meanwhile, knowing the self-same object in *his* way, gets easily lead to suppose that the thought, which is *of* it, knows it in the same way in which he knows it, although this is very often far from being the case. The most fictitious puzzles have been introduced into our science by this means" (p.196).

And this is my point here: unless we become sensitive to the manner in which our ways of speaking form and shape the topics of our discourse, we shall often be investigating *fictions* of our own devising without recognizing them as such. Psychologists are attempting to discover how people *would* perceive the world *if* it was as they depict it to be: as if full of 'things' and 'substances'. But is it? In an attempt to answer this question, I would now like to turn to a study of Whorf's (1956) writings, and in particular what he had to say a very different world from our's: the Hopi world of events and 'eventings'.

Metaphors We (SAE-speakers) Live By

In his chapter on "the relation of habitual thought and behaviour to language," Whorf (1956, p.138) explores two questions: (1) Are our concepts of 'time,' 'space,' and 'matter' given in substantially the same form by experience to all men and women, or are they in part conditioned by the structure of particular languages? And (2): Are there traceable affinities between a) cultural and behavioural norms and b) large-scale linguistic patterns? To both questions, Whorf answers "Yes." Let me turn first to what he has to say about our SAE use of nouns and noun phrases in talking about things in general.

As we have seen, Whorf (1956) claims that the world of SAE language is a world of matter, of things and substances – in general thought of as 'stuff'. We have two kinds of nouns for use in talking of such stuff:

individual (or count) nouns and mass nouns. Individual nouns are used in speaking of bodies with definite outlines: 'a tree, a stick, a man, a hill', while mass nouns are used for homogeneous continua without implied boundaries. However, as Whorf points out, we perceive few natural occurrences in this way, as unbounded extents: 'air, water, rain, snow, rock, dirt, grass, and sea' perhaps, but the distinction is more widespread in language than in the observable appearance of things. For, in the context of their occurrence we perceive most such substances as possessing a definite outline. However, their outline can be a different in different contexts. The mass noun has to be further individualized by the use of additional linguistic devices. This is partly done by the use of the names of *body-types*: 'stick of wood', 'piece of cloth',' 'pane of glass', and so on; but also by introducing the names of *containers*: 'glass of water', 'bag of flour', and so on. These very common container formulae, in which 'of' has an obvious, visually perceptible meaning ('contents'), influence our feeling about the less obvious body-type formulae, says Whorf: 'sticks', 'pieces', 'panes', etc., seem to *contain* something, a 'stuff', 'substance', or 'matter' equivalent in some way to the 'water', 'flour', etc., in the container formulae.

The formulae in both cases are similar: *formless item plus form*. Our ways of talking are such as to require us to talk of many things in terms of such a binomial structure; that is the only way in which they can be 'given', or 'lent' an intelligible character. Hence, says Whorf, for SAE people, the philosophical ideas of 'substance' and 'matter' are instantly acceptable as common sense; they represent in general the ways in which we already talk in particular 'about our reality'.

Nowhere is the power of linguistic analogy in the creation of imaginary entities more apparent than in the creation, among the stuff and substances of our universe, of the formless stuff we call 'time'. Such terms as September, morning, noon, and sunset are with us nouns, and they have little formal linguistic difference from other nouns, says Whorf. There is for us some 'thing' to which such phase-nouns, when we use them, seem to refer. In constructing it, we also apply here – in talking of 'a moment of time, a second of time, a year of time', etc. – the same linguistic formula of *formless item plus form* is used. We imagine that, just as 'a bottle' contains a quantity of liquid, so 'a summer' actually *contains* a quantity of time, marked out by 'beginning' and 'end' boundaries (which then puzzle us as to when exactly they occur). But in Hopi, all such phase terms , like 'morning', 'winter', etc., are not nouns at all but, says Whorf, a kind of adverb. Nor are these 'temporals' ever used as nouns, neither as subjects nor as objects. Thus they would not say, as we do, 'in the morning', but 'while morning-ing' is occurring. Indeed, as Whorf says, Hopi is a timeless language in the sense that, although it recognizes psychological time – the subjective sense of something being later or earlier that something else, or of things taking time to occur – this 'time' is quite unlike the objective, mathematical time we use to coordinate our practical affairs with each other. Thus what we feel must be explicitly recognized as features of the passage of time – the placing of events, for instance, in the past, present, or future – are not recognized as such in Hopi. Neither is there any 'thingifying' of time as a realm, region, extent, or quantity; nothing is suggested about it in Hopi, says Whorf, other than the 'getting later' or 'latering' of it.

How, then, do they talk of events occurring, as we see it, at different points in time – for conscious experience, even for us, does not obviously seem to contain a past, present, and future, but a complex unity: "EVERYTHING is in consciousness, and everything in consciousness IS, and is together," says Whorf (pp.143-4)? There is, however, a *subjective* distinction in consciousness between that with which we are in immediate *contact* (what we are seeing, hearing, touching) – the 'present' – and what is not a part of our immediate circumstances. Within that second category we may distinguish between what we can *remember* – the 'past' – and what we can *imagine*, intuit, believe, or fancy – the 'future'. All these: what we are in contact with, remembering, and imagining, are all in consciousness together. But whereas we order our conscious experience by talking of it in spatial terms, the Hopi make use of no such ordering devices; time for them enters into the above scheme by it *all* 'getting later' (or 'latering') together. As Whorf (1956) points out: "The timeless Hopi verb does not distinguish between the present, past, and future of the event itself but must always indicate what type of validity the SPEAKER intends the statement to have: (a) a report of an event; (b) expectation of an event; (c) generalization or law about events. [The situation][89] where the speaker and listener are in contact with the same objective field, is divided by our language into the two conditions, [one in which the speaker can see, now, the activity in question, and one in which he or she saw it happening, although it is now over], which it calls present and past, respectively. This division is unnecessary for a language which assures one that the statement is a report" (p.217). Thus what to us are differences in time, to Hopi are different aspects of *validity-forms* – where the different aspects of validity-forms denote different degrees of duration and different kinds of tendency *during duration*, and influence the degree to which listeners can feel confidence in basing their actions on a speaker's utterances.

But note here also the intrinsic connections, for them, between earlier and later events: everything which has ever been done is accumulated and carried over into the present event, while what it is becoming affects what it is also. It is, says Whorf, as if the return of the day was felt as the return of the same person (or group of persons, which in a sense, a practical sense, it is), not as 'another day' like the appearance of another and entirely different person.

Metonymical Forms of Talk

But are metaphorical forms always the basic shaping influences at work in all languages? Is it the same for the Hopi? Not quite, Whorf claims: While full of figures of speech, of course, their language has, he says, neither the need for nor analogies upon which to build a concept of existence as a duality of *formless-matter plus things-with-forms* (i.e., bodies and quasibodies made from, consisting of, or containing the basic substances of the world). The general character of the Hopi cosmos is marked out by the use of verb or predicator forms (if "verb" is the right term to use here in discussing a language not one's own), not by nouns and nominals. "The Hopi microcosm," says Whorf (1956), "seems to have analyzed reality largely in terms of EVENTS (or better 'eventing');" and he goes on to describe the different natures of the 'eventing' of events:

> "...events are considered the expression of invisible intensity factors[90], on which depend their stability and persistence, or their fugitiveness and proclivities. It implies that existents do not 'become later and later' all in the same way; but some do so by growing like plants, some by diffusing and vanishing, some by a procession of metamorphoses, some by enduring in one shape till affected by violent forces. In the nature of each existent able to manifest as a definite whole is the power of its own mode of duration: its growth, decline, stability, cyclicity, or creativeness. Everything is thus already 'prepared' for by the way it now manifests by earlier phases, and by what will be later, partly has been, and partly is in the act of being so 'prepared'" (p.147).

While 'planning for the future' is one of the central activities in *our* form of life, and is the activity towards which science is thought of as contributing, for the Hopi, Whorf claims, it is 'preparation'. Hopi preparation, however, is quite different from our planning. Both involve thinking. But we talk of our thinking as having to do with us constructing or formulating – as a result of a means-end, cause-effect analysis – a plan (or theory, or set of principles, etc.) which we then have 'to put into practice' in some mysterious way. The mysterious hiatus between theory and practice arises for us because, given our ways of talking, 'matter' is only changed and fashioned by other matter impinging directly upon it, and it is quite unnatural for us to think of our thought as pervading and as being able to affect the world around us directly in any way.

What is unnatural for the Hopi, however, is the thought that it does not! While our thought takes place in an *imaginary space* – 'in our minds', we say, 'somewhere privately within us', either 'in the forefront or the back of our minds' – the Hopi world has no such imaginary space. The corollary of this, as Whorf points out, is that thinkings and feelings to do with 'eventings' in the world, are located there, out in the world in which the eventing takes place – as a natural part of the whole into which they are responsively interwoven.

Thoughts and feelings are thus, for the Hopi, treated as directly connected to events in the world in some way: if one's thinking – about the health and growth of some plants, say – is good, then it will be good for the plants, if bad, then the reverse. But the kind of thought meant here is not 'theoretical' thought, the preliminary formulation of possibilities in imaginary space, but 'practical' thought, the invoking of the appropriate imagery, the thinking of oneself 'into' the context of the possibly required practical activities, the conducting of appropriate 'thought experiments', the attempt to increase one's awareness of what actually 'is', to rid oneself of goals irrelevant to the task in hand, and so on.

Such a form of activity – of working within a present situation, thus to accumulate within a part of it, a sufficient influence to affect an aspect of the whole – is, we might say, metonymical: a part is taken as representative, or as invoking the whole. But if, as Whorf implies, everything is in some sense everywhere in the Hopi world, then it is entirely reasonable to hold that what one does in one part of a field of interwoven activities, ripples out, so to speak, and affects what happens in the totality. In metonymic ways of speaking, a feather invokes the bird, an eagle's feather all the eagle's qualities, such that to possess such a feather gives one access to all the eagle's qualities in some way; just as we, being speakers of English (SAE) and possessing some of the requisite linguistic skills feel we possess access to English as whole. But there is, I think, more to it than that.

Practically speaking: 'withness' versus 'aboutness' thinking

The importance of preparing activities to the Hopi are indicative, as Whorf makes clear, of how their timeless notion of time influences what they take to be the relation of their mental activity to their surroundings – while we think of ourselves as viewing things around us form afar, as external observers, they are living, participants parts of the world around them. Thus: "It is no more unnatural [for Hopi] to think that thought contacts everything and pervades the universe than to think, as we all do, that light kindled outdoors does this. And it is not unnatural to suppose that thought, like any other force, leaves everywhere traces of effect. Now, when WE think of a certain actual rosebush, we do not suppose that our thought goes to that actual bush, and engages with it, like a searchlight turned upon it. What then do we suppose our consciousness is dealing with when we are thinking of that rosebush? Probably we think it is dealing with a 'mental image' which is not the rosebush but a mental surrogate of it. But why should it be NATURAL to think that our thought deals with a surrogate and not with the real rosebush? Quite possibly because we are dimly aware that we carry about with us a whole imaginary space, full of mental surrogates... The Hopi thought-world has no imaginary space" (pp.149-150). Their lack of need for such surrogates thus corresponds with their lack of need for analogies upon which to build their concepts of existence, thus the absence of metaphors from their figures of speech.

Earlier preparations for later developments

A corollary to this is, as Whorf points out, that Hopi do not locate thought dealing with things in real space anywhere else but in real space; nor do they insulate real space from the effects of thought. Thus Hopi naturally suppose that their thought (or they themselves) traffic with, say, the plants, animals, people, or other such events they are thinking of. The thought then should leave some trace of itself with the events in question. If it is a good thought, one about health and growth, it is good for the event; if a bad thought, the reverse. "The Hopi emphasize the intensity-factor of thought," notes Whorf (1956). "Thought to be most effective should be vivid in consciousness, definite, steady, sustained, charged with strongly felt good intentions. They render the idea in English as 'concentrating, holding it in your heart, putting your mind on it, earnestly hoping.' Thought power is the force behind ceremonies, prayer sticks, ritual smoking, etc. The prayer pipe is regarded as an aid to "concentrating" (so said my informant). Its name, *na'twanpi,* means 'instrument of preparing' " (p.150).

This not to say that, if we were to adopt this thought-style, that we should then hope to make plants grow or enemies change their ways merely by the power of our thought. But it does mean that by the use of vivid thought, guided by a concentrated focus on a particular entity, we can *prepare* ourselves, *sensitize* ourselves, to relating ourselves to it when we meet it in actuality, with the appropriate expectations and anticipations which, if they are fulfilled, will, in appropriate circumstances, enable me to say: "Yes, this is just what I would expect of this entity;" or, if they are not fulfilled: "No, that is not at all what I expected, something's missing." Thus, with my practical understanding of what a plant, animal, person, or event actually *is* in itself, I am able to anticipate at least the style of its unfolding, I can attend to its behaviour knowledgeably and interact meaningfully with it, even if I cannot predict the actual mechanical details of its unfolding. Indeed, those who gather around to smoke the pipe before peace negotiations, are already, in practice, halfway towards a more common, cooperative form of life – their smoking together is a *preparation* for the more explicit negotiations about to occur between them.

The 'trafficking' of thought with things: surrogational 'aboutness'-thinking versus 'withness'-thinking

This way of acting, then, guided by an inner, focused attention on a particular, concrete image of an entity, in which one's thought 'traffics' with the entity in question can be called *withness*-acting, to distinguished it from *aboutness*-acting, in which one guides one's actions by reference to a surrogate of the entity. I will outline it more fully in Chapter 9. Here, suffice it to say that all this implies that the answer to Whorf's first question – as to whether concepts of 'time', 'space', and 'matter' are given to all humankind in essentially the same form – is clearly: 'No'. The Hopi, in some sense, live in a space and time quite different from our space and time. Furthermore, whatever the space-time or time-space they do live in is, 'it' seems to be furnished quite differently from ours. It seems to be full of activities in which they can (to an extent) participate, rather than of things external to, and separate from, them. Such a form of life appears quite incomprehensible to us; we cannot easily assimilate it to any already familiar, *organized* common sense scheme of understanding. Indeed, our difficulties with it are manifested, as Harris (1980) says, in our modern theories of language, for they present "... a revealing anatomy of the difficulties inherent in an essentially literate society's attempt to conceptualize something it has forgotten, and which it cannot recall form its cultural past: what an essentially non-written form of language is like" (p.18).

We have forgotten what a language is like which consists only in *words in their speaking*, for, since Saussure's (1960/1911) pioneering work in general linguistics, we have studied only *patterns of already spoken words*, in short, written forms. And further, we have taken it that these written shapes or forms get *their* shape or form by standing in for things – for, without the ordering power of linguistic *forms* Saussure claimed, thought was simply a "shapeless mass" (p.55).

But, as Harris (1980) points out, Saussure's (1960/1911) thought drew from a much earlier past: "The concept of a language which survived as part of the intellectual inheritance of modern linguistics first took shape in Graco-Roman antiquity... The first of these strands which claims attention is the idea that words are essentially surrogates or substitutes for others things. Languages are thus surrogational systems, which provide the language-user with a set of verbal tokens which stand for, or take the place of, non-verbal items of various kinds" (p.33). And, Harris continues: "It is the surrogational concept of a language which sanctions the belief that a true proposition is a faithful representation of reality.. The validity of the argument is grounded in the assumption that something outside language guarantees the stability of verbal meanings. There must be things other than words for words to stand for" (p.59).

However, as we have already seen, this *surrogational* view, while intrinsic to SAE linguistic forms, is not the case in Hopi; and, as I see it, it need not be the case in SAE as well. For, when Wittgenstein (1953) remarks that: "A picture held us captive. And we could not get outside it, for it lay in our language and language seemed to repeat it to us inexorably" (no.115), it is precisely from our imprisonment by this 'picture' of language use that he is trying to release us. And by applying his remedy – of bringing "words back from their metaphysical to their everyday use" (no.116). In other words, as Wittgenstein suggests, it is much more prevalent in our official, written forms of language than in our everyday talk – and we can in fact find enclaves of language use within our own 'conversational realities' which appear to be very similar to Hopi uses.

Withness-thinking and withness-talking in SAE

In our everyday practical talk, rather than using the terms 'space' and 'time' like philosophers (to represent absolute and abstract entities), we often say such things as: (1) "There's no space in our relationship for such things,"(2) "I must make time for that," (3) "He's spaced-out man," (4) "We've too much time on our hands," and so on. In other words, we use the words 'space' and `time' in constituting actual and concrete features in and of the context in which they are used. We indicate by their usage, perhaps (to take the examples above in turn), that: (1) certain activities will invite sanctions, (2) that we're under pressure, that too much should not be expected of us, but we'll still try to do it, (3) that he's disorganized, that there is a lack of logical coherence in his behaviour and he is not to be relied upon, (4) we're bored, not engaged in anything interesting, so we're open to suggestions, and so on. In other words, how we live practically is not best described as taking place in a three-dimensional space of things in motion through *time* as a fourth, space-like dimension, but in a 'time-space' of 'nonlocatable' regions and moments, offering us various invitations and prohibitions, etc., *in relation to or relative to our current activity.*

It is difficult for us, however – when asked inappropriately formulated questions (see Chapter 5) – not to assign places in actual space somewhere, in which we feel the 'things' we speak of *must be* located. Yet as Wittgenstein (1981) says: "'I feel a great joy' – Where? – that sounds like nonsense. And yet one does say 'I feel a joyful agitation in my breast'. – But why is joy not localized? Is it because it is distributed all over the body? Even where the feeling that arouses joy is localized, joy is not....'Where do you feel grief?' – In the mind. – What kind of consequences do we draw from the assignment of place? One does not speak of a bodily place of grief...." (nos. 486 and 497). The answer will occur to us, he suggests (1989, I) if we ask: "But what does behaviour include here? Only the play of facial expression and gestures? Or also the surrounding, the occasion of the expression?..." (no.129). In other words, talk of place does not necessarily imply a *geographical* location, but is in fact to do with *the circumstances* surrounding our expression. For example, while we might say to someone "The love I feel for you is in my *heart*," that is not actually where we should look for the import of their statement. In practice, its implications are 'in' the subsequent context between that person and oneself that the statement helps to create, they are to found 'in' the subsequent interplay. In other words, the relevant circumstances can be intelligibly described perfectly well in the ordinary language available to us currently. Thus, the establishing of a special language for the description of 'eventing' is not as necessary as Whorf thought. What then is required?

Only, seemingly, the recognition and restoration to legal tender, so to speak, of some currency we in fact already possess in our ordinary, everyday talk – as well as the restoration of people's *poetic* rights to coin more, as and when they require it. The establishing of these new ways of sense-making is difficult, not because they are contrary to fact, nor because they are counter-intuitive, nor because they require description in a wholly new language, but because they require the reconstruction of our official accounting practices (our 'basic' ways of talking in terms of which we maintain our "official" forms of life). For it is these that currently rule ways of talking in terms of events and 'eventing' out of court, and reimpose talk of things and substances back upon us.

Intuition and 'recepts' from language

Given that, nonetheless, there are enclaves of understanding within our own 'reality' which appear to be very similar to Hopi ways as described by Whorf, why do we so easily fail to notice them? Why do the philosophical views characteristic of Western thought – especially Cartesian mind-body dualism – receive such massive support from our everyday, unreflective talk, while holistic, relativistic, and relational views of reality, similar to those of the Hopi (which have been argued for by philosophers and scientists, sages and priests, over and over again), remain mostly ignored in our more reflective moments, in our 'official' intellectual talk?

It is not because such views are refuted by *the* facts – indeed, as we now realize, there is no way in which 'facts' as such can ever in themselves 'refute' a way of speaking intertwined in with a form of life, for *it* determines what is to be 'accounted' as a 'fact' within that way of living. Nor is it because, contrary to what often is claimed, are they counter-intuitive. While Newtonian notions of space, time, and matter are often said to be intuitive, and relativity is cited as an example of how mathematical and scientific investigation can prove intuition wrong, is *that* actually what Einstein's discovery (invention?) of the theory of relativity proves?

Laying the blame on intuition, says Whorf, is wrong: "Newtonian space, time, and matter are no intuitions. They are," he says, using a special word, "*recepts* from culture and language. That is where Newton got them" (p.153, my emphasis). In other words – as recepts from language (to give the dictionary definition of the word) – they are mental images without an intellectual basis; they are fictions invented by us to satisfy expectations generated by our own badly formulated questions (see Chapter 5). What they represent as being 'in' the world is in fact 'in' our way of representing such matters to ourselves. They arose out of our current ways of speaking (of predominatingly of things and substances), and that is why – unlike Whorf's current awkward talk of "eventing", and "latering" – they were and are still so easily accepted back into these ways of talking.

As Whorf (1956) says, if intuition is not to blame, the reason why relativistic and relational views find it so difficult to gain acceptance, is that "they must be talked about in what amounts to a new language" (p.152) – one which, so to speak, seems to go against the grain of our current "fashions of speaking" (p.158). For our current fashions of speaking orient us toward already existing things and substances in space; they do not orient us toward entities in which various intensity factors influence the unfolding of certain tendencies in duration. To point ourselves in new directions, with new anticipations as what to expect next in our meetings with the others and othernesses around us, would seem to require, apparently, a language of verbs, a vocabulary of activities. Seemingly, we must talk in new terms in an attempt to make a new kind of sense. But must we? As I have already indicated, the turn I will take here will not be to coin new words – to *verb* nouns, to produce verbs like 'eventing', 'latering', or 'languaging' – but to follow Wittgenstein's (1953) lead in both "bringing words back to their everyday uses," and to coin new *poetic* meanings by the juxtaposing of ordinary words in extraordinary combinations.

Daniel Stern: the present moment

Daniel Stern (2004), working from a background of experience studying the mico-momentary worlds of naturally occurring mother-infant interactions, plus experience with choreographers and dancers attending to similar fleeting events, and from a long experience as a reflective psychotherapist, working with a collaborative group of other reachers and practitioners, has provided us with a book-length exploration of what he aptly calls "the temporal architecture of the present moment" (p.41). To repeat the point made in the epigraph quote used at the beginning of the chapter, Stern (2004) points out that we do not in fact make sense of and in the present moment retrospectively, only after it has already been completed as a discernable and categorizable pattern. It is made sense of as it "plays out a lived emotional drama. [And] as the drama unfolds it traces a temporal shape like a passing musical phrase" (p.4).

Thus, as Whorf outlines for the Hopi, we can be 'touched' by the specific temporal shapes unfolding in such moments in clearly discernable (and very memorable) ways. Stern (2004) gives a number of very nice examples: two from micro-analytic interviews, in which by simply asking clients, *And what happened then?*, he enables them to describe in profuse detail their own rich experience of seemingly banal events; a third about a handshake which changed the course of an entire therapy; and a fourth, which I will expand on now, about a reaction shared with strangers to a witnessed event.

The event in question was to do with watching a talented street mime who was surreptitiously mimicking the moods, postures, and walks of passersby to the amusement of onlookers. But one woman he chose to imitate realized what he was doing and upbraided him. But the mime simply continued to mime her upbraiding him; then she began to imitate his imitating of her. He went the next step until the two laughed, shook hands, and parted – while onlookers clapped. At that point, Stern stood up to go and so did a couple sitting near to him: "We looked at each other, smiling, raised our eyebrows, tilted out heads in a funny way, made some kind of indescribable facial expression, and opened our hands, palms up to the sky – all as if to say, 'It's a crazy, amusing world'. They went their way, I mine" (p.21).

We all have experience with such events. Even the simple event of acknowledging a stranger – with eye-contact and a nod of the head – as we pass them by. In such events we acknowledge and reaffirm our membership of a society of beings able mentally, physically, and affectively, to share such inter-subjective moments of meaning with each other.

About such moments, Stern (2004) notes that the unfolding events happening between people in such moments of meeting (1) create shared knowledge to do with their relations with each other that is often understood *implicitly*, and need not be talked about to have its effect. They also (2) enable each to sense the experience of the other, and to sense their own participation in the other's experience; thus there was, to an extent, an *interpentration of minds*; a unique state of intersubjectivity was created between them. Further, (3) while each such moment appeared quite spontaneously, its appearance was nonetheless *prepared* for by many preceding events in the experience of the individuals concerned. And also, (4) although each moment was very short, a 'story' unfolded – a directly experienced story, not one written or told, but a temporal structure with a beginning, middle, and an end to it. Thus, finally, (5) such moments are *memorable moments*, in that although they might not have been verbalized at all at the time, they can be recalled time and time again, and give rise to quite a number of verbal formulations. Indeed, it is just this quality of such moments – that they can be recalled time and time again and are amenable to innumerable verbal formulations – that makes them central to the methods of a *social poetics* developed by Arlene Katz and myself (Katz and Shotter, 1996; Shotter and Katz, 1996), discussed earlier, in Chapter 5; we call them 'striking', 'moving', 'arresting', or 'touching' moments.

Such moments seem to matter to us in that, in our lived *experience* of them, they unfolds in such a way as to accommodate novelty or to resolve a difficulty. In other words, in connection with what earlier we called *difficulties of orientation* or *relational difficulties*, such 'striking' moments seem to provide us with the kind of exemplars we need, in moments of disorientation on encountering something unexpected, to remind us ways of relating, or modes of orientation, or styles of address, that might be helpful in re-orienting us. See in this respect Wittgenstein's (1969) remark quoted in Chapter 5, on the importance of examples in establishing and teaching a practice. They can arouse in us the basic reactions that, in spontaneously 'moving' us to relate ourselves in *this* rather than *that* manner to a circumstance, can provide us with the sense in which we should respond to rule statements – without such exemplars to guide us, our attitude to rules would be left open to interpretation, to our imposition of a meaning to them.

This, Stern (2004) sees, is also a difficulty with our *narrative* accounts of temporally unfolding events: "Narratives select episodes of life and mark them in time: before, after, again, and so on. These episodes are then rearranged, not necessarily in historical order, but to tell the most coherent story about what life felt like. The narrative aims at life verisimilitude, not historical truth. In this way, narratives give us back the feeling of continuity in life (Bruner, 1990, 2002; Ricoeur, 1984-1988). They tame *chronos*, make the passage of time seem familiar and tolerable, and make us feel coherent along this infinite dimension. They do not, however, tame the present moment... *now* has no place in a narrative account except as a point of reference. In a narrative, the *now* that is being talked about has already happened. It puts past and future *nows* in relation. It is not a direct experience. Only the telling is happening *now*" (p.6, my emphases on 'now').

Attention needed to the 'architecture' of the moment of now, for it not only has a temporal dynamic within itself, but its importance lies in its relations other pieces of time, in the ways in which it is interwoven into them, not within itself. If each present "now" conceived of as like a bead on a thread, then these inter-relations are lost, and we are once again tempted to *impose* narratives upon life again, retrospectively, to give it form.

To avoid this, to avoid losing the dynamic phenomena available to us in the duration of the present moment, Stern (2004) draws our attention to the temporal contours of experienced events, to the dynamic time-shapes we can in fact vividly experience within them – he calls them "vitality affects." To get an idea of what he means here, imagine the time course of events as, say, a firework (a sky-rocket) shoots up into the sky, bursts, showers out, then crackles as each glowing fragment slowly falls to the ground. Imagine also the dawning and development of a smile, a piece of music, the unfolding of an utterance. "Vitality affects emerge as the moment unfolds," says Stern (2004). "This is captured in terms such as *accelerating, fading, exploding, unstable, tentative, forceful*, and so on" (p.36). These are, of course, just the same kinds of terms as Whorf (1956) called "tensors" in Hopi – parts of speech that convey distinctions in the sequencing and intensity of changes in time, as well as qualities of strengths, that we might express metaphorically in terms of rough, hard, flat or smooth. They relate also to what, as we have seen, William James (1890) called "*feelings of tendency*, often so vague that we are unable to name them at all" (p.254).

For Stern (2004) then, the moment of meeting is a key event in bringing about change. As we have seen above, particularly in relation to Bakhtin's (1981, 1984, 1986, 1993) work, the very nature of dialogically-structured events is such that those involved in them experience (or can experience) what Stern calls a "now moment" (p.166) – what above I called a striking or moving moment – moments when quantal changes in the conversational reality emerging between them occur. As a meeting between two people unfolds, Stern (2004) describes what occurs in such moments as a kind of micro-journey, lasting seconds, taken by them together, through time and space; he calls such micro-journeys, *shared feeling voyages*: "During a shared feeling voyage (which is the moment of meeting), two people traverse together a feeling-landscape as it unfolds in real time. Recall that the present moment can be a rich, emotional lived story. During this several-second journey, the participants ride the crest of the present instant as it crosses the span of the present moment, from its horizon of the past to its horizon of the future. As they move, they pass through an emotional narrative landscape with its hills and valleys of vitality affects, along its river of intentionality (which runs throughout), and over its peak of dramatic crisis. It is a voyage taken as the present unfolds. A passing subjective landscape is created and makes up a world in a grain of sand [to quote William Blake]" (p.172).

Such moments are crucial in that those who participate in them find that after them, their relationship is changed. There has been a discontinuous leap, a quantum jump. Certain distinctions have been 'redrawn', new dimensions of relation have been created, what was background becomes foreground, coherence and complexity have been enlarged. In the developed and developing event between them, they have co-created an expanded intersubjective reality that opens up new possibilities of ways-of-being-with-each-other. They are changed and are now related to, or oriented toward, each other differently for having changed one another.

This is why a shared feeling voyage is so different from just listening to a friend or patient narrate episodes of their life story – or, in Bakhtin's (1984) terms, why a dialogical relation to another is so different from a monological one. Because in such relations, one has a chance to get immersed in another's experiences, to become 'possessed' by their otherness. When this occurs, experience is shared as it originally unfolds. There is no remove in time. It is direct – not transmitted indirectly and retrospectively by 'aboutness'-talk solely in words. It is co-created by both partners and lived originally and directly by both.

Conclusions

Like Wittgenstein, then, Whorf (and Stern) can force us to see that our 'basic ways of being in the world' are not as basic as we had thought. They can be thought of, and talked of, in other ways: as a world of activities and events, rather than as of substances and things. Like Wittgenstein also, Whorf does this through 'grammatical' studies that explore what is felt by native speakers to connect with what. And, irrespective of whether his account of Hopi grammar is 'true' or not, like a good piece of science fiction writing, what he has to say enables us to imagine other ways in which we might make sense of our own forms of life. Indeed, they suggest to us, not so much the need for a change in our vocabularies, as a change in our orientation toward things occurring in our surroundings – we need to focus on 'eventings', on the changing relations occurring in our inter-activities, between ourselves and our surroundings, as they unfold over or through time.

Such 'eventings' are so simple and natural, so much an everyday part of our feelingful way of 'going on' with the others and othernesses around us, yet they are very hard to portray accurately in words. We need a language, one that does not yet 'officially' exist, that is oriented toward capturing the temporal dynamics involved. This is something of a paradoxical requirement because, as I have continually emphasized in the earlier parts of this book, all such experiences occur for *yet another first time*. To this extent, such experiences are all extraordinary events; they cannot be captured in any already existing categories. Yet, although they must always startle us, and are capable of changing our lives in irreversible quantum jumps (occurring in a sequence of small, controlled steps or in one big 'moving' moment), they are in fact a perfectly normal aspect of our everyday lives. As Bakhtin's (1981, 1986) work shows, we would be unable to understand the unique meaning of people's utterances without the occurrence of such 'eventings'. Indeed, as we noted in Chapter 3, the expressive efforts that speakers put into 'shaping' their voicing of their utterances, efforts that are manifested in what Bakhtin (1993) calls their "emotional-volitional tone," guide us in understanding how to *orient* or to *relate* ourselves to their utterances, i.e., to get a sense of their 'point' and 'purpose', the speaker's degree of commitment to them, and why he or she is motivated to utter them.

So, although currently in our 'official' talk we spatialize time, and talk of it as a fourth dimension of space that can be measured, and think of ourselves as living somewhere on that spatial dimension 'in' an historically changing world, Whorf's account of Hopi reality has some lessons to teach us. For, the Hopi (truly, or merely in Whorf's version) *dynamize* their space, and talk of it as space in which their thinkings and feelings are in a responsive, interactive contact with the influences at work in their surroundings.

For us to think of ourselves in this way – as like, say, a compass needle, thoughtlessly but sensitively registering changes in a surrounding magnetic field – goes against the grain of our thought about ourselves as the agents of our own actions. But we *can* think it, nonetheless. Indeed, in the relationally-responsive version of social constructionism I have outlined in this book, the supposed 'thinkings' and 'feelings' that we talk of as having to do with events occurring out in our world, have to be located out there, out in the world in which our talk in relation to them takes place – they are a part of the whole into which our talk is interwoven as an active *participant part* of that whole. To locate our 'thinkings' and 'feelings' in 'the mind' is to locate them in something imaginary rather than in reality.

By the same token, it is worth reminding ourselves of what Whorf said about the relationally-responsive power of language to create in us a seemingly incorrigible (but nonetheless, fictitious) sense of the 'reality' in which we live, a 'reality' that aspects of which our 'mind' can 'intuit'. What we talk of as our 'intuitions' are, he said, *recepts* from culture and language, i.e., they are present in our ways of talking to ourselves *about* our way of being 'in the world'. They are, in other words, 'rooted' in our current ways of speaking – whose primary function is the forming of different forms of life – and they work 'developmentally' to supplement, to specify, or to articulate these forms of life further.

But it is also worth noting, that it is only in working outwards, from within such intralinguistically constituted 'realities', that we can make intelligible contact with that which is due to *other than* our recepts from language. And it is this possibility – that of making contact with an otherness different from ourselves – that saves us from being wholly entrapped within intralinguitic realities of our own making. For, as we have seen, in dialogue with the others around them, different people can come to understand their differences. Thus, within a dialogical perspective, the problem of linguistic relativity takes on a quite different, nonvicious character. The different ways of being in the world of different peoples, although not easy to interlink, are not forever incommensurable.

This does not mean, however, that we are at last in a position to discover that final form of life that we all, as human beings, *should* live. For our task in the future is just as much a task of making as of finding. Each time we encounter a limitation upon our ways of knowing others (or ourselves) – as we did in revealing our entrapment by the traditional epistemological paradigm – we must try to identify it by contrasting our knowledge practices with alternatives, thus to respect the being of others (and ourselves) more effectively. And this is a process to which, of course, there is no foreseeable end, either in theory or practice. But distinguishing that which is due to our talk from that which is not becomes possible only if we can grasp the nature of our part in the construction of our own intralinguistic realities. And it is as an aid in this task that I think the value of Whorf's work lies.

Chapter Seven

IN SEARCH OF A PAST: THERAPEUTIC RE-AUTHORING

"Look, I've spent ten years trying to dispose of the past by committing it to paper. Uselessly, of course, otherwise I wouldn't be here" [says Fraser to his psychoanalyst] (Fraser, 1984, p.186).

We have now assembled a large number of 'tools', i.e., experience-distant concepts (Geertz), for use in making sense of events and processes occurring in the joint actions in which people produce between them various social constructions, various conversational realities. It is now time to demonstrate the use of some of them in action. In this chapter, then, what I want to discuss is the nature of 'living' dialogue, the nature of the unfolding process in which two unique human beings, occupying unique places or positions in the world, with two unique biographical projects, come together to make some kind of contact with each other, motivated by the very fact that, due to their differences, there is a possibility that they might fulfil in each other what singly they lack. And here, I want to talk of this process in the context of psychotherapy.

In a number of recent papers, Anderson and Goolishan (1988, 1990, 1992) have been critical of systems theory and constructivist approaches to family therapy for not providing a place anywhere for different people's unique experience, for ignoring the client's 'point of view'. They want to open up a 'space' for a form of conversation within which the 1st-person voice of clients can be heard, a space within which it is possible for clients to express 'who' they *are*, a space in which they can communicate in some way what it is like *to be* them and how they experience their uniquely troubled world. And with this concern, I am completely in agreement, for I shall take it that the basic practical-moral problem in life is not what *to do* but what *to be*; and, that the basic problem in psychotherapeutic dialogue is how to orient toward, or to relate to, or to address another person in a way appropriate to helping them reshape or re-author what they *have been* in the past, and to enable them to face what they *might be* in the future with hope rather than fear, dread, or despair.

As we have seen, such difficulties of orientation, i.e., difficulties of the will rather than of the intellect (Wittgenstein), are of a very different kind to those that have the form of problems that have a definite solution. More than just with the usual scientific virtues of the truth or accuracy, we must also be concerned with whether our accounts or portrayals of the life of the person before us is *adequate*, whether we have been what Lorraine Code

(1987) calls "epistemically responsible" in our formulations of it, i.e., with whether we know enough of the person in order to conduct our personal relationships with them 'well' – can we, for instance, judge whether *this* utterance will be hurtful to them, *that* will be supportive, while *this other* will *move* them to a reorientation toward their plight. It is simply epistemically irresponsible to claim, in virtue of one's expertise, ahead of time, that one already knows the rules for hurtful and supportive utterances, for utterances that will bring new orientations. Thus, what Anderson and Goolishan want is a way of portraying psychotherapeutic events which respects the *being* of their clients, an account 'in' which their clients 'can recognize themselves', in which their 'voice' can be heard.

But this concern with adequacy is not the only major change of emphasis we must make in turning away from purely scientific concerns to those of, what could be called, just ordinary, everyday reasonableness (Toulmin, 2001). We must also be concerned with the kind of interactional interplays, the whole background style of exchange we employ in therapeutic dialogues, and whether it affords or makes available the special kinds of moment that earlier I called "interactive moments," or what Stern (2004) has called "now moments" – moments in which therapists can share with their clients, not so much cognitively clear *understandings*, as *feelings*, thus to establish with them a shared sensory (or sensuous) basis in terms of which *both* can intelligibly contribute in their different ways to the joint authorship of a (new) *biographical account* of the significance of just those very feelings. For like Bakhtin (1981) – who, as we have seen, talked of our words as being shaped, both "in an atmosphere of the already spoken.. [but also] by that *which has not yet been said* but which is needed and in fact anticipated by the answering word" (p.280, my emphasis) – Anderson and Goolishian (1992) also note about therapeutic questions, that they "drawn from the future by as-yet unrealized possibility of a community of knowledge... Conversation in therapy is the unfolding of these 'yet-unsaid' possibilities, these 'yet-unsaid' narratives" (p.34). But it is only in special, dialogically-structured moments that an utterance "always creates something that never existed before, something absolutely new and unrepeatable... out of something given" (Bakhtin, 1986, pp.119-120). Thus, as we shall see in the cases discussed below, clients difficulties are not resolved "by giving new information, but by arranging what [they] have always known" – by a dissolving of "the bewitchment of [their] intelligence by means of language" (Wittgenstein, 1953, no.109).

Being 'touched' in one's being: some preliminary cases

The therapeutic task, then, if the remarks above are correct, is not that of bringing to light new facts, but to help clients re-orient toward the already existing facts of their lives in new ways, to help them change their expectations and anticipations of later (future) events on the basis of their earlier experiences – to enable them to face what *might be* in the future with, to repeat, hope, rather than with fear, dread, or confusion.

(1) In this connection, let me first mention a case discussed by Anderson and Goolishan (1992): A thirty-year old man, Bill, a so called 'revolving door treatment failure' who has been hospitalized on many previous occasions as a supposed paranoid schizophrenic, is asked by his new therapist (at the Houston Galveston Family Institute): "What, if anything, could your previous therapists have done differently that would have been more useful to you?" The form of his reply (which I will not give in full here) is quite revealing: "That is an interesting question," he says. "If a person like you had found a way to talk with me when I was going crazy... at all the times of my delusion that I was a grand military figure... I knew this [delusion] was a way that I was trying to tell myself that I could overcome my panic and fear... If you could have talked with the 'me' that knew how frightened I was. If you had been able to understand how crazy I had to be so that I was strong enough to deal with this life threatening fear... then we could have handled that crazy general" (p.25).

What I have cut from the conversation (that I will mention in a moment) is what Bill says about why previous attempts at therapy with him only made him feel even more panicked and frightened. But now, at last, it seems, he feels involved in a conversation that has a some chance of helping him in a way that 'touches' him.

But what is it in simply that one brief question that allows him to sense that the whole nature of the relation between him and his therapist is now different? What is special about the character of the therapist's talk *this time* that the talk of his other therapists lacked? This time, presumably, he feels that the conversation is open, so to speak, to his anticipations and expectations. No matter how bizarre and strange they may be, they can nonetheless play a part in 'shaping' its outcome. Thus, not only is *this* a conversation he is 'in', but his expectations and anticipations are 'within' it too. In other words, he experiences it as a conversation continuous with his being, a conversation in which he can be 'touched' in his very way of being in the world, and thus, potentially, it is a conversation capable of helping him cope with his madness. Bill's talk *shows* that he has *an acutely discriminative sense* (James) of the difference between talk of *this* kind, and other kinds of talk.

2) Talk of this kind can influence one in one's being, deeply. It is not just mere talk, but talk that can change a person's whole orientation toward themselves, that can, so to speak, help them 'find their way about' inside their own possible ways of being in a less confused manner. Let me illustrate the *depth* of what is involved here with another story, one from Oliver Sacks's (1985) book, *Man who mistook his wife for a hat*. In it, Sacks tells of Witty Ticcy Ray, a 24 year-old New Yorker, almost incapacitated by Tourette's Syndrome, a virtuoso jazz drummer, a brilliant ping-pong player, but

someone who was continually fired from his job due to his tics. Sacks first tried him on a minute dose of haldol – a dopamine antagonist that works to suppress the effect of neurotransmitters at the synapses of our nerves – Ray became virtually tic-free for a two hour period. So Sacks sent him away on an appropriate tree-times a day dose for a week. The results were disastrous. His timing of his movements, his way of being in the world was completely upset; he would jump from catatonia and Parkinsonism to Tourettism and twitching, and back again, without any happy medium. The trouble was, Ray said: "Suppose you *could* take away the tics – there'd be nothing left." He seemed to have little sense of his identity, who and what he was, except as a ticquer. You can almost imagine him saying: the trouble is, doc, I don't know how *to be* an ordinary person! On a much more grand scale, he must have felt something like, perhaps, we feel when try, say, to cut our own hair in the mirror and our hands just will not seem to move in the directions we intend.

Nonetheless, Sacks felt that Ray *did* have the possibilities within him to be cured, the possibility to be moved from his strange world into ours. He thus suggested that they meet for three months or so to explore the ways in which Ray could be ordinary: "This deep exploration was exciting and encouraging in itself and gave us, at least, a limited hope," says Sacks. "What in fact happened exceeded all our expectations and showed itself no mere flash in the pan, but an enduring and permanent transformation of reactivity. For when I again tried Ray on Haldol, in the same minute dose as before, he now found himself tic-free, but without significant ill-effects – and has remained this way for the past nine years" (p.94).

What happened here to produce that 'transformation of reactivity' of which Sacks speaks? Like a lover[91], Sacks sought out 'hints' of new possible ways of being that Ray expressed in his conversations with him, and, so to speak, reflected them back to him. And, in "three months of deep and painful exploration, in which (often against much resistance and spite and lack of faith in self and life)," he says, "all sorts of healthy and human potentials came to light: potentials that had somehow survived twenty years of severe Tourette's and 'Touretty" life, hidden in the deepest and strongest core of the personality" (p.94).

But why should mere *talk* in relation to these potentials make a difference? After all, the potentials, as Sacks says, were already there in him somewhere, weren't they? Seemingly, what Sacks and Ray did in the talk between them was not, perhaps, to go so far as to construct an explicit 'town plan' of Ray's potentials. But at least, by talking over their nature and possible interrelations, their meaning and use in everyday practical contexts, Ray got 'a feel', for whereabouts within himself they lay; he got to know in Wittgensteinian terms, as I mentioned above, 'his way about' inside the potentialities of his own being.

But can such talk really influence the action of drugs upon the nervous system – mind over matter? Yes, I do think that mere talk, that other people's and our own speech, can influence the effects that not only drugs, but many other aspects of our material surroundings, can have upon us. But it is not mind over matter. It is just that kind of talk to which Wittgenstein wishes to draw our attention, and to point out that we will completely mystify ourselves if we talk about the power of our talk in that way: for, if we think of matter as one kind of stuff and mind another, we might expect them to affect each other like billiard balls of two different kinds of material affect each other – by bodily impacts, by clashing up against each other. No matter how effective that way of thinking has been in other contexts, in this one, it is a way of thinking that *prevents* us from seeing the solution that Sacks saw to Ray's problem.

What led Sacks to anticipate, to hope, that by mere talk he could help Ray to develop a certain kind of knowledge of himself, an understanding of a way around inside of his own ways of being and talking, I don't know. But somehow, he seemed to understand that Ray was at odds with himself, that he intended an outcome and somehow it turned out other than he had expected, and he didn't know why... and that a problem of this kind, deep within a person's being, could be solved through talk.

Practical hermeneutics

In pursuit of this aim, in their attempts to understand the role of talk in the psychotherapeutic process, Anderson and Goolishan (1992) think of themselves as taking an interpretative, hermeneutical 'turn' – but one of a special kind. For rather than, as in many other forms of psychotherapy, including psychoanalysis (as well as in normal, everyday life activities) – where therapists make interpretations and construct stories against a background of what, on the basis of their professional or common sense knowledge, they think *ought* to be the case,given the facts of a client's life – Anderson and Goolishan have proposed what they call a "not-knowing" approach[92], an approach which allows the client to 'make', or to 're-author', a new biographical account of their lives. Thus, rather than having a narrative imposed on them of an already theoretically determined kind, a finished product supposedly 'discovered' for them by the therapist's 'scientific investigations', clients have the chance to explore the *narrating* of a new account of themselves within a back-and-forth, dialogically-structured exchange with their therapists – it is, as we shall see, the activity (a process) of narrating a new account, rather than in coming to possess an account with a new structure to it (a new product), that is crucial. For, to reiterate a now dominant theme in this book: it is primarily in the unfolding dynamics, in the back-and-forth 'movements' occurring in our interchanges, that the influences *orienting* us toward how next we might respond to our interlocutor's previous expression(s) become available to us. But different styles of movement are made available according to the different styles of address adopted towards clients.

Thus, in the relationally-responsive view toward language that I want to adopt in this book, the view of the human world that I shall take (a view that I also share with Anderson and Goolishan), is that the world in which we live our lives is best thought of as a whole 'multiverse', or 'social ecology', of unique but dynamically interdependent regions and moments of human communicative activity. And in such a multiverse (surprising though it may be to say it), language is neither primarily for the representation of the world, nor for the achievement of shared understandings: it is used much more practically. As I see it, in its spontaneously responsive workings, it is primarily for creating relationships, and within those relationships, different *ways of being* for the participants, according to how they *address* each other.

Orienting toward one's addressees as 'without rank'

In this connection, we noted earlier, Bakhtin's (1986) comment that: "An essential (constitutive) marker of the utterance is its quality of being directed to someone, its *addressivity*... Both the composition and, particularly, the style of the utterance depend on those to whom the utterance is addressed, how the speaker (or writer) senses and imagines his addressees, and the force of their effect on the utterance" (p.95). Here, I would like to expand that comment to include how Bakhtin (1986) sets out the range of potential addressees: "The addressee's social position, rank, and importance are reflected in a special way in utterances of everyday and business communication. Under the conditions of a class structure and especially an aristocratic class structure, one observes an extreme differentiation of speech genres and style, depending on the title, class, rank, wealth, social importance, and age of the addressees and the relative position of the speaker (or writer)... This addressee can be an immediate participant-interlocutor in an everyday dialogue, a differentiated collective of specialists in some particular area of cultural communication, a more or less differentiated public, ethnic group, contemporaries, like-minded people, opponents and enemies, a subordinate, a superior, someone who is lower, higher, familiar, foreign, [or of a different gender – js] and so forth... All these varieties and conceptions of the addressee are determined by that area of human activity and everyday life to which the given utterance is related" (p.95). As Bakhtin sees it, each one of these addressees influences the *style* of a speaker's speech, as style that shows up in their word choice, grammatical devices, pausing, pacing, emphases, and other aspects of their speech expressed in the temporal contouring of their utterances.

But of particular relevance here, are his remarks about "intimate" speech genres: "Finer nuances of style are determined by the nature and degree of *personal* proximity of the addressee to the speaker in various familiar speech genres, on the one hand, and in intimate ones, on the other. With all the immense differences among familiar and intimate genres (and, consequently, styles), they perceive their addressees in exactly the same way: more or less outside the framework of the social hierarchy and social conventions, 'without rank', as it were... Intimate speech is imbued with a deep confidence in the addressee, in his sympathy, in the sensitivity and goodwill of his responsive understanding. In this atmosphere of profound trust, the speaker reveals his internal depths" (Bakhtin, 1986, pp.96-97).

Thus, Anderson and Goolishian's "not-knowing" approach involves them, not only in the renunciation of the expert's standpoint, and along with it, the right to impose interpretations, narratives, etc., on their clients, but it also works to works to institute a form of partial togetherness – an intimate speech genre in which both client and therapist meet, as it were, 'without rank' – so, *in relation to or with the therapist*, clients are able to reveal their own unique otherness in their expressions. But for this to be fully possible, this mode of communication must, I think, as it unfolds be 'rooted' in certain 'special moments': moments in which therapists share with their clients, not so much cognitively understandings, as *moments of common feeling*.

Such moments of shared feeling can provide something of a common ground, a shared (sensory or sensuous) basis in terms of which *both* can intelligibly contribute in their different ways to the joint authorship of a (new) biographical account of the significance of just those very feelings. And the nature of these special 'moments' – in which "shared feeling voyages" (Stern, 2004) might take place – is one of the things that I want to discuss below.

Practical hermeneutics: the (chiasmic) interweaving of 'poetic' utterances into actions

However, if we are to understand their nature, we shall require more than the resources available in a solely hermeneutical, interpretative approach. For the hermeneutical approach – which in its application makes use of what is called 'the hermeneutical circle' – is concerned with a back-and-forth 'movement' between initial encounters with parts or fragments of meaningful behaviour, text, or utterances, and the fashioning of these fragments into a coherent, textual whole, a whole which, retrospectively, i.e., when you look back on it, is publicly intelligible text in itself. In other words, the back-and-forth movement ultimately gives rise to a *shared*, decontextualized, self-contained understanding on the printed page.

Such an interpretative hermeneutics has its place (and its dangers, as we shall see) in our biographical concerns. But our more immediate task, is that of trying to understand, prospectively and in practice, how conversation and dialogue can still proceed, *before* shared understandings (and the knowledge that goes with them) have been achieved! For, as we have already seen, in practice, genuinely shared understandings are infrequent, and only achieved with a great deal of special interpersonal work to do with their formulation, testing, judging and criticizing. For a truly shared understanding is not a simple, once and for all achievement. Indeed, as Anderson and Goolishan say, "...understanding is always a process 'on the way' and never fully achieved" (1988, p.378).

But what if, surprising though it may be to say it, it is not necessary for therapists to *understand* their clients in order to help them therapeutically? What if, paradoxically, the therapist's task is simply to help clients understand themselves better, to come – like Sacks' Witty Ticcy Ray – to know their own way around inside their own potentials better? Then the practical-hermeneutic task faced here takes on a rather different character.

Earlier, we discussed Geertz's (1983) account of the anthropologist's task as that of gaining a grasp of what others "perceive 'with' – or 'by means of', or 'through'...or whatever the word should be" (p.58), and of how we can gain that grasp by placing their, unfamiliar to us, experience-near concepts by placing "them in illuminating connection with experience-distant concepts theorists have fashioned to capture the general features of social life" (Geertz, 1983, p.58). A part of this task is the familiar hermeneutical one of "hopping back and forth between the whole conceived through the parts that actualize it and the parts conceived through the whole that motivates them" (1983, p.69).

Here, in our much more practical concern with helping an individual gain a more elaborate sense of the *possible* relations between aspects of their own experience than they have at present, it would seem that we need almost the reverse of this process: For our task is *not* that of arriving at an understanding of *their* already inter-related network of concepts, images, and methods of understand themselves and their world in *our* terms, in *our* experience-distant concepts (and other terms of art) with *our own ends in mind*. Our task is to help them use *their* means to *their* ends – to help them make new connections, to see new relational-dimensions, devise new images, etc, *through* which they themselves can make a new sense of their lives. For this, rather than an interpretative approach, we need a practical hermeneutics.

In the essentially noncognitive approach toward our use of language that I want to outline here, then, our different *ways* or *styles* of speaking become important because I am assuming that the primary function of speech is not simply to give listeners a 'picture' of an already existing state of affairs that was unknown to them. But that it's function is to help them 'give shape' to a circumstance that they are now 'in' but bewildered by, and further, to give such a shape to it that they are able to overcome their bewilderment and to 'go on' with their lives. But to do this, the relevant talk must come from the therapist at an appropriate moment. In an interpretative hermeneutics, it is usually the cases that all the relevant fragments are already available and the task is to arrange them into an intelligible whole. While in a practical hermeneutics, in which relevant fragments are still unfolding, and many may still exist in only an inchoate form, the *timing* of the therapist's talk, and its *style*, would seem to be crucial – as we shall see in the Fraser case discussed below.

Poetic forms and shared feelings

It is here, with regard to the *style* of therapy-talk, that the poetic function of language becomes most relevant. There are two aspects to poetic forms of talk that I want to emphasize, the first is much less familiar than the second: (1) The more unfamiliar aspect is related to its function as *poesis* (Greek for 'making'), to do with 'creating' a *first form* for what otherwise are in fact only vaguely or partially ordered feelings and activities. And it is this, that even in the face of the vague, indescribable, open, fluid, and ever changing nature of human life, language can work to give appearances a sufficiently well ordered and structured form for us to be able to 'go on' with our actions in relation to them. Seeing events in our surroundings *through* our words (Geertz, Vygotsky) affords or makes available to us various expectations as to what might occur next as the events unfold. Thus it is its form-giving or form-creating aspect that is, for us, I think, its most important characteristic. However, (2) the most familiar aspect of poetic speech, is its capacity to 'move' us, to affect our behaviour and perception in some mysterious, noncognitive way. It is its capacity to affect people's 'feelings' in a spontaneous and immediate way that we shall also find below to be of great importance.

To illustrate this second aspect, and how a mere, brief utterance can create 'a moving moment' that can re-orient us in relation to our own lives, I want to make use of a line from Samuel Beckett's *Endgame* (Beckett, 1986, p.118). It is Hamm's vehement, angry, accusatory, but also self-pitying line, which comes after his account of why he had offered only minimal help to a poor man in the snow. He loses his patience with the man for still retaining a hope for a better future, and he says to him (and also to us all): "Use your head, can't you, use your head, you're on earth, there's no cure for that!" – a powerful line, I think you'll agree. But what does it mean? What does it do? For clearly, it doesn't tell us anything we didn't in some sense already know.

It imparts no new knowledge. But it does 'move' us in the sense of morally 're-positioning' us in relation to our own situation, so that we come to 're-see' it in a new perspective. It breaks the flow of our mundane thoughts and interests, and, in contrasting with them, confronts us afresh with a realization, a consideration, an occasion, perhaps, for a re-evaluation of our lives. In Wittgenstein's terms, it does not so much 'say' anything as 'show' us, or 'remind' us of, something that we already perfectly well know about ourselves. It reminds us of something that – because of being distracted by other more mundane issues – we are ignoring. Reminding us of it clashes with and thus problematizes (or 'deconstructs') our everyday circumstances. Thus its utterance thus provokes us into seeing them as being 'other than' what at first they seemed to be, into seeing new (but in this case tragic) possibilities within them. And if Hamm were a real person, it would also tell us something about him. As it is, we feel it tells us something about Beckett the writer – about his tragic vision, about what his world is like for him.

This, then, is one of the functions of what earlier I called a *social poetics* (Shotter, 1998; Shotter and Katz, 1996, 1998; and Katz and Shotter, 1996) in our forms of talk and writing in the social and behavioral sciences, and in philosophy: their role is to put our routine ways of talking on '*freeze frame*', so to speak, and then move us to search over the details in that *freeze frame* for ways in which to relate, or re-relate, ourselves responsively to aspects of it that we might not otherwise have noticed. Such utterances, due to their unexpected, extraordinary nature, can, in striking us also arrest us, and produce a delay between the moment of perception and the moment of action. And in that moment of delay, they can produce a special kind of experience where, seemingly, everything-of-relevance is present to us all-at-once. The greater this delay or 'zone of indeterminacy' becomes, the greater the listener's or reader's access to alternative possibilities for their next step in the orchestration of their own inner 'movements' becomes.

In other words, as I suggested in Chapter 3, in 'arresting' what might otherwise have been a next step in a more monological sequencing of our utterances, in that moment, a 'call' for the other voices existing within us to respond can occur.

But what is the nature of our being such that we can be moved like this? If as theorists, as thinkers and writers seeking to make sense of the nature of these 'arresting' and 'moving' utterances, we must do more than just formulate some new concepts; we must also practice a bit of conceptual psychotherapy upon ourselves, and allow ourselves to be a little bit changed in *our own* being: Thus our 'psychotherapeutic' task, is to recognize the deeply embedded, implicit metaphors lodged in the language in terms of which we currently unthinkingly think, and to replace them with others: for instance, we hardly need Rorty's (1980, p.12) reminders – about pictures and metaphors being more important than propositions – for it to be 'clear'(?) to us that much of our talk about our ways of thinking and knowing, makes use of a vocabulary of 'visual' terms. But what if, instead, we were to imagine ourselves blind, and as having to make sense of our surroundings by feeling our way forward like blind people, through the use of long canes? Then, for instance, we might find talk about knowledge – in terms of 'knowing our way around' (Wittgenstein, 1980, I, no.549); or, as being able 'to go on' (Wittgenstein, 1980, I, no.446) without stumbling or meeting insurmountable barriers – as not metaphorical, but as literally what having knowledge is for us.

In wanting to talk in this way about our mental lives, as I have already made plain, I have been greatly influenced, among others[93], by William James (1890) who, in his famous 'The Stream of Thought' chapter, talks of "*signs of direction* in thought, of which we nevertheless have an acutely discriminative sense, though no definite sensorial image plays any part in it whatsoever" (p.244). So when I talk of feelings here, it not simply to a feeling-in-itself that I refer, but to feelings of tendency – "a feeling of what thoughts are next to arise, before they have arisen" (p.247) – to quote James yet again. This aspect of feelings connects with what some other philosophers might call the *intentionality* of our mental activities: the *sense* that they contain an intrinsic interconnectedness with all else around them. And indeed, it is precisely this kind of language of 'feeling' – of being able to feel the 'shape' of the 'othernesses' around us through the use of various 'means' and 'devices' – that will help us to understand why narrative constructions can be such powerful psychotherapeutic instruments.

Thus let me emphasize again what I think is crucial for us to recognize here – an activity common to all the cases I have mentioned so far, and crucial too in the Fraser case discussed below – is the bringing of such 'feelings' back into the special, conversational or dialogically-structured realm of human interaction, in which they had first originated, and in which now, new possibilities for their re-formulation, new ways in which new words can be interwoven into them, can be created. This, indeed, was what was different about the talk that Bill got from his therapists, this time, that made it special: his therapist, in asking what kind of talk "would have been more useful to you?," allowed Bill right away to focus on his own disturbed feelings, and allowed him to begin a more dialogically-structured exploration of them.

So, what was the kind of talk he had encountered previously that seemed to prevent this? Some words of his that I omitted above can give us a clue here: what else he said was, that "rather than talk with me about this [his panic and fear], my doctors would always ask me what I call conditional questions." To which the therapist inquired: "What are conditional questions?" And Bill replied: "You [professionals] are always checking me out... checking me out, to see if I knew what you knew rather than find a way to talk with me. You would ask, 'Is this an ashtry?' to see if I knew or not. It was as if you knew[,] and wanted to see if I could... that only made me more frighten, more panicked." Such a form of talk, of course, did not have the loose-jointedness, the playful openness, of ordinary conversation. It was the monological, means-ends, problem solving talk of professionals intent upon applying their 'theories', and, on the basis of their 'observations', of coming to an accurate 'picture' of Bill's supposed 'inner mental state'. Where, it is hoped, of course, that the possession of such a 'picture' will provide the knowledge of what 'caused' his mental state, thus to re-cause it in a new and better configuration.

But this is a form of talk *external* to Bill's involvement in it, in which he had no constructive part to play in creating any of the new possibilities for being that might become available within it; if any new possibilities did come into existence at all, none felt continuous with his being, none were linked to any of his expectations or anticipations. It was a professional or scientific knowledge that was being sought.

Fraser: in search of a past

To make this issue less abstract – of how a poetic utterance, an utterance that 'strikes' us by confronting us with an unusual combination of words and in so doing can 'move' us from 'inner talk' of a monlogical kind to dialogical talk – let me mention another particular case: For some time now I have been both moved and intrigued by an account of his own (successful) psychoanalysis, written by the British oral historian, Ronald Fraser (1984) – he is well known in England for his 1979 book *Blood of Spain*, recording peoples' experiences of fighting in the Spanish Civil War (Fraser, 1984). When he was three [in 1933], Fraser's Scots father and wealthy American Mother went to live in a Manor House in the South East of England (the Home Counties) where his father embarked upon the life of the energetically idle rich: fox-hunting, shooting and entertaining, whilst his mother began to have love affairs. The account is intriguing, because he combines oral history material gathered in the early 1970's from the servants of the estate amongst whom he grew up [the period 1933-1945], with accounts of his psychotherapy sessions.

At the beginning of the analysis, 'P' (the analyst) asks Fraser "What exactly are you hoping for?" And Fraser replies ""Mmm... To consign – no, to recreate an uncertain past..." [pause] "With sufficient certainty to put it behind me." He wants just to be rid of the trouble it causes him. He describes his initial conflict, his unease, the dis-ease within his self or selves that his life on the estate produced within him as follows:

> "F: It's not surprising, perhaps, because there were two worlds, two houses within those same walls... Two Manors, under different roofs,... the old at the rear... where servants, nanny and children [Ronald and his brother Colin] lived; and the superimposed and imposing new Manor at the front, which belonged to the parents... 'I belonged without yet belonging'" (pp.4-5).

That, at least, was his initial, general formulation of his problem.

But as the analysis progresses, it seems to be rooted in a more specific feeling, one which *at first* he formulated as that of his mother as having abandoned him – but which, as we shall see, indicated that something else was at stake, something much more to do generally with sources of security and a sense of belonging. But the feeling, when he thinks of it as being directed toward his mother, was expressed thus:

> "P (the analyst): You've never forgiven your mother for leaving you with Ilse [the German nanny], have you?
> Fraser: No! I've never forgiven her for not being the kind of mother I wanted – an island in the sea from which a child can set sail on its own,

always sure there's a refuge to which to return to" (p.97).

He said this after what I think is the crucial analytic exchange. It goes like this:

> "F (Thinks: Since her [his mother's] death I have hardly thought of her, and says): 'I mustn't tell Ilse I love my mother for fear I may lose her, Ilse... Does that make sense?... What's it mean to be looked after by someone who isn't your mother while your mother is actually there?
> (long pause)
> P: Having two mothers, I suppose..."

"The words strike me with great force," says Fraser, and indeed, these are *poetic* words: to talk of a person as having 'two mothers' is, of course, unusual; it is to put some ordinary words into an extraordinary combination.

> "F: 'Two mothers! Split between each, neither sufficient in herself. Why have I never seen this?...' 'Two mothers and I'm torn between them...'
> P: '... you split them – into the good and the bad mother.'
> F: 'Oh...' (long silence) 'I split them! Not they me...'"

What the analyst does here, is to 'move' Fraser to confront himself with the objective fact that although his mother didn't help him as much as she might have done, and that, in fact, others on the Estate looked after him much better, they too placed demands upon him to judge her: and that in response to these demands, *he* split Ilse and Janey, not they him. The analyst's remarks draw Fraser's attention to facts that are at odds with Fraser's own initial conviction that he is merely a victim of circumstances. He can only 'bridge' this 'gap' intelligibly by bring his own agency into the foreground from its unnoticed place in the background.

This is the beginning of his 'cure', of him 'beginning to know his own way around inside himself', the beginning of his recognition of the degree to which he has been, and can be, a creative agent in his 'construction' of himself. In the conversational exchanges occurring in the 'analysis', the feeling of disquiet, or disorientation within himself that brought to the psychoanalyst – that he had first formulated as being 'split', and then as 'as having been abandoned', then as 'as having been a traitor', and then as 'as having been "disformed" by a past now out of his agency to control', and so on – is brought back into the special, conversational realm of human interaction in which it arouse in the first place. But now in a way in which he can become a little more aware of his own agency within the overall process of social construction. "I split them! Not they me... " He did not at first know *how* to accept this. The practicalities of it made no sense to him. As Fraser later said to P about his mother: "I wanted to love her, not destroy her..." (p.184). He had wanted to have her in a central place in his life; she was the one he had tried to be an 'I' for; she was the one for whom he had tried to be someone. And 'How can one write about one's past without an 'I' as the focus?' he had asked P earlier (p.90).

And this, I think, is crucial. It is to do with how Fraser thought of himself as 'placed', 'positioned', or 'situated' in relation to all the others around him: objectively, he was someone who was abandoned, someone who did not belong. Thus, in trying (as he thought) to be someone for his mother, he was trying to attain a 'feeling of belonging' – where 'belonging' means, I imagine, something like possessing the confidence possessed by the members of a ruling class, where whatever you might do wrong, you never lose your membership – they look after their own. While 'not belonging' means, I think, something like this: the carrying around of a hidden weight of anxiety that one is going to be judged and not only found inadequate, but, as a result, banished from further participation. Thus, he had set himself an impossible task: he was trying *to be* was someone who, from the position of not belonging, was trying to re-collect the fragments of his biography as someone who did belong. Thus, if not for her, for whom else could he *be* someone?

To 'move' him from this original, seemingly objectively true position, required a poetic use of language, the provoking of a dialogically-structured, 'arresting' moment. In the next session he says to his analyst:

> "F: I've reached the bottom line: to accept the destruction and start again...

(And he writes) "In the inner darkness I look across the years in silence until I hear him say:

> P: Without accepting it you wouldn't find parts of the lost ones in you again. It's like mourning..." (p.184).

And the analysis begins to draw to a close when Fraser begins to understand how his quest *to be* someone can, perhaps, be satisfied by other formulations. And he realizes how – not to be rid of his past – but to begin to *reconstitute* his biography (making use of all the events already 'inscribed' or 'embodied' in his being as the person he is) as body of knowledge he feels he can now rely upon. Instead of being confused and disoriented within it, he can now begin to find his 'way around' within it.

> "F: Yes, I seem to have made my peace with the house [he says].
> P: Well, your people live on in you perhaps more than you want to believe. Your mother, father, Ilse...
> F: Perhaps they do... ...and silently I feel them gathering, coming together, until they fill the emptiness around me...

> P: It was the unity of love you yearned for.
> F: Instead of the fragments, yes. The dead live on in us, despite everything, don't they? *Like people in books whom you can return to time and again...*
> P: Sure...[pause]" (p.186, my emphasis).

And that, I think – the phrase "like people in books you can return to time and again" – is the clue we need to understand what has actually happened to Fraser in his analysis, and I shall make more of it later. But, just for the moment, if we were to ask Fraser himself, 'How did the testimony about your mother (and all the others with whom you were involved) help you in "coming to terms with" your past?', then, at one level, he gives us a very nice answer. I would like to quote it here, because it emphasizes what we usually fail to notice. For, as he says to his analyst:

> "F: But all we've done here is to examine the fragments. We've never seen the totality, the causal relationships between them.
> P: [and his analyst replies] I doubt that one can ever be so precise... You want to be the subject of your history instead of the object you felt yourself to be.
> F: The subject, yes, – but also the object. It's the synthesis of the two, isn't it?
> P: The author of your childhood then, the historian of your past.
> F: That's what I intend – to write about it from the inside and out..." (p.187).

And that is, of course, what he does in the book. In other words, what he says here emphasizes – in talking about wanting to be both the continuing subject (the author) and the (developing well crafted) object of his own history – is not that the child is the father of the man, but just the opposite: that people who feel free (of the anxiety of 'not belonging') and are able to orient toward the future with hope and confidence, are themselves the authors of the children they once were (Crites, 1986). In short, the man is (or can be – to disagree with Freud) the author of their own childhood. And Fraser was able (with a little but very necessary help, and much work) to remake his 'I', the 'position', the point of view from which he can now recollect ('re-collect') the fragments of feeling he will require as a *resource* in his future biographical projects.

But let me emphasize once again what I think is crucial for us to recognize here: that central to the therapeutic exploration occurring in his conversations with his analyst, is the continued focus on Fraser's *feelings of disquiet within himself*, his inability to feel 'at home', so to speak, in any of his own forms of life, not on his 'formulations' or 'interpretations' of that disquiet. Each of these was an attempt to formulate a difficulty of the will, a difficulty of orientation or relationship, as a difficulty of the intellect, as a *problem* that could be solved by merely by taking thought. The beginning of his 'cure' – and here we begin to make contact with an activity common to all the cases discussed above – is the bringing of this 'feeling' back into that special, conversational realm of human interaction, in which it had originated, and in which now, new connections, uniquely new "relational dimensions" can be *dialogically* created between already existing fragments that were not previously in existence.

In other words, it is not simply the construction of a new narrative to replace the old that has happened here. If that were the case, then we might expect that a few years later, that too would become another imprisoning straightjacket. What has happened is that Fraser has become an *author* of all such narratives, with no single narrative being dominant over all the others, and with all being drawn, as and when necessary, from the real fragments of experience he embodies within himself.

Biographical fragments as a practical corpus

The comments above, clearly, bear on the current turn from logical, theoretical frameworks to 'narrative accounts' (Sarbin, 1986; White and Epston, 1989). For, if the living of a life does involve a situated, temporal working out of conflicting forces, it is all but impossible to represent the tensions and the movements, the 'motivations' and the 'desires' at work in such a process, in terms of a set of timeless theorems derived from abstract, context-free principles. We ways of depicting, or portraying, the dynamics at work in the unfolding of our activities. Thus, instead of theoretical structures, there is a turn to storied forms, to see, not only if they can function as the required intellectual device for collecting together an otherwise disconnected, fragmentary set of events into an intelligible whole, but also – just as 'theories' were thought to play a central role in how we made sense of ourselves and the events occurring around us – to see whether, as many now suggest, it is the stories that we tell ourselves about ourselves that 'instruct' our lives.

Can we now look at Fraser's new way of being in this way? Is it true to say that he has now re-storied his life? For clearly, instead of being able to 'get rid of' his past, as he had first thought, he ended by re-relating himself to it in quite a new way. I think not. He has done more than the mere re-storying of his life.

To grasp what I am trying to get at here, let us return to the classical hermeneutical approach outlined in a number of placers above, but now, to bring out one of its central dangers, what Donald Spence calls (1986) "narrative smoothing." It is a danger because a nice coherent, well organized narrative, with everything in its place, *prevents* the appearance of alternative *circumstantial* possibilities, amongst which, if we are to be the authors of our own lives, we must be free to judge. It ignores those dialogically-structured moments when, in a pause, in a moment when the next logical step is interrupted, other voices within us can be 'called out'. In other words, the very coherency of the narrative can divert our attention away from the fact that in our practical-moral activities, we are embedded in an ever changing sea of other possibilities from which we must continually select. Our attention is diverted, because, in a hermeneutical construction, all the fragments which have occurred are decontextualized, and made into a *orderly or systematic whole* – with, as Freud put it, the often insertion of the "missing portions" which *must* have 'originally' been there if things are to be orderly. This is the 'finding' or 'discovery' of a narrative by an expert, trained in expert skills – and Freud, as we all know, used the archeological metaphor[94]. Once we have found this correct whole, people's past actions can then be thought of as taking on their *proper* or *real* meaning within *its* context.

But this, I think, is absolutely wrong. What their actions take on there is not so much meaning as *intelligibility*, i.e., they become capable of being grasped reflectively and intellectually. The order has been *constructed* and the missing portions supplied, by drawing upon a 'grammar' implicit in our life and language, by drawing upon features implicit in our 'accepted' ways of coordinating our actions with one another – and to the rational intellect, such a grammar gives the appearance of a proper meaning. But it is, I shall say, a 'counterfeit' version. It has been 'minted' wrongly; it has the wrong origins. For it has issued from a desire for a single, particular way of ordering social life – which for Freud, concerned as he was with psychoanalysis as a natural science ("What else can it be?") was in terms of individuals achieving mastery and possession of essentially socially produced resources. This is what it debases: its own proper minting and currency in the 'hurly-burly' or 'bustle' of practical, everyday life events (Wittgenstein), in which there is no order, no one single, complete, proper or true order. "A faithful account of... of the context of discovery will very likely have the appearance," says Spence (1986), "of a disconnected series of fragments strung together. Surprise, bewilderment, and faint glimmers of understanding probably all circle around one another during the average [analytic] hour in much the same way as they appear during a dream state..." (p.231).

But if this is so, the *true* meanings of the events in the living of our lives cannot be properly understood within the confines of any coherently ordered account, narrative or otherwise. They are only to be found in the not wholly orderly, practical living of our lives. And this was Fraser's discovery: that if he was to be a 'maker', an 'author' of narratives – the author of his own childhood, the historian of his past – he had to find a new 'position' for himself, to re-orient himself in relation to his own past. What he needed to do was *not* just to carry *the* narrative of his past into the future, as if it were the only proper one, but to be able to draw together the fragments of his own past, as and when he pleased, to re-collect from them enablements (and constraints) of moment by moment relevance in judging how at present to best proceed in the realization of who he felt he should be in the future. This is why I emphasized his account of how he now felt about those he had known, that they were "like people in books you can return to time and again." No longer imprisoned within a single narrative, he realized he could treat his own biographical fragments as, to use a phrase of Alan Blum's (1970, pp.301-2), "a practically conceived corpus of knowledge." That is: rather than his embodied practical-moral experience remaining unnoticed in the background as a prison, he could now begin to bring into the foreground to use as a *resource*.

Conclusions

Thus, to sum up, first for Fraser and then for the therapist: (1) From Fraser's new position, as now the author of himself, his life now becomes an 'eventing' (Whorf), a sequence of still developing now-moments (Stern), and is now understood by him as such, that is, as an ongoing, two-way, back-and-forth process of 'construction', or of 'authorship', in which he is a prominent (but not the only) agent. It is a dialogically-structured process that oscillates, among other tasks, between the task of formulating two interlinked aspects of a narrative: one a retrospective, re-collective, hermeneutically constructed narrative aspect of *where* at present he *is*, and the other a prospective, pro-jective, poetic or dialogically formed narrative aspect of where at present he might *go next* – two quite different narrative aspects, each modifying or playing into the other, and each only ephemeral or momentary. For it is a mistake to think that the kind of understanding we seek is the final, 'proper', fixed narrative of our past lives, or, that we need a single well ordered script to carry us into the future. Each prevents us from being present at that moment of judgment when, in contact with the actual circumstances around us, we must recollect just those aspects of our past relevant for our future, at *this* moment in time. If we are to continually re-constitute our past in terms of the 'lure' of our future projects, we must be prepared, at least to some extent, to *continually* reconstitute ourselves (Crites, 1986).

Thus the 'I', who at any one moment we *are*, is poised in that tense bridging position (the 'present' moment), and must link an indefinite number of remembered episodes from that present point of view, while also being oriented toward a future project, while noticing as well... and it is this which we all forget ... the uniquely new opportunities also made available to us in our actual current circumstances. Fraser's problem was that he could not live with what he himself had so far made of his own biography; it did not make sense to him, or, for him; he could not easily use it; it limited rather then liberated him; he did not feel at home in it; it did not enable him clearly to 'see' how to 'project' himself into the future.

(2) This was Frazer's problem: but what was it like for the psychotherapist? If we ask: What *practically* happened in Fraser's analysis? Then I think we must reply along the following lines: (a) That to begin with, the analyst afforded Fraser the expression of his central feeling of insecurity and dis-orientation, the feeling that was at the heart of Fraser's 'dis-ease' with his life (expressed by him at first a *problem* of belonging yet not belonging). (b) But in not accepting that *this* was in fact Fraser's *problem*, but that is was an expression of something still *not yet said*, the analyst also afforded Fraser the opportunity to discover that the well-formed narrative he had fashioned from the fragments of his past history to 'explain' his disquiet (in terms of his 'belonging yet not-belonging') – together with his wanting to be an 'I' for his mother – not only made it impossible to *solve* his problem, but made the biography practically unusable.

Up until this point, the analyst could be said to be facing the task of 'finding' *the* all too well-made narrative within which Fraser had entrapped himself. (c) But as the analyst continues, and Fraser begins to offer other and very different formulations of his disquiet, the analyst's task changes to that of responding to the biographically engendered source *feeling* which these different narratives each, indeed accurately, but in fact inadequately, formulated. (d) At this point, the analysts's task changes from, primarily, a practical-hermeneutical to a poetic task: he now to 'move' Fraser to a new 'position' from which to make sense of his own biographical data. And he does this by firstly leading him himself to discredit his old position ('You split them'), and secondly by helping him to 'make' a new 'position' and thus a new biography for himself ('I split them, not they me').

In all of these activities, narrative instruments are in use in one way or another: hermeneutically and narratively. However, because there is no principled way in which we can decide which should have priority over the other, I want to end by emphasizing again the importance of the poetic, the 'dialogical doings' occurring in the telling of a narrative, rather than the final achievement of a new narrative – for it has not so far been given sufficient prominence in our theories of language. In moving away from the merely representational use of language (for monological use in communicating a 'picture' of a static state of affairs), and in beginning to focus on the myriad uses of the more dynamical forms of influence at work in our more dialogically-structured forms of talk – that we can begin to see at work *through* the experience-distant terms made available to us from our studies of Wittgenstein, Bakhtin, Vygotsky, etc., etc. – we can begin to gather around us the resources we need to 'see' the 'movements' involved in 'doing' communicating. They can enable us to 'see' the movement between the retrospective and prospective aspects of the process of understanding at work; to 'see' the differences between attending to what has already been said and the context to which it gives rise, and attending to the activity of saying something further, in which one person materially 'moves' or 'affects' another by their utterances *in that context*. By 'moving' us to new 'positions' in relation to our own story telling, they can enable us to 'see' how... we might 'move' ourselves to new positions by our own storytelling... which is, of course, one of the great powers, and one of the great dangers, of all storytelling. But, to repeat, it is only in the *narrating* of our stories that these movements happen; once the story has been told, the dynamical forms that produced its 'movingness' disappear.

Chapter Eight

HEARING THINGS IN THE TEMPORAL CONTOURS OF PEOPLE'S TALK:

TRANSITORY UNDERSTANDINGS AND ACTION GUIDING ANTICIPATIONS[95]

> "I begin to understand a philosophy by feeling my way into its existential manner, by reproducing the tone and accent of the philosopher. In fact, every language conveys its own teaching and carries its meaning into the listener's mind... There is thus, either in the man who listens or reads, or in the one who speaks or writes, a *thought in speech* the existence of which is unsuspected by intellectualism" (Merleau-Ponty, 1962, p.179).

> "Understanding a sentence is much more akin to understanding a theme in music than one might think" (Wittgenstein, 1953, no.527).

Much of the material in this chapter was first written in a paper in a symposium entitled: *Evolving Perspectives on this Thing Called Psychotherapy*, convened by Harlene Anderson at the Taos Institute, Oct 7th, 2005. In convening the symposium, she noted: *"This 'thing called psychotherapy' is becoming more and more medicalized and problem-saturated in today's marketplace. Pervasive is the language of best practices, evidence based practices, and techniques. These trends speak from an authoritarian or expert voice. The client's voice is left behind."*

In these comments, Harlene is responding to a move which we can now see, I think, being made by administrators everywhere in the Western world – in England under 'New Labour' governments, it is simply being called: 'modernization'. It involves the 'rationalization' of existing practices to make them both 'accountable' (in a budgetary but not in an ethical sense) and 'controllable' (by central government). It rests on the easy and wholly unexamined assumption that, what in the past has been done rather haphazardly in different ways in different local conditions, and thus in what *must*, inevitably, be in wasteful ways, can now be done more 'effectively', 'efficiently', and 'controllably' by practitioners having to satisfy externally imposed criteria in their practices (all in the service, of course, of tax cuts for the rich – for the poor everywhere are getting poorer). Thus at the beginning of each new administrative year, the program for the year is yet more cuts. But as far I have been able to establish, there is no "stop rule," i.e., no criterion of when enough cutting will have been done!

Central to such a process, is the assumption that all human activities can be made more efficient by the elimination of all irrelevant activities, as doing something for the second or third or fourth time, is no different from doing it for the first time. This easily made but never tested assumption is, I think, in almost all human affairs, utterly wrong. Indeed, it has been and is a central in this book that, in almost all human affairs, everything we do is continually being done for a yet another next first time. It is the uniqueness of the situations we deal with that everywhere is being lost. While individualism thrives, there is a contempt for uniqueness and individuality. A one-size-fits-all mentality seems prevalent everywhere.

Harlene Anderson in her introductory comments about the symposium, noted the loss of the client's own unique voice and personal experience. And as I have continually emphasized, and will continue to emphasize in this book, it is only by paying attention to a client's expressions and by allowing ourselves to be 'moved' by them, that we can get any sense of what their inner lives are like for them. But what can also be easily lost, in my estimation, is the psychotherapists's own unique use of their own spontaneously expressive being in responsive relation to their client's expressions. For what should occur every time afresh – for yet "another first time," as Garfinkel (1967, p.9) so nicely puts it – are the embodied, expressive utterances of the psychotherapist as she or he speaks in a way that is spontaneously responsive to the unique, embodied, expressive utterances of a client. For it is only in this atmosphere, the spontaneously responsive atmosphere of a truly dialogically-structured exchange, that possibilities for novel ways of acting, uniquely relevant to participant's concerns, can be created. They cannot be created according to deliberate pre-planned moves imposed on clients by the therapists.

Thus there is something very special, I think, that people can do in their haphazard (seemingly wasteful) collaborations with each other that they cannot do apart. But the uniquely new possible ways of going on in their lives together with the others and othernesses around them that they can create between them is only made possible by them, as living embodied beings, being spontaneously responsive to each other. This much, as we will see, is basic to our being in any kind of *open* dialogue with each other.

But what seems to me especially distinct about psychotherapeutic dialogues is that in them, therapists both speak to and listen to their clients in certain special ways – ways that are often *poetic* ways – and in so doing, ensure that many of the new ways of going on created are fashioned from their clients's own resources. New ways forward are fashioned in *their* terms, not in *our's*. So what I want ultimately to discuss here today are the understandings and anticipations that can be generated in us by certain features in the ongoing micro-dynamics of therapeutic encounters –

intonation contours, bodily postures and movements, patterns of breathing, etc. – that might make this focus on *their* potentialities possible.

As some of you may know, very much under the influence of Tom Andersen's emphasis on noticing and treating as significant the spontaneous occurrence of fleeting bodily events – as well as the writings of Wittgenstein, Vygotsky, and Bakhtin and Voloshinov – Arlene Katz And I (Katz and Shotter, 1996; Shotter and Katz, 1996; Katz and Shotter, 1996a) have begun to outline a non-systematic set of methods, the methods of what we call a "social poetics," for making sense of, as Bakhtin (1993) puts it, "once-occurrent events of Being" (p.2). Tom Andersen (1996) describes his interest in such events thus: "The listener who sees as much as he or she hears will notice that various spoken words 'touch' the speaker differently. The speaker is touched by the words as they reach his or her own ears. Some words touch the speaker in such a way that the listener can see him or her being moved" (p.121).

So, if I was allowed only one word to sum up this section of this chapter, it would be the word "responsive" – only if our acting is continually responsive to the expressive movements of the others around us can we remain in *living contact* with them. But if was allowed a second word, it would be the word "spontaneous" – for our reactions must not issue from any deliberations on our part. They must issue from the embodied ways of spontaneously giving meaning to the expressions of those around us *that we have grown into* (Vygotsky, 1978, p.88).

Spontaneously responsive listening and listening with intention

If one is speaking and listening to another in accord only with an internalized general schematism of one's own – speaking in terms only of one's own systematic logic, and listening only for opportunities to apply it – it is easy to ignore, to bypass, one's capacity to notice and to be spontaneously responsive to the kind of subtle events mentioned by Andersen.

Roger Lowe (2005), who has explored just this tension between "listening in order to speak" and "speaking in order to listen" – a distinction he took from Lynn Hoffman (2002) – gives a nice example that came to light on looking at the video-tape of one of his own therapy sessions: Beth is a 39 year old woman who has struggled for many years with debilitating panic attacks. He begins by following a systematic solution-focused sequence in an attempt to build a sense of evolving purpose and possibility, and he asks her to reflect on what would be a clear sign to her that things were improving:

> "**Beth**: I'd be able to go shopping with my husband in a strange store without having to check out where the nearest medical facilities are first.
> **Therapist**: How would that make a difference for you? *(a typical follow up in this sequence)*

> **Beth**: I wouldn't feel so helpless. I wouldn't be clinging onto his arm for dear life . . . (pause) *(as I hear these words, I immediately think of a typical "well-formed goal" question: what would you be doing instead? I begin to rehearse the wording of this question in my inner conversation* and tune out *to the end of Beth's sentence which continues,...* and he wouldn't have to cling on to me any more. *(Beth's voice goes very quiet and her expression turns sad as she almost whispers these final words.* But I do not attend to this *as I have already begun to ask, "What would you be doing instead?")*" (p.70, his italics, my emphases).

Lowe goes on to comment that because at this point he was "listening in order to speak," he ignored the expressive force of the spontaneous changes occurring in Beth's bodily demeanor and tone as she talked, which, if he had been more responsive to them, might have taken the conversation in a more significant direction. This comment is very apposite, as later in the session – while still resolutely following "well-formed goal" questions – Lowe went on to question Beth about yet further possible events that would signal her increased confidence. And, after having said that not caring about having a panic attack while with a friend, in answer to yet another possible-events-question from Lowe, Beth said that a difficult step would be for her to allow this to happen when she was with her husband. "*Noticing her pensive look, I invited elaboration*," says Lowe (2005, p.73, my emphasis). Suddenly her utter resentment at being so dependent on her husband bursts out. "The intensity of her own reaction surprises her and she reflects that, irrespective of the severity of the attacks, her marriage, in some fundamental way, may be over. Staying with these reflections seems more important than the prosaic pursuit of further signs of change. Exploring the unanticipated resonance of a single question takes precedence over the completion of a sequence," says Lowe (2005, p.74).

In other words, rather than Lowe using his expertise to direct his own exploration of Beth's impulses and other spontaneously aroused feelings, by inviting Beth to conduct her own further explorations, in her own terms, of her own spontaneous expression – her pensive look – he is 'inviting' Beth herself to answer the 'call' in her expression to which he feels 'called' to respond. This small change in who responds to the 'calls' exerted on us by both other people's expressions as well as our own, is crucial. For, while Lowe might all to easily have been tempted to offer an 'interpretation' of it, or a response in *his* terms to it, his invitation to her to elaborate on it, afforded her the opportunity to respond to it in *her own* terms.

Now I noted above the tension between "listening in order to speak" and "speaking in order to listen." But this is just one small aspect of a major tension in the whole of western thought that I have remarked on over and over again in this book: that between things we ourselves as individuals desire, want, and do, and things which just happen to us. As we have seen, the great power and attraction of Descartes' philosophy in his *Discourse on the Method of Rightly Conducting the Reason, and Seeking Truth in the Sciences* of 1637, is that it promised us that if we followed his method, we could not only be "masters and possessors of Nature" (Descartes, 1968, p.78), but also that "there can be nothing so distant that one does not reach it eventually, or so hidden that one cannot discover it" (p.41). In other words, we inherited both the idea that what we did deliberately and voluntarily was centrally significant in our lives, and that our deliberate control over the conditions of our lives could be expended indefinitely. Hence the cultural shock to the West with Freud's insistence on the unconscious influences in our lives, a shock, it seems to me, that we have still not got over – for we are still searching for mastery in our own terms within our professional lives, rather than seeking to be sensitive and knowledgeable participants in, and beneficiaries of, processes spontaneously occurring very largely beyond our agency to control.

Be all that as it may, what I want to emphasize here is not the shock to Western thought, but the fact that whether we like it or not, if we are participants in, and beneficiaries of, processes spontaneously occurring very largely beyond our agency to control, then a first task we face is that of portraying to ourselves what is in fact our relations to our surroundings. This task, this concern, is well put, I think, by Gadamer (1989), when he notes that his concern in his dialogic philosophy is with "not what we do or what we ought to do, but what happens to us over and above our wanting and doing" (p.xxviii). And I want here to underline this, for it is not at all easy to pay attention to what is just happening to us, spontaneously, in the background to our lives.

But this is precisely, I think, the great power of the philosophies of Wittgenstein, Bakhtin, Vygotsky, Merleau-Ponty, Mead, William James, Bergson, Bateson, Goethe, and many, many others. Rather than a focus on command and control, on visible, mechanistic forms of cause and effect activity, on events that can be pictured, they direct our attention differently, toward in Bergson's (1911) terms "the inner becoming of things" (p.322), toward the unfolding temporal contours of continuously evolving and developing events – think here of a tone of voice, a piece of music, the style of a person's walk, a firework bursting in the sky, note here also, Lowe's comment about Beth's "pensive look" – these are all events with a real and distinct but invisible *relational-structure* to them that can only be, a distinctive *time-contour* that, we say, can only be 'intuited' or felt. But note that Lowe takes it absolutely for granted that we all know what a pensive look looks like, and that he also knew it and could sensitively respond to it when he saw it too – that it is something we have all *grown into* being responsive to in growing up into our own particular culture. Indeed, if there were no shared spontaneous beginnings of this kind for our understandings, all our communicating with each other by spoken and written words would be impossible.

These issues were all explored extensively in Chapter 6. As we saw there, there is something very special about *living movement*, about what we can call *expression* that we have failed to attend to in our official philosophies, something that makes it very different from the mere physical or locomotive movement of things and objects in space. Elsewhere, I have tried to bring these differences out into the open (Shotter, 1975, 1984, 1993a&b), but there is insufficient space to outline them fully here.

Suffice it to say here that, rather than simply being the re-arrangement or re-configuration of separately existing parts which, at each instant in time, take up a new configuration (according to pre-existing laws or principles) in space, *expressive* movements are quite different. They are the movements of indivisible, dynamic, self-structurizing, unitary, living wholes, each one utterly unique in itself. Thus, besides their moving around in space, such living wholes can also be sensed as moving *within themselves*. Indeed, such expressive movements, such gestures, can be sensed as occurring through time, even if the bodies of the relevant living beings stay steadfastly fixed in space – they breath, they make noises, they wave their limbs about, and so on. In so doing, they seem to display both short-term expressive 'inner' movements – smiles, frowns, vocalizations, and other such gestural movements – both the expressions of a 'thou', i.e., expressions of their own living identity, as well as more long term 'inner' movements, i.e., manifestations of their growing up, maturing, and aging.

In other words, although not necessarily moving around in space at all, all such living processes, inevitably, are always irreversible 'motions in time', and such living motions are *expressive* of their own unique identity, their own unique way of 'coming into being' and of 'becoming older' within their surroundings.

If urged to sum up this section very briefly, then, I would choose two words: My first word would be "unique," for unlike current inquiries in science, we must concern ourselves with unique, unrepeatable, once-off, invisible, fleeting events. And my second word would be "creative," for each such unique event, if it is to be a relevant event appropriate to the conditions of its occurrence, it has to be created for yet another first time – it cannot 'produced' or 'manufactured' by the setting in motion a mechanism or by deducing consequences from a logical schematism.

'Transitory understandings' and 'action guiding anticipations': problems and re-orientations

In turning now to events occurring between us in our everyday use of language, we find that Bakhtin (1986) nicely captures some aspects of the special nature of what I have called the "spontaneous responsiveness" at work in our untroubled ways of understanding each other. In such circumstances, he suggests that: "All real and integral understanding is actively responsive... And the speaker himself is oriented precisely toward such an actively responsive understanding. He does not expect passive understanding that, so to speak, only duplicates his or her own idea in someone else's mind. Rather, he expects response, agreement, sympathy, objection, execution, and so forth..." (p.69).

In other words, we do not have to wait for speakers to complete their utterances before we can understand their speech sufficiently to respond to it in practice. For present to us in our spontaneous bodily responsiveness to their voicing of their utterances as they unfold, are *action guiding anticipatory understandings* of what they might possibly say next. For again, as Bakhtin (1986) notes: "The utterance is related not only to preceding, but also to subsequent links in the chain of speech communication... [F]rom the very beginning, the utterance is constructed while taking into account possible responsive reactions, for whose sake, in essence, it is actually created... From the very beginning, the speaker expects a response from them, an active responsive understanding. The entire utterance is constructed, as it were, in anticipation of encountering this response" (p.94).

And all these *relationally-responsive*, "transitory understandings" happen spontaneously, as a result no doubt of the countless hours of training we have had in our prior involvements in our culture. We do not have to 'work them out', self-consciously and deliberately. Indeed, in always being fashioned in a responsive relation to local circumstances they can never be merely mechanical repetitions of previous utterances. They can be heard in the unfolding temporal contours of a person's talk. As Voloshinov (1986) puts it: "The task of understanding does not basically amount to recognizing the form used, but rather to understanding it in a particular, concrete context, to understanding its meaning in a particular utterance, i.e., it amounts to understanding its novelty and not to recognizing its identity" (p.68). It is not its precise repeatability that is important but its "specific variability" (p.69) – or in Bateson's (1972) terms, it is "a difference that makes a difference" (p.286) that matters. And it is this that allows us to move on from what a speaker's words mean generally, to what uniquely a speaker means by their use of them.

Indeed, it is precisely these unique transitory understandings (that give us a sense of 'where we stand' in relation to the others around us) and action guiding anticipations (that give us a sense of 'where we might go next' in relation to them) that give us our *orientation* in expressing our own unique, once-off, creative responses to them, that are lost when we re-fashion our responses as in accord with a rational schematism as wilfully planned de-contextualized actions. What originally occurred as a unique 'answer' to a unique 'question' coming to us from our surroundings, is re-composed into an action that can be executed by any isolated individual, anywhere, at anytime, irrespective of the needs and requirements of our surroundings.

Following Bakhtin (1984), we can call these one-way relations – in which we "constrain nature to give answers to questions of reason's own determining" (Kant, 1781/1970, p.20) – monological forms of relation, for, as we have seen: "Monologue is finalized and deaf to other's response, does not expect it and does not acknowledge in it any *decisive* force" (p.293). While those relations in which our expressive-responsive activities are spontaneously intertwined or interwoven with those of the others with whom we are engaged or involved, we can call *dialogically-structured relations*, for: "To live means to participate in dialogue, to ask questions, to heed, to respond, to agree, and so forth. In this dialogue a person participates wholly and throughout his whole life: with his eyes, lips, hands, soul, spirit, with his whole body and deeds" (p.293). As Jaakko Seikkula (2002) puts it: "Monological dialogue refers to utterances that convey the speaker's own thoughts and ideas without being adapted to the interlocutors. One utterance rejects another. In dialogical dialogue utterances are constructed to answer previous utterances and also to wait for an answer from utterances that follow. New understanding is constructed between the interlocutors" (p.268) – this is a major condition for the possibility of Open Dialogue.

In other words, in adopting the orientational stance of knowledgeable professionals, intent upon bringing our professional expertise to bear on the circumstances in question before us, we can be tempted to *un-relate* ourselves to the people before us as the unique individuals they are, and instead of relating to them in terms of *who they are* and to *their needs*, we begin to treat them merely as instances of a type. But, as I indicated above, only if we can allow ourselves to respond spontaneously to the unique expressions they spontaneously express, can we *re-relate* ourselves to them in such a way that they arouse in us the uniquely appropriate transitory understandings and action guiding anticipations that can enable us to 'go on' to respond to them in an appropriately therapeutic manner. But what does that entail?

Lowe (2005), quite rightly in my estimation, suggests that what has proved most appealing about the use of structured methods, is that "they provide clear direction and a sense of purpose," and that they are "definable and teachable" (p.67), and they provide a "vocabulary... of directionality and stepwise movement as particular themes are developed and enriched" (p.68). This is clearly true and important, but, as I have already suggested, the transitory understandings and action guiding anticipations continually arising in our exchanges with others can give us a moment-by-moment shaped and vectored sense both of how things 'hang' for us and where we might 'go next' in our ongoing coping with the world around us. In other words, the need for a sense of direction and stepwise movement can, at least partially, be satisfied in other ways – and I will return in a moment to how those steps might be therapeutically directed.

What I want to point out here, is something else that is also true of structured methods, but is usually so taken for granted that it is not usually remarked on: All such structured methods are seen as *problem-oriented* methods – or as *problem-saturated* approaches, as Harlene Anderson put it in setting the scene for the symposium in which the first version of this chapter was given as a paper. And this is understandable: for if it's not problems we face, what do we face? Well, this is exactly what I now want to question: Is it appropriate to talk of the difficulties we face as "problems," as circumstances that can be overcome by "solutions"? I think not. Indeed, as I have suggested above, in Chapter 4, we should, perhaps, talk in more general terms of difficulties, and then talk of difficulties of the intellect that can be solved as problems, and difficulties or orientation or relating which can be resolved by the development of a line of action.

Interestingly, although Lowe adopts the vocabulary of problems and solutions in his theory-talk, in both the cases he discusses in his paper – Beth and Wayne – he does continue his discussion in the way the logical grammar of problem talk would lead him. Instead, he talks of them as *struggling* with something, Beth with debilitating panic attacks, and Wayne with peer pressure at school; he also talks of himself as "struggling to engage Wayne in a question sequence" (p.73).

I think this is significant. I think Lowe's sense of logical grammar here is very apposite: struggling to overcoming a difficulty is an activity with a very different grammar, a quite different set of implied expectations associated with it, than those linked with the activity of solving a problem. Instead of simply choosing among an already existing set of logically independent elements to combine them into an appropriate sequence, a struggle involves *navigating* within an often overwhelming sea of unique details – each one only becoming sensed as something to move on from, or back from as one encounters it – and somehow to create a unique course of action related to them all.

In dealing with the kind of circumstances both Beth and Wayne face, and in trying to engage Wayne in a question sequence – i.e., to engage him in a way that involves him so deeply that he is 'moved' or 'touched' and thus changed in his very being by at least some of the events occurring in the engagement – there is nothing comparable to the solution of a logical or mathematical problem. For in such problems, we have to cudgel our brains to devise ways of working out something unknown from what we already clearly know about the situation in question. Problems of that kind can be solved by 'calculation' because they are already well defined as such. Thus, "problem solving" of this kind entails the application of what Schön (1983) calls a "technical rationality."

But, as all these cases make clear – Lowe's own difficulty with engaging Wayne included – what is involved is not the conducting of a process of producing a result from a set of rational calculations, but a *struggle*, the process of creating an appropriate form of action in the first place. In short, a struggle is resolved only by the development of a clear line of action, and only once it is over, can we look back to describe it in terms of the turns we took and to conjecture some reasons for taking them.

The 'emotional-volitional tone' of an expression

Mainstream theory-driven research thus portrays practitioners as people who simply choose and reflect (or reflect and choose) in the performance of their actions. It fails to portray them as participants already caught up in a ceaselessly ongoing process who – in the face of the constraints and limited resources it affords them, as well as the responses it 'calls for' from them – must produce *from within* that ongoing process, both recognizable and accountable utterances and actions, recognizable and accountable sounds and movements. In moving on inside a world that is making them whilst they are making it, they are not able to reflect on that world as a finished object: they know *what* they are doing, i.e., they can account for it to others if challenged; they know *why* they are doing it, i.e., they have a reason for it; but what they still don't yet know, is *what* their doing *has done* – they must live with the anxiety that it may, in the end, all turn out badly. An overall evaluation of the outcome of their actions is possible only on their final completion (whenever and whatever that may be!!).

Theory-driven research, however, approaches the process of people acting as a sequence of already completed actions, and reflects back on them with the aim of mastering their rational reproduction. In so doing, their sequential unfolding is represented as a sequence of static, well-defined, already existing states or positions, occurring juxtaposed with each other like beads on a string (with time being seen as a fourth dimension of space). It fails to account for the myriad situated details to which an actor must attend and respond in their struggles to creatively produce their actions in the first place.

Indeed, as we have already seen, a major failure is the failure to take into account the anticipations aroused in us by the voicing of utterances, other people's as well as our own. Indeed, so pervasive are the anticipations we arouse in our talk, that they can be seen as the 'glue' – albeit, at each juncture, a very locally specialized glue – holding a complexly organized chain of utterances together as an intelligible conversation or discourse of some kind. As workers in conversational analysis (CA) put it, the *first pair-part* of an *adjacency pair* establishes a *conditional relevance* in terms of which, whatever is said in response to it, will be inspected to see how it can possibly serve as the *second pair-part* of the relevant adjacency pair[96]. In other words, we not only hear the sounds made by another person as *a response* to our sounds, we hear them as *sounds of agreement*, of *objection*, of *compliance*, and so on. We have both a *transitional understanding* of what they have said (the semantic aspect of their utterance) and an *action guiding anticipation* of how to respond (the orientational or relational aspect of their utterance).

But our sensibility in such exchanges is even more subtle and shaded than this. If the sounds we hear are sounds of *agreement*, we can hear them as *sympathetic agreement*, as *patronizing agreement*, as *hurried agreement*, as *inconsequential agreement*, as *reluctant agreement*, as *unexpected or surprised agreement*, and so on. Similarly with all other heard responses[97]. They are all subtly shaded, nuanced, or intonated in such a way as to enable us, mostly, to 'go on' with those to whom we must respond in reply, with at least decorum and courtesy, and sometimes, to 'go on' in ways appropriate to more complex aims: "... the word does not merely designate an object as a present-on-hand entity, but also expresses by its intonation my valuative attitude toward the object, toward what is desirable or undesirable in it, and, in so doing sets it in motion toward that which it yet-to-be-determined about it, turns it into a constituent moment of the living, ongoing event. Everything that is actually experienced," says Bakhtin (1993), "is experienced as something given and as something-yet-to-be-determined, is intonated, has *emotional-volitional tone*, and enters into an effective relationship to me within the unity of the ongoing event encompassing us" (pp.32-33, my emphasis).

Even if we are unmoving in space, as I intimated above, we can be sensed by others as making – indeed, as *struggling* or as *effortfully* making – expressive movements over time, expressive movements that, in an anticipatory fashion, reach out toward the future.

Thus, in his use of the expression "emotional-volitional tone," Bakhtin is suggesting that at every moment, as we voice an unfolding utterance, there is the possibility of a degree of personal freedom as to the different turns we might struggle to take, a struggle expressed in the intonational time-contours of our utterances. So, although "the word in language is half someone else's," he notes (Bakhtin, 1981). "It becomes 'one's own' only *when the speaker populates it with his own intentions*, his own accent, when he appropriates the word, adapting it to his own semantic and expressive intention. Prior to this moment of appropriation, the word does not exist in a neutral and impersonal language (it is not, after all, out of a dictionary that the speaker gets his words!), but rather it exists in other people's mouths, in other people's contexts, serving other people's intentions: it is from there that one must take the word, *and make it one's own*" (pp.293-4, my emphases).

Indeed, what makes a person's words *their own words*, are the efforts (struggles) they exert, and that we can sense them as exerting in their speech, to make their talk conform to 'a something' they are *trying* to express – we can hear these *efforts* 'in' their utterances, in their time-contouring of the emotional-volitional tone of their expressions. Thus, as Bakhtin (1993) puts it: "The answerably performed act is the final result or summation, an all-round definitive conclusion. The performed act concentrates, correlates, and resolves within a unitary and unique and, this time, *final context* both the sense and the fact, the universal and the individual, the real and the ideal, for everything enters into the composition of its answerable motivation. The performed act constitutes a going out *once and for all* from within possibility as such into *what is once-occurrent*" (pp.28-29).

So, as I intimated above, if we can allow ourselves to be spontaneously responsive to the others around us in a dialogically-structured manner, the conversation itself will provide us with a sense of where to go next. For everything that occurs will be sensibly connected to everything else – nothing can come into the conversation from the 'outside', so to speak, without being in response to, in answer to, events occurring within it. Thus the emotional-volitional tone of a person's utterances is not something just tacked onto them as an optional extra, but is crucial to organizing the pragmatic conduct of all our communicating – one cannot give another person a piece of information (without insulting them) until one has set up an *information giving relationship* with them, negotiating an expectant orientation with them toward something yet to come (Schegloff, 1995). Indeed, all complex human activities which involve in their organization both the sequencing and the simultaneous combining of a whole multiplicity of different, (often) individually performed activities, requires – as in the performance of a piece of music by an orchestra – the continually re-orienting and re-relating of these many different activities with each other, the 'orchestration' in oneself of a complex 'inner movement'.

In other words, what we face in practice are not problems presenting themselves as something already well-defined in relation to the kind of technical ingenuity required for their solution, but situations in which a *struggle* to realize an effective outcome in the face of often unpropitious circumstances is required. And it is appropriate to call it a struggle, for, as we have already seen, in expressing each sequential movement in an ongoing course of action, we have to *negotiate* a passage within an often overwhelming sea of unique details, and to somehow take them all into account in the unique course of action we actually take.

Yet, surprisingly, as we have already seen, in the global but unitary responsiveness of our bodies to the relevant circumstances surrounding the voicing of our utterances, the bodying forth of our utterances is in some way (that is quite undescribable but which we can nonetheless discriminate) expressive of all these factors. For, to repeat: "The performed act concentrates, correlates, and resolves within a unitary and unique and, this time, *final context* both the sense and the fact, the universal and the individual, the real and the ideal, for everything enters into the composition of its answerable motivation" (Bakhtin, 1993, p.29).

Thus, as we saw above, in Jaakko Seikkula's (2002) account of Open Dialogue (OD), it is only if "utterances are constructed to answer previous utterances and also to wait for an answer from utterances that follow" (p.268) that genuine Open Dialogue as such is possible. For then, everything that occurs will be sensibly connected to everything else – nothing can come into the conversation from the 'outside', so to speak, to disconnect the web or network of elements making up the indivisible complexity of the conversation as a whole from each other. Nothing should occur within the conversation without it being in response to, in answer to, events that have already occurred within it. Nor, to go further, should any "conversations or decisions about [a] case [be] conducted outside the presence of the network," i.e., the network of agencies involved in a case. These are some of the major conditions set by Jaakko Seikkula for the conduct of Open Dialogues (see also Seikkula and Arnkil, 2005). But while this gets us into *Open Dialogue* (and the creative power for all kinds of other projects that becomes available within such exchanges), it still doesn't give us direction in how to be therapeutic in our dialogical exchanges. Something else would seem to be needed: a special kind of enraptured, a not-yet-satisfied pre-occupation with the nature of an other or otherness.

Love

Here, I'm going to draw on some comments about the nature of *love*, by Max Scheler, that I first drew on many years ago when my main focus was in child development and I was interested in a mother's attention to her child. Now I'm aware of Maturana's long standing claims, also, that love is what makes the world go around. But for our purposes, an account of love that states that: "Being in love means making a space for one another so that each becomes part of the domain of existence of the other, and within their continuous recurrency of interactions they form a system in which they have a co-ontogeny" (Maturana and Varela, 2002), doesn't do it for me. Somehow, it doesn't make a difference to me that matters. We need an account that gives us some direction, that 'moves' us, that works in practice, both to direct our attention toward what, in another person's behaviour, is relevant to their further growth and development, and to help shape our responses to them. As I see it, Max Scheler's (1954) account *does* help us in this regard. He says:

> "If we love any human being, we certainly love him [sic] for what he is; but at the same time we love him also for what he *might* be, according to the possibilities of perfection inherent in his being. Our eyes are fixed upon his ideal image which we grasp in, through and behind his

> empirical traits; yet we are indifferent as to how far it is reflected and realized in his actual state. At the same time, our love is the most potent force that can lift him from one to the other. It carries before him his own purified, and, as it were, redeemed and transfigured likeness, as a challenge to follow and to reach it; it is like a voice calling: become what you are! become in reality what ideally you are in design!" (p.153).

In other words, what another person can do that is crucial to a child's development, to a sports-person's development, or to help a disoriented or disturbed person to feel more 'at home' in the world, is to notice and be responsive to *the possibilities of perfection inherent in his or her being* – to be the voice calling: "*Become in reality what ideally you are in design*!"

But to be able to do this, either to become this kind of voice, or – which is perhaps more important – to introduce to the client another voice or other voices that can exert that kind of influence on, or in, them, we must attend to their behaviour, he suggests, not objectively, not just in terms of its observable and countable aspects, but in terms of what it is *gesturing* toward, what it is *points* toward as a possibility for the future. "Love does not simply gape approval, so to speak, at a value lying ready to hand for inspection," he says.

> "It does not reach out towards given objects (or real persons) merely on account of positive values inherent in them, and already 'given' *prio*r to the coming of love. For this idea still betrays that gaping at mere empirical fact, which is so utterly uncongenial to love. Love only occurs when, upon the values already acknowledged as 'real' there supervenes a movement, an intention towards potential values still higher than those already given and presented. In so doing, love invariably sets up an *'idealized' paradigm of value* for the person actually present" (p.153).

And it is the unique transitory understandings (that also give us a sense of 'where they stand' in relation to us), as well as the unique action guiding anticipations (that also give us a sense of 'where they might go next' in relation to us) that can only arise in our spontaneously responsive, dialogically-structured relations with another person – understandings and anticipations that are *unique* to that other person – that can give us the possibility of being that the voice (or of introducing another voice) that calls to them: "*become what you are? become in reality what ideally you are in design*!"

But these unique transitory understandings and unique action guiding anticipations only arise out of fleeting, "once-occurrent events of Being" (Bakhtin, 1993, p.2). Or,, as Tom Andersen (1996) puts it: "... the life in which we therapists are particularly interested in comprises meanings and feelings which shift all the time; they are there for a second and have passed away the next second" (p.119); thus: "Life is... "composed" of small events, which each happen only once" (p.122).

Thus, if *Open Dialogue* is to turn into *therapeutic dialogue*, to become a healing dialogue, a dialogue oriented toward making a person an integrated 'whole' again, then, it seems to me, there is a need to introduce into it a voice or voices that notices and responds to these fleeting hints in a person's behaviour, a voice that 'arrests' the routine next step a person is about to take in accord with their own 'rational' logic, and which introduces to them another possibility – but not just any old possibility, but one already clearly inherent in his or her being. This is Peggy Penn's move, to quote what she said in this symposium, in aiding her client to "introduce a chosen protective figure into the flashback, which has the effect of interrupting the old scenario." And in her "participant text" paper with Marilyn Frankfurt (Penn & Frankfurt,1994), they also shows how introducing new voices, and reorienting clients toward addressing these new voices, "opens a space for felt meanings" (p.230). Harlene Anderson (1998) also remarks: "I want to create and facilitate a learning environment and process where participants can access, elaborate on, and produce their own unique competencies" (p.66). While White and Epston (1990) focus, of course, on what they call "unique outcomes." In other words, all these very notable therapists work not with beginnings given them by other theorists, therapists, or thinkers, but with beginnings given them by their clients.

Jaakko Seikkula (2002), in his strikingly successful crisis intervention team approach to the treatment of psychotic episodes, also notes the necessity to see psychotic reactions "as attempts to make sense of one's experience and to cope with experiences so difficult that it has not been possible to construct a rational spoken narrative about them... An open dialogue, without any preplanned themes or forms seems to be important in enabling the construction of new language in which to express difficult events in a person's life... [and] to allow different voices to be heard concerning the themes under discussion including the psychotic experience" (p.264). In other words, he also sees the very language that seemingly served to get the patient/client into trouble, also as providing the beginnings for new ways to 'go on' that leave the old troubles behind.

Thus what seems to me to be common to all these different approaches, is that the resources for change emerge, or arise out of, the unique answering responses from an *other* to the unique responsiveness of client's in those of their expressions related to their distress. It is "the 'otherness' [of the other] which enters into us makes us other," says Steiner (1989, p.188). But it is precisely these unique understandings and anticipations that arise only in our spontaneous responsiveness to the others and othernesses around us that are lost if we re-fashion our responses as wilfully planned de-contextualized actions to accord with a rational schematism.

Conclusions

Arlene Katz and I (Katz & Shotter, 1996, 1998, 2004) have tried to capture the general style of all of these approaches in terms of a focus on "arresting, moving, striking, etc., moments," and the idea of a set of "social poetic" methods – methods derived very much from Wittgenstein's (1953) later philosophy. But I want to add here, that our concern in our articles has been not just to draw attention to the 'workings' of such striking moments in people's communications with each other, and how they create shared understandings to do with people 'going on' with each other. We have also experimented with a certain style of 'instructive' or 'formative' writing – in terms of such moments – which we think of as also itself an aspect of a research practice.

Indeed, we can already find some aspects of this new style of writing in Wittgenstein's (1953, 1969, 1980) later works. Indeed, there is much use now, as Geertz (1983) has put it, of "blurred genres," in which meanings are seen as "performed meanings" (p.29), which are achieved by writers leading readers through a sequence of movements as they "tack back and forth between ludic, dramatistic, and textual idioms" (p.33), and in which explanation is regarded more "as a matter of connecting action to its sense rather than behavior to its determinants" (p.34). We can call it an 'instructive' or 'formative' style of writing in that exerts its influence on us, not by depicting a true state of affairs to us in our thought, but by 'moving' or 'striking' us in such a way that, not cognitively but perceptually, we 'grasp' or 'see' something in our surroundings entirely new to us. In other words, we achieve that kind of "understanding which consists in 'seeing connections'," says Wittgenstein (1953, no.122). And it does this by "tacking back and forth" between understandings from experience-distant, academic language games – especially from Wittgenstein, Bakhtin, and so on, because they are also concerned in their own different ways with those crucial 'poetic' moments when one is 'moved', 'arrested', or 'struck' by the working of certain words within oneself, and in conversation with others – and our more experience-near, everyday understandings.

Thus, this style of writing is not straightforwardly an 'interpretive' or 'theory informed' style of writing, in the sense of introducing formal academic theorizing through which to view 'empirical' data. Nor is it a social constructionist style of writing, to do with trying to infer things about the world through language (Gergen, 1999). Nor is it of the kind inspired by critical theory where the ideological influences structuring the text becomes a part of the text itself (Parker, 1992). Nor is it simply instantiation of Tannen's (1989) "involvement strategies." It works by juxtaposing – in a carefully timed, hermeneutical back and forth as outlined by Geertz (1983) – experience near accounts from the field with experience distant insights from these writers which works to 'arrest' or 'interrupt' our usual, critical way of reading academic articles. For usually, we read them as arguments to which we must continually raise objects and offer counter arguments. Instead, I invite readers to read my writing here dialogically – *with* various other particular writings in mind as *reminders* (Wittgenstein (1953) – writings that offer suggestions for the possible beginnings of new language games, beginnings to which readers can spontaneously respond, thus to create within themselves the appropriate transitional understandings and action guiding anticipations that might enable them to sense how to 'go on' in the situation depicted.

As depicted here, my approach is primarily "practice rooted," not "theory rooted," and all the questions of concern to me, and to which I seek answers in my juxtaposing of concrete events occurring in a particular practice with pieces of academic literature that might illuminate them, are also particular and detailed questions, not general theoretical ones. But the results of such work as it is presented here – in terms of suggestions, offers, possibilities and other *first parts* of a dialogical exchange – has its consummation in the *second part* replies that such first parts invite. It is in the reader's own responses that (possible) transitional understandings and action guiding anticipations relevant to a reader's own difficulties and struggles, but not to their problems, might be created.

Currently, however, as I begin to consult more with health care practitioners and managers and suchlike, I begin to discover more and more that their practices are becoming "administratively rooted." In other words, rather than their practices being constitutive of their actions, their actions are being shaped more and more by administrative frameworks and category systems – CAFs, KPIs, APAs, OPMs, etc... No doubt commenting on the coming age of Stalinism in Russia, Voloshinov (1929/1986) captured our current age of command and control, of formalism and systematicity, brilliantly well. He describes it as follows: "The typical distinguishing marks of [this] kind of thinking [is that it is] focused on a ready-made and, so to speak, arrested object... Characteristically, what undergoes systematization is usually (if not exclusively) someone else's thought. True creators – the initiators of new ideological trends – are never formalistic systematizers. Systematization comes upon the scene during an age which feels itself in command of a ready-made and handed-down body of authoritative thought. A creative age must first have passed, then and only then does the business of formalistic systematizing begin – an undertaking typical of heirs and epigones who feel themselves in possession of someone else's, now voiceless word. Orientation in the dynamic flow of generative process can never be of the formal, systematizing kind... Formal, systematic thought about language is incompatible with living, historical understanding of language. From the system's point of view, history always seems merely a series of accidental transgressions" (p.78). And as we can all see at the moment, much of the writing now becoming available to us – in manualized versions of family therapy[98], for instance – is leading us all in exactly this direction.

But as I have already indicated, it is precisely these unique understandings and anticipations that arise in our spontaneous responsiveness to the others and othernesses around us that are lost if we re-fashion our responses as wilfully planned de-contextualized actions to accord with a rational schematism. And there is no way to get these back, except in a return to the original everyday, conversational relations from which our formalisms and systems arose in the first place.

Chapter Nine

TWO KINDS OF RESPONSES TO AN 'EXPERIENCED DIFFICULTY': 'ABOUTNESS'-THINKING VERSUS 'WITHNESS'–THINKING

"... it is not that before you can understand it you need to be specially trained in abstruse matters, but the contrast between understanding the subject and what most people *want* to see. Because of this the very things which are most obvious may become the hardest of all to understand. What has to be overcome is a difficulty having to do with the will, rather than with the intellect" (Wittgenstein, 1980a, p.17).

A central theme in this book – which is related to Wittgenstein's remark quoted above – depends, as we have seen, on the distinction he draws between difficulties of the intellect and difficulties of the will. And in this book, instead of with the difficulties associated with the solving intellectual problems, I have been mainly concerned with the task of understanding what is involved in overcoming difficulties of the will.

Difficulties of the will and difficulties of the intellect

Currently, the will is a very unfamiliar concept to us in the context of modern philosophy and psychology, inquiries essentially concerned with the workings of 'the mind'. Indeed, just at the moment, when almost every sphere of psychological study is modified by the adjective '*cognitive*', it is the supposed 'inner workings' of a generalized, individual mind that is almost in every case at issue in the investigations being discussed. So, although Vygotsky (1966, orig. pub., 1930-31) remarked long ago: "It is surprising to us that traditional psychology has completely failed to notice this phenomenon which we can call *mastering one's own reactions*" (p.33, my emphasis), we need not be at all surprised, either that this *was* the case long ago, or that it is still the case today. Issues of this kind are still not on the agenda of mainstream psychology. Perhaps the nearest we come, currently, to referring to such issues, is in talking of people's *mind-set*, the idea that they have certain fixed mental attitudes which dispose them to respond to or to verbally describe events and circumstances in characteristic ways. But this is to locate the issue once again inside the mind of the individual.

In the this book, I have adopted the idea that such difficulties of the will are best called *difficulties of orientation* or *relational difficulties*, difficulties in which we need to *resolve* a *line of action*, a *style* or *way* of approach *in relation to* the others and othernesses around us. And such difficulties as these need not be due just to an individual's attitudes or opinions; they can be to do with attitudes, inclinations, tendencies, or *ways* of orienting ourselves towards the phenomena that concern us that are implicit in the metaphorical nature of much of our language-intertwined activities (Rorty, 1980, Lakoff & Johnson, 1980). As Rorty (1980) comments, "it is pictures rather than propositions, metaphors rather than statements, which determine most of our philosophical convictions" (p.12), and, as he sees it, it is a picture of the mind as a great mirror, containing representations – some accurate, some not – that has shaped and made sense of many of the major projects in modern philosophy and psychology, the urge, say, to seek single, accurate, systematic explanatory theories of phenomena of our concern: "Without the notion of the mind as mirror, the notion of knowledge as accuracy of representation would not have suggested itself" (p.12). Indeed, it is our feeling that other kinds of knowledge, for instance, the implicit practical knowledge(s) embodied our skilful activities as practitioners, is not, so to speak, *proper* knowledge, has stood in the way of our thinking inquiries into their special natures as at all worthwhile. Wittgenstein (1953), as we have seen, describes the kind of difficulty we face here thus: "A picture held us captive. And we could not get outside it, for it lay in our language and language seemed to repeat it to us inexorably" (no.115). In other words, without our being aware of it for, in shaping and guiding our thinking and talking, such images, metaphors, or 'pictures' are not the focal topics of our talk or thought, we are not thinking *about* them; we are only *subsidiarily* aware of them (Polanyi, 1958, 1963).

This is a part of why such difficulties are so hard to deal with. But they are also difficult to deal with as they have their source in the dialogically-structured nature of our joint, language-intertwined, actions. For, as we have seen, when people spontaneously interlace their responsive reactions in with those around them, they remain deeply ignorant of quite *what* they are doing, not because the *intentions* supposedly informing their conduct are too deeply hidden to be brought out easily into the light of day, but because people's pre-planned actions, their stated desires, etc., are not and cannot be the major influences on their conduct in the moment of their acting – unless, that is, they are acting a completely non-human way toward the others around them. The time contours of invisible, dynamic events spontaneously occurring *between*, and *only* between the participants are the relevant influences – indeed, the focus on such ephemeral, invisible events is another central feature of this book. As matters of the will, not the intellect, they manifest themselves only in our practical actions, in our spontaneously expressed, embodied anticipations of what next we expect to occur in our exchanges with those around us. This is why, as I said earlier, I cannot agree with those who suggest that joint action is best understood in terms of our *coordinating* our activities with each other. For a major feature of joint action is its creation of once-occurrent outcomes, *unintended* by any of the participants, and it is the creation of these ephemeral entities which can provide us both with *transitory understandings* and *action guiding anticipations* of what next might happen that can help us coordinate our activities, but which can equally well lead us also into 'bewitching' ourselves with our own words – it is this second feature of joint action that is lost if we focus only on coordination.

If we are to understand the unintended, unplanned and unplannable, noncognitive nature of our interactive conduct further, we must, firstly, turn to a focus on our own and other people's spontaneous bodily reactions, and on the intertwining of these reactions with particular events, occurring in particular circumstances. Secondly, this requires us to focus on essentially *invisible* events, events that have their major properties in the *time contours* of their unfolding, in the dynamics of the relations between people. And thirdly, such a focus requires an orientation toward the everyday practical difficulties that arise in people's attempts to devise and implement, to maintain and elaborate, or to attempt to correct or enrich their own, local practices. In other words, all these foci require sensitive attention not only to the subtle details of briefly occurring, unique events, but also to the *possible relationships* between such events themselves as well as their possible relationships with other features in their surroundings – close attention to unique particularities rather than generalities.

All these new orientations would seem to be a turning away from those thought to be the proper foci of scientifically oriented psychologists: (1) the first would be a turn away from the mind to the body (thus to trespass into the province of the physiotherapist or sports-coach, etc.); (2) while the second would be to seriously trivialize the more general aims of authentic scientific research, for it requires attention not only to very specific details, but also to the precise, situated relations of these details to their surroundings, at the moment of their occurrence. Wittgenstein (1981) characterizes the kinds of disquiet we can feel when seemingly facing insoluble problems in our thought as follows:

> "Disquiet in philosophy might be said to arise from looking at philosophy wrongly, seeing it wrong, namely as if it were divided into (infinite) longitudinal strips instead of into (finite) cross strips. This inversion of our conception produces the *greatest* difficulty. So we try as it were to grasp the unlimited strips and complain that it cannot be done piecemeal. To be sure it cannot, if by a piece one means an infinite longitudinal strip. But it may well be done, if one means a cross-strip. –

> But in that case we never get to the end of our work! – Of course not, for it has no end. (We want to replace wild conjectures and explanations by the quiet weighing of linguistic facts) (no.447).

In other words, he is re-orienting us here towards the kind of detailed, practical inquiries I have been discussing in this book. These, as he sees it, and I agree, must replace the self-appointed mission that academic and research psychology has pursued in recent times of discovering final, general answers to the big, longitudinal-strip questions, not the temporary answers to the little cross-strip questions arising in particular concrete practices. What has been left to practitioners to tackle piece-meal now becomes our central concern.

Indeed, the attempt to go further and to try to build periods or regions of critical reflection into our everyday practices, such that they might become self-investigating and self-portraying, thus also to become self-critical and, as a consequence, continually self-developing and self-determining, has been considered by very few as an important project for the present time (e.g., Gustavsen, 1992; MacIntyre, 1990; Spellmeyer, 2003; Spinosa, Flores, and Dreyfus, 1997). It is, however, the whole point and purpose of *this* book.

The lack of attention to such projects in current, scientifically oriented, academic psychology, as I see it, to put it perhaps over strongly, exhibits, as I see it, an implicit contempt for the fact that ordinary people, in their own everyday and ordinary circumstances, still encounter the everyday events occurring around them, continually, for yet another first time. And that in so doing, they are *creating* an understanding, and a potential source of new knowledge of use to the rest of the community should anyone else come to occupy a similar place in reality to the place uniquely occupied now by the unique individual in question. Thus, in line with another overall theme of this book – that we have been concerned with things happening for *yet another first time* – the issue, as we shall see, comes down to that of whether it is our task in our inquiries to discover samenesses or differences.

Two ways of responding to difficulties: samenesses and differences

In our current 'scientistic' approach to the difficulties we face, there is a tendency to treat *all* the circumstances we find bewildering or disorienting, or *all* the events that are strange and new to us, as posing a *problem* for us, i.e., as difficulties of the mind or of the intellect. Thus we often respond to such events by trying to *explain* them. However, as I hope is now very clear, there is an altogether different way in which we might respond to such difficult situations: we can 'enter into' a dialogically-structured relationship with them, and, as we 'dwell' *on* them, or *within* them, or *with* them for a while, we can gradually gain an orientation toward their 'inner natures' as they become more familiar to us – much, say, as we get to know our 'way around' inside a city which is at first unfamiliar to us by exploring its highways and byways according to the different projects we try to pursue within it.

In becoming more familiar with something in our surroundings in this way, we come to know 'it' not just in terms of its inert, objective nature, but to know it in terms of a whole realm of possible responsive, living relations that we might have toward it. We can come to orient toward it in terms of its yet-to-be-achieved *values*; we can come to appreciate the (grammatical) 'calls' it can exert on us to 'go on' with it in one way rather than another. Indeed, Bakhtin (1993) makes this point very clearly:

> "This world-as-event is not just a world of being, of that which is given; no object, no relation, is given here as something simply given, as something totally on hand, but is always given in conjunction with another given that is connected with those objects and relations, namely, that which is yet-to-be-achieved or determined; 'one ought to...', 'it is desirable that...' An object that is absolutely indifferent, totally finished, cannot be something one experiences actually. When I experience an object actually, I thereby carry out something in relation to it; the object enters into relation with that which is to-be-achieved, grows in it – within my relationship to that object... Insofar as I am actually experiencing an object, even if I do so by thinking of it, it becomes a changing moment in the ongoing event of my experiencing (thinking) it... Or, to be exact, it is given to me within a certain event-unity, in which the moments of what-is-given and what-is-to-be-achieved, of what-is and what-ought-to-be, of being and value, are inseparable. All these abstract categories are here constituent moments of a certain, living, concrete, and palpable (intuitable) once-occurrent whole – an event" (p.32).

The development of a sensitivity to such calls, to the *uniqueness* of the other, is clearly not a part of the problem-solving process, concerned as that is with samenesses. It is an aspect of the process of 'entering into' a dialogically-structured relationship with them, thus to know how to 'go on' with them. Wittgenstein (1981) describes the unusual nature of this kind of inquiry as follows: "... the difficulty – I might say – is not that of finding the solution but rather that of recognizing as the solution something that looks as if it were only a preliminary to it. 'We have already said everything. – Not anything that follows from this, no, *this* itself is the solution!' This is connected, I believe, with our wrongly expecting an explanation, whereas the solution to the difficulty is a description, if we give it the right place in our considerations. If we dwell upon it, and do not try to get beyond it. The difficulty here is: to stop" (1981, no.314). In other words, again, it is a matter of the will, i.e., a matter of what we unquestioningly *expect* of ourselves in a particular circumstance that misleads us into taking an inappropriate approach to the difficulties we face.

Instead of treating *some* of the difficulties we face as difficulties of orientation, at the moment we seem to them *all* as difficulties of the intellect. Below I will set out, briefly, some features relevant to these two stances. First, I will explore the two very different sequences of steps involved in these two very different ways of responsively relating ourselves to our surrounding circumstances; then, I will set out the properties of the two processes; and finally, I will discuss the effects of conducting the process on the self of the investigator.

(1) Problem-solving: the continual monological rediscovery of sameness – on being able to talk "about" the other

First, the *sequence of steps* involved: (1) treat the newness or strangeness as a problem to be solved, as something that can be fully known to us; (2) analyze it into identifiable elements; (3) find a pattern or order amongst them; (4) hypothesize an agency responsible for this pattern or order (call it, say, "synergy" or "coordination," or some other such 'stuff'); (5) find further evidence for its 'workings'; (6) enshrine these workings in a theory or theoretical system; (7) manipulate features of the strangeness (now known to us in terms of the theory) to produce a advantageous outcomes; (8) call these 'the solution' to the problem; (9) turn 'to apply' the theory elsewhere.

Let me now turn to the *properties* and *outcome* of the process: (1) it is a search for repetitions or regularities; (2) it establishes a single order of connectedness among certain, selectively perceived aspects of our circumstances; (3) occasionally, such 'solutions' can occur to us 'in a flash of insight'; (4) they work wholly within the realm of what is already known to us to elaborate it internally, i.e., they do not introduce any new categories into our already established ways of thinking.

Finally, I want to outlines the effects of such a processes of inquiry on *the self of the investigator*: (1) the *self* remains unchanged in the process; (2) we remain *outside* the other or the otherness we are inquiring into, we are 'set over against' it; (3) we are not engaged or involved with it; (4) we acquire extra *knowledge* about it in the form of facts or information; (5) as a result, we gain *mastery* over it (Descartes' aim). In other words, the difference the process makes to us essentially an *epistemological* difference. We are not changed in our way of being in the world, only in the degree of competence or expertise that we carry out our basic way of acting. We view objects in terms of what-is-given in them, but not it terms of what-is-to-be-achieved in our relations to them.

(2) Entering into a dialogical relationship "with" an other: beginnings and beginnings and beginnings, but no endings

The sequence of *steps* involved in this *dialogically-structured* process is very different from the more *monlogically-structured* process outlined above: (1) we begin by treating the other or otherness as radically unknown to us, and furthermore, as not every fully knowable; (2) we then 'enter into' dialogically-structured relations with it, become involved or engaged with it; (3) we must 'open' ourselves to being spontaneously 'moved by it; (4) we must relate to it responsively and responsibly – this is crucial: we always know when a person is 'with' us or not, say, when at a party they are responsively 'following' us (i.e., anticipating' us), or whether they are looking over our shoulder to find others they want to be with; (5) this sense of contiguity, of contingency, of the other's responses to us being contingent on our own toward them, is very basic – present even in new-born children; (6) but to 'enter into' dialogically-structured relations with another requires 'tact', 'courtesy'; (7) we must not only 'follow' the other, but also provide opportunities for them to 'follow' us; (8) the other 'calls on' us – and in doing so, comes both to be 'with' us, as well as to 'call out' responses from us; (9) the other can affect us, move us – their meaning for us in the responsive movements they 'call out' from us; (10) we are 'answerable (partially) to' their calls as they are (partially) to ours – we do not reply to every aspect of their influence upon us; (11) an 'it' appears between us: produced neither solely by 'me' or by 'you'; (12) the 'it' is *our* it: there is *poiesis* at work between us – the sensed creation of form; (13) the form has a shaped and vectored sense to it; (14) central to giving shape to our actions is our *sensitivity* or *sensibility* to the particular details of the other's responsive activities; (15) as we 'dwell on, with, or within' the other, there is a gradually growth of familiarity with its 'inner shape'; (16) we have a sense of the *value* of its yet-to-be-achieved aspects – the prospects it offers us for 'going on' with it (see Bakhtin, 1993, p.32, quoted above); (17) we gain orientation, a sense of 'at homeness', we come to find our 'footing', to know our 'way about' in relation to it.

Turning now to the *properties* of the process: (1) "once-occurrent events of Being" are crucial – single, unique events that make a difference, and we talk from within the process in terms of what we are 'struck by'; (2) we establish a multiple, complexly ordered *sense of connectedness* among the perceived aspects of the other or otherness: a "synopsis of trivialities"[99]; (3) our familiarity with it grows only gradually and is never finished; (4) it works at the boundaries between the radically unknown and the realm of the known to expand its boundaries.

Finally, turning to the effects of such a process of inquiry on *the self of the investigator*: (1) the investigator's *self* is changed in such encounters; (2) we become involved with, immersed in, the 'inner life' of the other or otherness, indeed, we came to internalize an aspect of the other within ourselves; (3) everything we do is partly shaped by the other in being a response to what it might do; (4) at first wholly 'bewitched' by its 'voice', as our familiarity with it grows, its voice becomes one voice among the many other voices with us; (5) rather than *knowledge* of its nature, we gain *orientation* toward it, i.e., we grasp how to 'go on' with it; (6) but we can never gain mastery over it – others and othernesses can always surprise us, no matter how familiar they might become to us. In other words, the difference the process makes to us essentially an *ontological* difference. We *are* changed in our way of being in the world; our basic ways of acting are enriched, and they become enriched by our now being able to *relate* to, or to *orient toward* events in our surroundings by making use of a *style of address* guided by the new object with which we have now become familiar. We view objects, not only in terms of what-is-given in them, but also in terms of what-is-to-be-achieved in our relations to them.

From Descartes' methods to Goethe's way of science: from dead to living things

The Cartesian world is a dead world, a world of mechanical movement, a world of forces and impacts in which change is thought of as changes in the spatial configuration of a set of separately existing parts. Many changes in the human world, however, are of a very different kind. Rather than changes taking place *within* an already fully realized reality, instead of changes of a quantitative and repeatable kind, i.e., *ordinary* changes, they are unique, irreversible, one-off changes, novel changes of a *qualitative* kind, i.e., *living* changes, changes *of reality* itself. And as living changes, such changes are creative, developmental changes, changes making something possible that before was impossible. Such changes – against a Cartesian background – strike us as changes that happen unpredictably, unexpectedly, not according to any laws or principles, but capriciously dependent on circumstances. Indeed, such changes can be surprising and can strike us with amazement or wonder, for they are *extraordinary* changes. And it is with such moments of wonder that – as both Aristotle and Plato thought – that we must begin our inquiries. For, being 'struck' by wonder is for them (as for Wittgenstein in his inquiries), not a state to be dissolved but a beckoning to be followed. For we are already 'in' the place, the situation in which we need to be, to find the way out of our difficulties; there is no necessity to 'go beyond' our present circumstances, to get 'behind appearances' – for the way to 'go on' can be found 'here', where we are now.

Elsewhere (Shotter, 2005), I have explored in some detail Goethe's approach to science. Many of the conclusions I have arrived at above resonate with those set out by Goethe in the late 18th and early 19th centuries. In particular, in quoting with approval an account by someone called Hienroth (who commented on of his way of thinking), he said that Hienroth "observes properly: that my faculty of thinking is 'objectively active' [*gegenständliches Denken*], whereby he means to say that my thinking does not separate itself from its objects; that the elements of the objects, the concrete intuitions (*Anschauungen*) enter into that thinking and are most inwardly permeated by it in form; that my way of seeing (*anschauen*) is itself a thinking, my thinking a way of seeing – a procedure said friend [i.e., Goethe] does not wish to deny his approbation" (Goethe, HA, 13: 37, quoted in Brady, p.97).

In other words, like our active responsive understandings of people's utterances – that arouse in us an anticipation of the not-yet-said – so our thinking of certain objects (especially of those associated in some way with living processes) can come, as in Goethe's thinking, to arouse more in us than merely their currently given characteristics. They can also arouse in us anticipations of how next they might change, move, or otherwise express themselves. Thus, as Goethe puts it: "Every new object, well contemplated, opens up a new organ of perception in us" (Goethe, SS, p.39, quoted in Amrine, p.47; Cottrell, p.257) – that is, it *can* open up a new organ of perception in us if we are prepared to enter into a dialogical, rather than a monologically-structured form of engagement with it. It gives rise, then, to a kind of perceiving-thinking-acting in which, instead of our first thinking *about* something, some unknown *object* – by comparing it with an inner representation (theory) already in our possession devised as a result of studying other such objects, in order to decide on a course of action regarding it – we *resolve* on a course of thoughtful-action with *it* in-forming our acting in the course of our interacting with it.

What is different here from our classic forms of inquiry into objects, is that the object in question is a *living being* and can thus give rise to the presence, in our interactions with it, of dynamical events distinctive to us only in the 'shape' of their unfolding time contours. Thus, instead of our investigation it solely in *our own* terms, we can begin to investigate it, either in *its* terms, or in terms that *we* (i.e., ourselves and it) have fashioned between us.

Bakhtin (1986) puts this difference usefully and well, as follows: "The exact sciences constitute a monologic form of knowledge, the intellect contemplates *a thing* and expounds upon it. There is only one subject here – cognizing (contemplating) and speaking (expounding). In opposition to the subject there is only *a voiceless thing.* Any object of knowledge (including man) can be perceived and cognized as a thing. But a subject as such cannot be perceived and studied as a thing, for as a subject it cannot, while remaining a subject, become voiceless, and, consequently, cognition of it can only be *dialogic*" (p.161).

But this *dialogic* way of relating to an other is only possible if we stay in movement, but not so much in locomotive movement as in a dynamic inter-active, expressive-responsive relation with the others and othernesses in our surroundings. For, as we have seen, something very special occurs on those occasions when two or more of us bodily approach each other, face-to-face, and engage in a *meeting*, in a dialogically-structured or chiasmically-organized encounter. In such meetings, our actions cannot be *accounted as* wholly our own, for they are partly 'shaped' by being *spontaneously responsive* to those of others. Thus in all such circumstances, our actions are neither mine nor their's. They are truly 'ours'.

This kind of activity cannot be explained! It cannot be explained as people's *actions* can be explained: by giving their *reasons*; nor can it be explained as simply *behaviour*: in terms of regularities and causal principles. It constitutes a distinct, *sui generis*, third sphere of first-time, unique activities, which cannot be explained, but which do in fact have their own distinctive properties.

As already mentioned, I have called this third sphere or realm, the dialogical, or the chiasmic: It involves a special kind of nonrepresentational, sensuous or embodied form of *practical-moral* (Bernstein, 1983) understanding, which, in being constitutive of people's social and personal identities, is prior to and determines all the other ways of knowing available to us. What is produced in such chiasmically-structured exchanges is a very complex intertwining or 'orchestration' of not wholly reconcilable influences – as Bakhtin (1981) remarks, both 'centripetal' tendencies *inward* toward order and unity at the center, as well as 'centrifugal' ones *outward* toward diversity and difference on its borders or margins with other active, indivisible wholes.

Let me repeat the nature of their distinctive properties again here: Activities in this sphere lack specificity; they are only partially determined. They are a complex 'orchestration' of many different kinds of influences. They are just as much material as mental. They are just as much felt as thought, and thought as felt. Their intertwined, complex nature makes it very difficult for us to characterize their nature. They have neither a fully orderly nor a fully disorderly structure, neither a completely stable nor an easily changed organization, neither a fully subjective nor fully objective character. They are also non-locatable – they are 'spread out' among all those participating in them. They are neither 'inside' people, but nor are they 'outside' them; they are located in that space where inside and outside are one. Nor is there a separate before and after (Bergson), neither an agent nor an effect, but only a meaningful whole which cannot divide itself into separable parts. But, as living activities, they have a 'style' and 'point' beyond themselves toward both events in their surroundings, and what can come next in the future.

Indeed, it is precisely their lack of any pre-determined order, and thus their openness to being specified or determined *by those involved in them*, in practice – while usually remaining quite unaware of having done so – that we can take as their central defining feature. And it is precisely this that makes this sphere of activity of empirical interest to us, for at least the three following reasons: We can investigate in practical detail 1) how people actually do manage to 'work things out' in their *responsively interconnected* activities; 2) the part played by the ways of talking we interweave into the many different spheres of practical activity occurring between us, and the different functions of these different forms of talk; and 3) how we might refine and elaborate these different spheres of activity and extend them into novel spheres as yet unknown to us.

We can, perhaps, now begin to see why a nonrepresentational, allusive, gesturing or groping form of talk – a form of talk that is both indicative and mimetic – is required if we are to capture the nature of such developing but always unfinished, indivisible wholes. And we can also, perhaps, begin to see why some of our current ways of talking, in terms of well ordered systems and structures, in terms of separable and 'picturable' component parts, are quite inadequate to the task. For, as I have tried to make clear above, under both the influence of our separateness from each other within the "individualism" of the day, and the "logical atomism" into which we have been trained in most of our more academic practices, we 'picture' the systems and structures, the processes of which we talk, as objective entities, as assemblages of externally related parts. And we seem to think that if we possessed their 'blueprint', we could build them from the ground up, so to speak, piece by piece. Indivisible wholes, as we have seen are quite different. They have a life of their own (in actuality or at least in essence)! Thus, what kind of talk, what kind of thinking, might be of use to us in our inquiries into their basic nature, and in our inquiries into how we might influence *changes* in their nature?

'Withness-thinking' and 'aboutness-thinking'

As we have seen, if we can enter into living, dialogically-structured relations with such beings, events, or circumstances, and allow them to call out spontaneous reactions from us, then an engaged, responsive understanding becomes available to us *from within* the unfolding dynamics of such relationships – a kind of understanding that is utterly unavailable to us if we adopt only a monological approach to them and treat them as dead forms. As I hope has now become very clear from the preceding chapters, I have tried to clarify the differences between these two forms of talk, these two very different ways of relating ourselves to our surroundings, in terms of the difference between 'aboutness-talk/thinking' and 'withness-talk/thinking' – a difference, in other words, that can be expressed in terms of what it is to relate ourselves to the others and othernesses around us, intellectually or in a living, embodied fashion.

The experience of 'withness-thinking'

Lacking in our purely intellectual relations to our surroundings, but central to our experiences in withness-thinking, is the '*shaped*' and '*vectored*' sense of our moment-by-moment changing *placement* or *position* within our current surroundings to which it can give rise. Indeed, just as we can gain in our practical perceptions, as we move around within a situation, a sense of *where* we now are within the circumstances with which we must deal, along with both anticipations as to what might next happen to us as well as with certain 'action-guiding anticipations' as to what actions we next might take, so can we do this within our thinking. This is, I think, what Wittgenstein (1953) means when he says that the kinds of difficulties that concern him have "the form: "I don't know my way about" (no.123), and the criterion of them being overcome, is a person both being able to say, "Now I can go on," and in fact being able to go on in a way others can recognize as appropriate.

But there is another crucial aspect of withness-thinking just as important, if not more so, than this: It is that, instead of our always acting in terms of tendencies already well known to *us*, we can come to act in terms of tendencies coming to us in the expressions of *others*. This is very important. Let me approach it step-by-step.

First, we need to remind ourselves that it is only through a process, essentially, of creative discovery that, when we experience a need, we do not at first know what it is that will satisfy it. We must cast around to discover, while being guided by variations in the degrees to which we feel satisfied, what in fact will alleviate it. Thus this cannot be found by comparing an objectively represented, desired state of affairs with objective in one's surroundings – for no such well-defined, desired state of affairs exists. It is thus a specific, concrete, bodily felt need that structures our first-time explorations, and it is the satisfaction of this specific need that is experienced as the discovery of what we needed all along. But, as Todes (2002) points out, it is a retroactive understanding which shifts our attention away from the fact that we were unable to make our need determinate, i.e., give ourselves a name for it, without first being able to gratify it.

Next, we need also to remind ourselves that much of our casting around in our efforts to relate ourselves appropriately to our circumstances is, as in our thinking, language-influenced – it is only through their expressive forms that people can gain an experience of how things stand for them[100]. But finally, as (Geertz, 1983) notes, with respect to the anthropologist's task of making sense of people who act in ways very different from one's own ways of acting, "the ethnographer does not, and, in my opinion, largely cannot, perceive what his informants perceive. What he perceives, and that uncertainly enough, is what they [his informants] perceive 'with' – or 'by means of', or 'through'... whatever the word should be" (p.58). In other words: "Whatever sense we have of how things stand with someone else's inner life, *we gain it through their expressions*, not through some magical intrusion into their consciousness. It's all a matter of scratching surfaces..." (Geertz, 1986, p.73, my emphasis). Thus anthropological understanding is not a matter of extraordinary empathy, but a matter of working out from their readily observable expressions, the influences at work in shaping or informing a person's or a people's activities in their everyday lives.

It is our special capacity to be influenced, dialogically, by the tendencies, the anticipations, in other people's activities that can give us the chance to learn something utterly different from all the human things already known to us. And, to repeat, we can gain a sense of the 'depths' in other people's lives from a close attention to what is visible *on the surface*.

Thus, as I see it, although abstract and general theories have been of tremendous importance in the physical sciences and engineering, they are of little help to each of us in the unique living of our unique lives together. When it is a matter of our changing our *relations* with, or *orientations* toward, events occurring around us, or of our developing new such relations, that is at issue, whether we face that task as ordinary people and as professional practitioners, general and abstract theories are not only of no help to us, they can often stand in the way of our realizing what *is* of help.

This is not, however, to say that the turn away from the study of 'mind' to the study of human practices, need in no way lessen the quality of the thought, nor the quality of the scholarship, needed to make sense of how effective practices are developed, instituted, maintained, corrected and refined. The tasks entailed are all far from trivial. The high Enlightenment ideal of the universities as the repository of the best and the brightest intellects, and of the highest and best forms of scholarship and inquiry, which has motivated the opening of more and more universities everywhere, is still an awesome ideal – realms of explorative reflection, so hard to come by in the cut and thrust of for-profit business and industry – are of crucial importance. So the question I want to begin to end this book with, is the question of how can researchers, professors, lecturers, and students in universities begin to create new knowledge *in interactive cooperation with practitioners out in the surrounding world*, without reducing the intellectual quality of their traditional work: teaching, and research? In other words, how can the universities begin to carry out *three* different tasks to the best of their abilities? What *institutional* changes are required to make it possible? And what changes in thought-styles are required? It is this last question that I have not only tried to pursue in this book, but have also tried to implement in the very style of thought and expression (style of writing) I have employed in it.

For, as I see it, one way in which we can still draw on the important work of scholars, is to switch our attention from the supposed 'content' of their words (their writing) to their actual use of words, to *their* uses, to *their* expressions. So that we can begin to school ourselves in a style of thinking *'with' an other's voice, with their utterances, in mind*: Here, I want to suggest, we can begin to see another way in which what we call 'theory' can be influential – in a way, quite often, unintended by its original author. When confronted by unknown, bewildering events, instead of turning away from them to *think about* them in terms of this, that, or some other theoretical schematism appropriate to responding to them later, in *its* terms, we can use some of their words, literally, in 'instructing' ourselves in our practical actions out in the world of our everyday, practical affairs. For after all, almost all theorists propose their theory on the basis of noticing people express important reactions to events unnoticed by others – Freud: *sexual* reactions; Bateson: *metacommunicative* reactions ('This is play'); Festinger: *cognitive dissonance* reactions; and so on.

As beneficiaries of all these 'noticings', instead of turning away to think about the events before us, as I suggested above, we can turn ourselves responsively toward them immediately, and begin an intensive, i.e., in detail, and extensive, exploratory, dialogically-structured interaction with them, approaching them *this* way and *that* way... 'moved' to act in *this* way and *that* in accord with the 'reminders' (as Wittgenstein, 1953, no.127 calls them) issued by others to us, as a result of their explorations.

In other words, seeing *with another's words in mind* can itself be a thoughtful, feelingful, way of seeing, while thinking *with another's words in mind* can also be a feelingful, seeingful, way of thinking – a way of seeing and thinking that brings us into a close and personal, living contact with events in our surroundings, with their subtle but mattering details. This is a style of seeingful and feelingful thought that can be of help to us not only in our practical daily affairs, but also in our further explorations of our own human lives together – in our everyday interpersonal communications, in psychotherapy, in intercultural communication, management, administration, government, etc., and, in fact, in science, in understanding how 'aboutness (monolgical)-thinking' actually works and its reliance on a community of those trained in scientific practices. But it is crucial to bear in mind that, quite unlike the general, decontextualized statements occurring in science, the specific words of another person must be uttered at a timely moment within an actual ongoing practice, if they are to function as a 'reminder' as to a possible next step within that practice, or as 'pointers' oriented toward openings for its development and refinement.

Thus, following Goethe's comments above, while resonating also with Wittgenstein and Bakhtin, we can outline a distinction between 'withness-thinking' and 'aboutness-thinking' as follows:

— *Withness (dialogic)-thinking* is a form of reflective interaction that involves coming into living contact with an other's living being, with their utterances, their bodily expressions, their words, their 'works'.
— It is a meeting of outsides, of surfaces, of two or more kinds of 'flesh'

(Merleau-Ponty, 1968), such that they come into 'touch' with each other.
— All involved both touch and are touched, and in the relations between their outgoing touching and resultant incoming, responsive touches of the others, the sense of a 'touching' or of a 'moving' difference emerges.
— In the interplay of living movements intertwining with each other, new possibilities of relation are engendered, new interconnections are made, new 'shapes' of experience can emerge.
— Thus this kind of thinking does not give rise to a 'seeing', for what is 'sensed' is invisible; nor to an interpretation (a representation), for our responses occur spontaneously and directly in our living encounters with an other's expressions.
— Neither is it merely a feeling, for carries with it as it unfolds a bodily sense of the possibilities for responsive action in relation to one's momentary placement, position, or orientation in the present interaction.
— Instead, it gives rise to a *'shaped'* and *'vectored'* sense of our moment-by-moment changing placement in our current surroundings – engendering in us both unique anticipations as to what-next might happen along with, so to speak, 'action-guiding anticiptions' as to what-next we might do.
— In short, we are spontaneously 'moved' toward specific possibilities for action in such thinking.
— It is the kind of thinking we require in gaining an initial, first-time, orientation towards a subject matter, towards a difficult person or situation.

By contrast:

— *Aboutness (monologic)-thinking* is unresponsive to another's expressions; it works simply in terms of a thinker's 'theoretical pictures' – but, even when we 'get the picture', we still have to interpret it, and to decide, intellectually, on a right course of action.
— Thus, in aboutness-thinking, "(in its extreme pure form) another person remains wholly and merely an object of consciousness, and not another consciousness... Monologue is finalized and deaf to the other's response, does not expect it and does not acknowledge in it any *decisive* force" (Bakhtin, 1984, p.293).
— In other words, it works simply in terms of 'pictures', thus, even when we 'get the picture', we still have to decide, intellectually, on a right course of action – "The cat sat on the mat, the mat was red, the cat was black – get the picture?" "Yes, but so what?"
— It is the kind of thinking we indulge in 'problem-solving'.

The beginnings of 'withness-thinking'

So where do we begin, what is our point of departure for such a style of thinking, for such a mode of inquiry? How can we begin to teach ourselves, to change ourselves not in our intellect but in our will? How can we ourselves learn to master our own impulses more effectively, without a classroom teacher to 'instruct' us?

As we have already seen, the kind of learning involved here begins by our being spontaneously "struck by" an event. As Wittgenstein (1980a) noted: "The origin and primitive form of the language game is a reaction; only from this can more complicated forms develop..." (p.31); or, as Bateson (1979) puts it, it can begin with our noticing, "differences that make a difference" (p.453) – although I would like to add to this formulation of Bateson's the phrase, "a difference that matters to us." In other words, if we are struck by a difference that makes a difference to us, then it is by a difference that strikes us or surprises us because it makes a difference in our very way of being in the world – it is distinctive *for us* given *who* we are, or would like to be. And it matters to us, as I made clear in Chapter 8, because it is a kind of learning to do with the degree to which we, so to speak, know our 'way around' inside ourselves, inside our own capacities and impulses, inside our own habits and inclinations. For it is only when we have at least some degree of such an understanding of ourselves, can we cease to be victims of our own obsessions, compulsions, and impulses, and become an independent, autonomous, and self-determining individual.

Indeed, with respect to the question of which kind of knowledge is more fundamental – what we call "scientific" knowledge or this more ontological kind of knowledge – we can say without hesitation: this kind of ontological knowledge. For, it is only because people can distinguish between events occurring as a result of their intended actions or whether they are just happening, outside of the control of their agency, that they can do science at all. Further, people must be able, when acting in accord with theories of what the world might be like, whether the results of our actions accord with or depart from the expectations engendered by the theories. If they could not, then they would never be able to put their theories to empirical test – for this is the only way of establishing the nature of a theory's purchase on reality. In other words, besides being crucial in everyday life – in which we mus be continually *answerable* (Bakhtin, 1986) in our actions, such a distinction is crucial in the conduct of science, absolutely crucial: no other more fundamental basis for deciding the truth of empirical matters exists; nor will one ever be found – in the organizational complexity of matter, say, as some have proposed – for how could it ever be established as a true basis?" (see Shotter, 1975, p.86).

Other colleagues and I have set out some of the features of this approach in terms of the methods of a "social poetics" (Katz and Shotter, 1996; Shotter and Katz, 1996; Katz and Shotter, 1996a; Shotter, 1998; Cunliffe, 1999). This work explored its use within reflective, collaborating groups in developing not only a sensitivity to subtle and fleeting events of importance in their shared practice, but also in developing an appropriate vocabulary for creating and sustaining such appropriate 'ways of looking', i.e., of paying attention, among members of the group. Here is not the place to review this work in details, but in brief, within such self-reflecting and self-developing practices:

(1) Researchers (therapists, consultants) become co-practitioners, and practitioners (clients, patients, workers) become co-researchers, as each are 'struck by' uniquely new, first-time events that occur in the unfolding process, and they each begin to intertwine new language-games into such events.

(2) Both researchers (therapists, consultants) and practitioners (clients, patients, workers) alike are engaged in creating sense about lived experience. This sense emerges in the collaborative dialogical activity between them. As a result, practice, teaching, therapy, and research are all become enfolded with each other, as one in-forms and creates the other in a evolving, generative fashion.

(3) Both inquiry and learning in this process becomes a matter of "practical authorship" in which teachers and students, managers and workers, researchers and practitioners, all co-construct both what is that they create and learn together, as well as "re-authoring" themselves, i.e., reorienting they way of being in the world.

(4) And in such creative/learning conversations, participants may develop "practical-descriptive theory" together (see Chapter 3) – Goethe: "The highest thing would be to comprehend that everything factual is already theory... One should not seek anything behind phenomena: they themselves are the theory" (quoted in Brady, 1998, p.98, HA, p.432).

A case: Tom Andersen and a client's expression of the word "independence"

A case of Tom Andersen's (Andersen, unpub), a Norwegian family therapist, may illustrate how, by 'going into' people's expressions in great detail, and by 'calling out' yet further explorations from them through one's responsive listening, people can be helped in such 'inner explorations' to re-orient or to re-relate themselves to past experiences that till now have disabled them in some way. (I have been working closely with Tom for the last three years and have had his work in mind to think 'with' during the whole re-fashioning of this book). Central to the case is a "reminder" that he uses to orient himself in his interactions with clients: "The listener (therapist) who follows the talker (the client), not only hearing words but also seeing how the words are uttered, will notice that every word is part of the moving of the body. Spoken words and bodily activity come together in a unity and cannot be separated. The listener who sees as much as he or she hears will notice that various spoken words 'touch' the speaker differently. The speaker is touched by the words as they reach his or her own ears. Some words touch the speaker in such a way that the listener can see him or her being moved..." (Andersen, 1996, p.212). The case concerns Mary, who had been sick and has been trying to take care of herself. ("T" is Tom Andersen; "*M*" is *Mary*).

> "T: How do they.. your family.. see you? Do they see you as a person who should never ask for something...or do they see as a person who deserves to ask for something for yourself... How do they see you? *M: I am not sure.. I.. uhm.. I don't think that they look in terms of that ... I think that ... you know ... look at ... I guess that the family I grew up in ... we were supposed to be self-reliant .... independent was the big word in my family ...* Self-reliant? *What?* Independent? *(nods) yes. Independent was the really big word. And ... You know I feel that I got the message there. I* am sorry, you feel that ... *I feel that I got that message there... right ... and I feel that that was something I did really incorporate in my life....... I have ... no ... as soon as they were not responsible for me, it became... there was no longer an issue, I mean they don't talk of that any more, you know... ...* but it is still there ..."

The word "independent" had been mentioned two times, and as she said and heard the word her voice went down, and a sad look came over her face. It was as if she was hit and moved by the word. Andersen determined to investigate that word further. In other words, he begins a new language game, a new way relating both himself and Mary to the word "independence," in response to his being 'stuck by' her being so strongly 'touched' by this word. After having had to wait, since she wanted to say something first, he then asked:

> "How was that word independent expressed? Was it in the open or was it implicit? Or..? How was it expressed? *Well.. it was verbally* Verbally? The word independent? *Yes* In the way you should be independent or independence in general, or..? *We should be independent. They wanted us to be independent.. and we should be independent. They wanted us to be independent.. and...* So how... along the route when you came to be acquainted with the word and let that word be part of yourself .. what do you see in that word if you look into the word independent? *I don't like it. I personally don't like that word very much. Partly ... (she starts to move on the chair)* Do you see thing that ... say more, what don't you like when you see into the word, or look into the word? *Well I see (she starts to cry)... talking about loneliness is so hard for me ... you know I just... this was something I tried to not to think too much about.. uhm... I guess the word independent does mean staying alone... and for me that is gotten to be lonely... being alone uhm ... that's what the word...*

> *we used to talk about being independent and I finally said; don't use that word about me anymore. It is reinforcing something that I really don't like. Having to do everything myself Having to ... I have always felt it has been forced on me... for me ... what I would like to do is just ...I don't think independent is a virtue. I don't think so at all. I mean staying alone ... uhm .... (she is slightly bend forward as if she falls together and one hand holds the other hand.) Having to cope with things myself .. uhm....I just don't.. I don't think... I don't think I treat other people like that... but I treat myself like that... I feel that I treat other people as ... I try to provide support at least when I can... When it comes to me I...it's like I don't seek support... instead of... maybe I do ... I think about a year ago I finally realized that thing independence about me ... I constantly used that to describe me and I finally ... I am not independent, no I am not independent like you think I am ... I may have grown up with the idea that I should be, but that is not what I believe in now ... (she stretches her back and moves her hands to the sides and opens the upper part of the body again) ... I believe that people shall be supportive, I believe in being cooperative. You know always strong all the time. So that is something that I feel I ... it is really worth for me coming here and talking about things I wouldn't talk about.* If your mother was to look into the word independent, what would she see? *She would see strength ...* And you father? *Also strength (she paused for a while and laughed) ... that was interesting, because he will see another kind of strength than my mother ...* And your sister? *She will see what I see.*

As Andersen (unpub) sees it, two of the questions he asked above were of crucial importance: (1) 'How was it (the word "independent") expressed?', and (2) 'In the way you should be independent or independence in general, or...?' For he was able to sense in the *way* she answered these questions that she could *stay* with the word 'independence', and was ready to investigate it further – and was thus ready, herself, to come to a felt understanding of its role in her life, by connecting her felt expression of it with the current, general conditions of her life. But if she had answered the questions with an expression of disgust – 'that word destroys me' or 'I hate that word' – then, as he makes clear, he would not have 'called' her to 'go on' further with her investigations into its 'shaping' influences in her life. Andersen was able to sense, i.e., to anticipate in the unfolding 'shape' of her expression, how to 'go on' with her with respect to this crucial word.

In doing this, Andersen is not so much exploring *his* understanding of Mary, as sustaining a dialogically-structured activity in which Mary can explore *her own* understanding of herself. He does this by responsively "answering" to what he can hear/see in her utterances, spontaneously, i.e., not just in words but, due to his bodily engagement in the exchange with her, with all his bodily expressions. This kind of *answerability* (Bakhtin, 1986)

– not simply the giving of an answer to the asking of a question, but the kind of responsive responding to *tendencies* sensed by a listener in another's utterances – can give to that other the chance to sense and to respond to these tendencies themselves, and as a result, to 'go on' to take further steps and make further connections in relation to what they have just uttered. Thus Andersen's responsive 'answers' to Mary's utterances did not function *cognitively* as a response in words to a question asked, nor was he offering any explanations for the causes of her 'problems' or interpretations as to how they might be related to her past experiences. Instead, in his spontaneous responses to what she had just uttered, he was maintaining and nurturing the 'dialogical' relations between them, or, in other words, making sure their relations did not become monological. For, as Bakhtin (1984) puts it: "Monologism, at its extreme, denies the existence outside itself of another consciousness with equal rights and equal responsibilities, another *I* with equal rights (*thou*). With a monologic approach (in its extreme pure form) *another person* remains wholly and merely an *object* of consciousness, and not another consciousness... Monologue is finalized and deaf to the other's response, does not expect it and does not acknowledge in it any *decisive* force"(pp.292-293). In short, instead of responding to who *they* are, and thinking and acting *with their uttered words* as our guides, we respond to them in terms of who *we* are, *with our own words* as our guides.

Conclusions

Those of us trained in academic disciplines have been trained us into a certain style of 'rational' thought, modelled on thinking in the physical sciences, aimed at discovering a supposed 'reality' hidden behind appearances. When confronted with a perplexing, disorienting, bewildering, or astonishing (!) circumstance, we take it that our task is to analyze it (i.e., dissect it) into a unique set of separate elements, to find a pattern among them, and then to try to invent a theoretical schematism, functioning in terms of rules, laws, or principles, to account for the pattern so observed. In the social sciences, we express this method by seeking a supposed hidden agency responsible for the observed patterns in our behaviour; in the arts, we seek 'the content' supposed to be hidden in the 'forms' before us, by offering 'interpretations' to 'represent' this content. In short, we formulate the circumstance in question as a 'problem' requiring a 'solution' or 'explanation' that those, sitting in classrooms or seminar rooms, can 'see' or 'picture' as 'matching' or as 'fitting the facts'. But, to the extent that this style of thought is based in mental representations *of our own creation*, it leads us into adopting a certain relationship to the phenomena before us: Instead of leading us to look over them or into them more closely, from this way and that way, it (mis)leads us into first turning ourselves away from them, while we cudgel our brains in the attempt to construct an appropriate theoretical schematism into which to fit them. We only turn back toward them again when we have an action in mind suggested to us by our theoretical representation of their nature.

Clearly, this is a violent procedure that ignores all the intrinsic *living relations* already in existence in virtue of which living things grow, develop, flower, and die, only to reproduce others of their kind, to continue the unbroken stream of life on our planet. It is aimed at a very limited, selective account of nature – one, in fact, that is oriented toward, as Descartes (1968) put it in 1637, the "mastery and possession" (p.78) of nature. In it, living wholes are torn asunder ("We murder to dissect" – Wordsworth). The living activities spontaneously occurring between us all, and between us and our surroundings, are excluded from our considerations. Indeed, it is a style of thinking that completely ignores the expressions of living bodies, and the fact that people's meanings and understandings are *in* the relations between their responsive expressions.

But if our aim is not that of mastery and possession, but is merely that of desiring to be an unconfused *participant* within a larger scheme of things, most of which we cannot control but to which we must respond appropriately, we need to know how to gain orientation toward it, not a knowledge of facts, of it nature. We need to know how *to be*, to live out our existence, in relation to it. Our task is not that of *matching* static 'pictures' to static facts, but of gaining a sense of the unique 'inner lives' of those around us by allowing ourselves to be *both* 'moved' by their expressions, *and* by the events around them to which they are responding, thus to come to an understanding of *how* they are relating themselves to *their* circumstances. In short, we find the *life* they have put into their expressions by connecting them with the life around them – to produce that "just that understanding which consists in 'seeing connections' " (Wittgenstein, 1953, no.122).

Thus a reflective encounter of this kind is not simply the 'seeing' of a object, for what is sensed is in fact invisible; nor is it an interpretation (a representation), for it arises directly and immediately in the dynamics of one's living encounter with an other's expressions; but neither is it merely a feeling, for carries with it as it unfolds a bodily sense of the possibilities for responsive action in relation to one's momentary placement, position, or orientation in the present interaction. It is a style of seeingful and feelingful thought, of seeingful and feelingful action, that can be of help to us not only in our own, everyday, practical affairs, but also in our further, more focussed explorations of our own human lives together – in psychotherapy, intercultural communication, management, administration, government, etc., and also, in fact, in science itself, in understanding how 'aboutness (monological)-thinking' actually works, to judge whether in fact a Theory of Everything (TOE) is a realistic possibility, or a seriously mistaken fantasy, a result of our 'bewitchment' by language.

While it might seem somewhat ludicrous to suggest, as I did above, that we are and have remained deeply ignorant of quite *what* it is that we are doing to and for ourselves in our living, embodied encounters with each other, especially when we seem to have such clear intentions in all our actions, that is a major conclusion of this book. As I suggested above, our ignorance of the consequences of our interactions is not because the *intentions* supposedly informing our conduct are too deeply hidden to be brought out easily into the light of day, but because our plans and stated desires, etc., are not, and cannot be, the major influences on our conduct. Invisible, dynamical influences are at work in the moment of our acting – and to ignore these influences is to act in a non-human way toward the others around them.

Biff, Willy Loman's son, in Arthur Miller's *Death of a Salesman* (1949), wishes he had a different, more successful father. Linda, his mother and Willy Loman's wife, says to him:

> "Then make Charley your father, Biff. You can't do that, can you? I don't say he's a great man. Willy Loman never made a lot of money. His name was never in the paper. He's not the finest character that ever lived. But he's a human being, and a terrible thing is happening to him. So attention must be paid. He's not to be allowed to fall into his grave like an old dog. Attention, attention must finally be paid to such a person" (Linda, Willy Loman's wife, in Arthur Miller's *Death of a Salesman*).

Everyone is unique, someone to whom *attention must be paid.* This book is written in the hope that, by learning what is involved in paying attention to others, particularly to their *means* of expression, we can get a living, moving sense of *their lives* in *their terms* – and not think we have understood them simply because we have found a way to 'fit them into' *our* ways of making sense of them.

Epilogue:

ON THE EDGE OF SOCIAL CONSTRUCTIONISM – SOME FINAL WITTGENSTEINIAN REMARKS

> "Now if it is not the causal connections which we are concerned with, then the activities of the mind lie open before us. And when we are worried about the nature of thinking, the puzzlement which we wrongly interpret to be one about the nature of a medium is a puzzlement caused by the mystifying use of our language. This kind of mistake occurs again and again in philosophy; e.g. when we are puzzled about the nature of time, when time seems to us a *queer thing*... St Augustine says in the *Confessions*: What then is time? If no one asks me then I know; if they as, I know not"... We are most strongly tempted to think that here things are hidden, something we can see from the outside but which we can't look into. And yet nothing of the sort is the case. it is not new facts about time which we want to know. All the facts that concern us lie open before us. But it is the use of the substantive 'time' which mystifies us" (Wittgenstein, 1965, p.6).

Four themes have been central in this book: (1) One has been the focus on people's spontaneous, living, bodily responsiveness to the expressive movements of the others around them, and the creative nature of the dialogically-structured nature of the events occurring in the meetings between them. (2) This gave rise to a second: the fact that events occurring with such living processes of growth and development always occur for *another next first time*. No living patterns are ever perfectly repeated; there are always unique variations that are responsive to, and expressive of, aspects of the pattern's surroundings. Living time is irreversible. (3) This emphasis on uniqueness was associated with a third theme: the fact that, because of their unique, always creative nature, developing in response to events in their surroundings, all such processes cannot be understood in terms of mechanical repetitions, in terms of focal entities exhibiting regularities or patterns in their behaviour *unrelated* to their circumstances. And a final theme, of great importance, (4) is that our actual use of words, our voiced utterances as we body them forth, can exert a directive, motivational, and anticipatory influence both on the others around us, as well as on ourselves.

Taken together, these four features necessitated a fundamental reorientation toward the kinds of difficulties we face in our inquiries into communicational and relational difficulties. Instead of seeking to solve problems of knowledge, our task became the much more practical one of continually *struggling* to create uniquely new 'pathways' within those regions that are on the very edge, on the horizon, of our living out our lives together. For it is at the edge, on the horizon, that we must 'break new ground', for we cannot rely here on already established conventions or rules: we cannot assume that by "the world's future, we always mean the destination it will reach if it keeps going in the direction we can see it going now" (Wittgenstein, 1980a). The path into the future is often "not a straight line but a curve, constantly changing direction" (p.3). Thus the task we face here, on the edge, cannot be planned ahead of time, for the relevant features influencing each step only become present to us as we take each step, as we bodily move around within our surroundings. Thus, we must always create the relevant, sequentially unfolding *ways of relating* ourselves to events in our circumstances for another next first time from within what I have called "the interactive moment."

Proceeding with our practical inquiries in this fashion, however, is very different from our past ways of conducting our more reflective inquiries. In the past, with the mind being more central in our inquiries that than the body, we have seen most of our difficulties as being difficulties of the intellect – difficulties that we have tried to overcome by finding suitable ways in which to *think about* them, difficulties that we have sought to *solve* as problems. Clearly, the explorations in this book have been oriented in a quite different direction: toward overcoming orientational or relational difficulties – difficulties that we have to overcome, perhaps in a step by step manner, but certainly *in the course of* creating (dialogical) ways of 'going on' with the others around us, when we are all (both they and us) are oriented toward finding ways to *resolve* a unique practical difficulty we happen to face at a particular moment in the living of our lives together. Indeed, central to the whole *dynamical* approach I have adopted toward these kind of difficulties in this book, both the precise character of each, unique relational difficulty, and the relation of each of our actions to its resolution, only become apparent to us *within* the unfolding time course of events occurring as a consequence of our engaged involvement with our surroundings. As soon as our engaged involvement ceases, both these dynamically unfolding senses cease.

Our engaged involvement is crucial, and it is this that makes the methods of inquiry set out in this book quite different from the more problem-oriented methods of inquiry – to do with us seeking rules, patterns, orders, laws, or principles in our own human activities as a preliminary to planning a course of action – that, on encountering a difficulty, we always have resorted to in the past. The impulse to stop our activities, to step out of the flow and to take the standpoint of an external observer is very strong in us. But, as we have seen, it is not an appropriate impulse upon which to act in every case. In some cases we have to make that seemingly impossible effort to 'catch ourselves in the act'. Thus some difficulties, difficulties of the will rather than of the intellect, require us to work on ourselves, to work "on one's way of seeing things. (And what one expects of them)" (Wittgenstein, 1980a, p.16). Indeed, it is in Wittgenstein's working on himself, on his impulses, his temptations and wants, his own spontaneous inclinations and compulsions, that he brings to light the invisible, dynamical role of the anticipations and expectations spontaneously aroused in us by our training into our use of our language in influencing, not only each other in our practical affairs, but also, quite unconsciously, but also ourselves in shaping our own actions. So here, I would like to provide an epilogue that allows Wittgenstein to state succinctly, in his own words, the nature of his overall approach.

How we can so easily 'bewitch' ourselves in our own use of our words

First, let me draw attention to a number of his remarks to do with how some of the very first 'innocent' steps we take, in talking amongst ourselves about many of the difficulties in human relations we face *as problems that can be solved*, can lead us into 'bewitching' ourselves with our own linguistic constructions. Right from the start, we inevitably formulate such 'problems' in terms of supposedly hidden entities, things which none of us have actually ever seen – we talk of thoughts, ideas, of mental processes, of states of mind, attitudes, etc. – and set out 'the problem' in theses terms: "In wonder how we can change those people to change their attitudes?" I wonder what was going on in his mind when....?" "I wish I knew how to get everyone to agree to...?" "If only we knew how to explain why people get so disturbed at these thoughts... ?" "I wonder what processes are going on in his mind when he hits X like that?" Etc., etc. About such problem-formulations involving reference to such, as yet undetermined, invisible processes, Wittgenstein (1953) remarks:

> "How does the philosophical problem about mental processes and states and about behaviourism arise.? – The first step is the one that altogether escapes notice. We talk of processes and states and leave their nature undecided. Sometime perhaps we shall know more about them – we think. *But that is just what commits us to a particular way of looking at the matter*. For we have a definite concept of what it means to learn to know a process better. (The decisive movement in the conjuring trick has been made, and it was the very one that we thought quite innocent.) – And now the analogy which was to make us understand our thoughts falls to pieces. So we have to deny the yet uncomprehended process in the yet unexplored medium. And now it looks as if we had denied mental processes. And naturally we don't want to deny them" (no.308, my emphasis).

The point Wittgenstein is making here is that when we formulate a difficulty as a *problem*, few of those we are talking with (at least, to begin with) object to our formulation of it. We almost all feel that we can specify in more precise detail the nature of the 'as yet unknown things' we assume to be causing the problem later. Indeed, that is precisely the aim of our inquiries, so we can now begin to take the first step in our search for a solution. However, the very terms in which the problem is formulated, can easily (mis)lead us into looking in the wrong place with the wrong expectations for the solution (the outcome) we desire.

This point, however, is very easy to misunderstand. So let me explore it a little further for, as Wittgenstein emphasizes, it might seem that he wants completely to deny that any significant 'inner events' – call them "mental processes," or "mental states," or what you will – are occurring at all. For we all feel the need to reply to his objections by saying: "But there must have been a mental process occurring in me when I remembered ...." Surely *something* special happens when we remember something or understand something? And he does not want to deny this. But what he does want to ask is: On the basis of such utterances, where next do we go in our inquiries? What kinds of anticipations do such utterances engender in us? Do we start trying to look inside people's heads for usually hidden things, or do we start to look at the *relations* between their expressions and the relevant surrounding circumstances, i.e., at events occurring between them out in the open, in the world? If our concerns are scientific ones, it will most likely be the former; but if our concern is with overcoming a more practical confusion or difficulty, it must be the latter.

Indeed, with respect to the issue of whether we are seeking to *explain* 'hidden' processes or simply to *describe* what is out in the open between us, Wittgenstein (1953) claims that, if we were to ask: "How do sentences manage to represent?" – and answer that one might give could be: "Don't you know? You certainly see it, when you use them." And he goes on to claim that this is the case because: "Nothing is concealed... Nothing is hidden" (no.435). If it was, then we would only be able to grasp a small proportion of what in fact we do grasp, and then not spontaneously but only by labouriously trying to 'work it out'. Although "it all goes by so quick," descriptively, there is no in principle difficulty, everything we need to attend to if we are to understand the practicalities of how understanding works is out in the world present to us.

In making this claim, however, that "nothing is hidden" (no.435), that everything we need to understand the working of our utterances is present to us out in the world around us, Wittgenstein could easily be accused of being "a behaviourist in disguise" (no.307), accused of saying that mental events are 'nothing but' sequences of various stimulus-response (S-R) contingencies. But again, what would we be doing in making such an accusation? What would we expect to happen next? That he will deny the role of *all* inner processes? Or: that he will just pay attention to S-R sequences and ignore their relations to their surroundings?

Let us look at what he says in relation to these two possibilities: With respect to the first, if someone were to say to him: "Surely, you cannot deny that in remembering, an inner process takes place?," he would reply: No, of course not. But what gives you the impression that we want to deny something *like that*? He does want to deny something, but its point is quite different. What he wants to deny "is that the picture of an inner process gives us the correct idea *of the use of the word* 'to remember'. We say that this picture stands in the way of our seeing the use of the word as it is" (no.305, my emphasis).

His concern here is with what we are doing, practically, in our particular uses of words at particular points in our interactions with each other. It is a very specific concern, and a quite legitimate concern, and what is more, a concern that orients us toward specific activities with respect to specific kinds of difficulty.

It is this also – the way we must always interweave our activities into events in our surroundings, and must continually struggle to create new 'pathways' on the horizon of our living out our lives together – that prevents Wittgenstein from being a simple behaviourist: "Take the various psychological phenomena: thinking, pain, anger, joy, wish, fear, intention, memory, etc., – and compare the behaviour corresponding to each. – But what does behaviour include here? Only the play of facial expression and gestures? Or also the surroundings, so to speak the occasions of this expression? And if one does include the surroundings as well, – how is the behaviour to be compared in the case of anger and in that of memory, for example? " (1980b, I, no.129). The task of thinking through the different kinds of inquiry required here, of thinking through in slow-motion, so to speak, the unfolding steps involved in describing different particular cases of a person being angry at someone (or some thing) and of a person remembering something, while in principle possible, still leaves us with much work to do – work that we always have to do for ourselves, for another first time. For, to repeat, from our place always on the edge of breaking new ground, we cannot hope to mechanically and blindly repeat our past successes.

Enchantment and disenchanted, self-deception and becoming unself-deceived

Modern philosophy has always been in the thrall of science. It is only by following "the secure path of a science," said Kant in his *Critique of Pure Reason* in 1787, that philosophy can become more than "a merely random groping" (Kant, 1970, p.17). And even now, we are still under that spell, the belief that there is a form or pattern of reasoning, a methodology, that we must follow if we are to overcome the difficulties we face in our lives. Wittgenstein's (1953) great achievement in his later philosophy is to have broken the spell, to have made it very clear to us that many of our difficulties are not of the form of *problems* which, by the application of a science-like methodology, one can solve by reasoning. They are difficulties of a quite different kind. They are not "empirical problems," they can be overcome "by looking into the workings of our language, and that in such a way as to make us recognize those workings: in despite of an urge to misunderstand them. The problems are solved, not by giving new information, but by arranging what we have always known. Philosophy is a battle against the bewitchment of our intelligence by means of language" (no.109).

If this is the case, as I said above, the task of slowly thinking through the unfolding steps involved in describing the different temporal and spatial relations between our talk, our actions, and their responsive relations to their surroundings, is not easy. It is work that we have to do for ourselves, always for another first time: "There is not a philosophical method, though there are indeed methods, like different therapies" (1953, no.133).

His project then, is not simply to *replace* all scientific inquiries to do with our human affairs with his own philosophical/grammatical ones. Science is fine in its own proper place. But what he does want to do is to bring us to a realization that we often we think that our difficulties are scientific ones when in fact they are not. Understanding the *causes* of a person's mental disturbance in a psychotic crisis is of no help to us in guiding us toward first responding to him or her in a calming fashion, and then in suggesting to us further utterances, gestures, and expressions that might help them to become more well oriented within themselves. To insist that there must always be an inner process of some kind to be discovered when we face such (orientational or relational) difficulties, and that until we have discovered it we cannot begin to take any adequate measures to overcome them can, not only divert our attention away from the kinds of inquiry that might help us resolve appropriate lines of action, but can also divert us very easily into enormously expensive projects to do with brain scans, building the appropriate electron microscopes, etc., which, in the end, still leave us bewildered in the same way as before as to how to act for the best in a disorienting circumstance.

To undo the influence of such problem-structured utterances (often uttered within the confines of academic seminars or colloquia, or institutional planning committees), is not easy. It requires our working on ourselves, on our expectations, our ways of seeing things. All of our western institutions contain rooms and times set aside for such meetings, we take for granted that problem analysis and solution planning talks are an essential part of our institutional lives together. Thus, in such circumstances, in making use of words in our utterances, we almost all take it for granted that our words are *about* something, and that that *something* can sooner or later be brought into view if required, but until then, we take it that our ability to provide a 'representation' (picture) of it in words is sufficient for us all to have a sense of *what* we are talking *about*.

But to understand the 'bewitching' power of our own talk upon us here, the power of pure talk alone to create a taken-for-granted sense of reality, it is perhaps necessary to explore a little further what it is about certain forms of talk that allows them to exert such influence on us. For clearly, not just any old way of talking will be taken seriously by others as representing (giving us a picture of) actual states of affairs.

As I see it, our feeling that a linguistic representation is a representation of a *real* thing is due to the fact that, as our linguistic competency increases, we become more and more adept at constructing a linguistic context, a network of *intralinguistic* references, into which to direct our next utterances. And in doing this, instead of always needing to refer to things and events within the immediate surroundings of our speech, we can move toward a reliance on references to what has already occurred, to what is already well known to everyone within the shared context of our talk. In other words, as long as we take the trouble to *justify* to the others around us as to why they should treat what we are saying as true, i.e., as representative of reality, then we can move away from a reliance upon a referent in the immediate, shared context, and, in accord with the *syntactical* relations between words, move toward a reliance upon links between what has already been, or with what might be, said. We have to develop methods for warranting in the course of our talk (i.e., for giving support to) our claims about what 'might be' as being what 'is' – we must learn to say, for instance, when making a claim about a state of affairs, that others saw it that way too, and so on. By the use of such methods and procedures, we can construct our statements *as* 'factual statements', and thus come to use forms of speech that can function with a large degree of independence from their immediate context. But, as I hope is now clear, in the decrease of reference to what 'is' and consequent increase of reference to what 'might be', the danger of referring only to a hermeneutically constructed *imaginary* or *theoretical* world is considerable.

Nowhere is this danger more intense than in our philosophy and other academic seminar rooms, in our conferences, in our institutional analysis and planning rooms, committee rooms, board rooms, and governmental meetings. We all think – when we use such words as thought, idea, meaning, language, society, person, neurosis, psychosis, attention deficit hyperactivity disorder, bipolar personality, market trends, staff unrest, leadership, etc., etc., in such rooms – that we are all talking about *things* that exist, and that we are all talking about the *same* thing. Our qualm-less trust in the power and worth of pure talk, and in the ultimate *reality* of the things all our 'big words' refer to, is amazing, and, no doubt, in many spheres of life, quite justified.

But it is Wittgenstein's (1953) claim that in philosophy – and, I want to claim that in many of our more practical difficulties in life, in which we are acting at the edge of human affairs, always for another first time – we cannot just rely on the syntactic conventions that we have developed in the past to try to ensure *real* references for our talk. We must be bring our talk back into a living connection with the circumstances that gave it its life in the first place – especially when it comes to talk in which 'big words' play a prominent part. Wittgenstein wants to bring such words back into an everyday context in which they can play a specific role as a result of their specific intertwining into a specific practical activity: "When philosophers use a word – 'knowledge', 'being', 'object', 'I', 'proposition', 'name' – and try to grasp the essence of the thing, one must always ask oneself: is the word ever actually used in this way in the language-game which is its original home? — What we do is to bring words back from their metaphysical to their everyday use" (no.116).

It is when we say to ourselves or to each other: "What is X?," where we might fill in for X the name of a supposed hidden entity that plays an important role in shaping our activities – words such as 'mind', 'thought', 'memory', attitude', 'meaning', etc. – that we can so easily get ourselves into trouble, and can send ourselves off on a search for chimeras, for grotesque nonexistent monsters: "The questions 'What is length?', 'What is meanings?', 'What is the number one?' etc., produce in us a mental cramp," says Wittgenstein (1965). "We feel that we can't point to anything in reply to them and yet ought to point to something. (We are up against one of the greatest sources of philosophical bewilderment: a substantive makes us look for a thing that corresponds to it.)" (p.1). Let me repeat this last sentence with a special emphasis: a substantive *makes us* look for a thing that corresponds to it. In other words, a certain style of talk, with a certain of intonation, etc., can spontaneously arouse in us, bodily, a certain expectation, a certain motivation to 'go on' to carry out a next act. It is not easy to accept that language can have this power over us.

Thus by bringing the use of such words – words that we can very easily think of as the names of hidden inner processes or states, or of special hidden agencies responsible for the patterns we think of as occurring in our actions – back into this or that particular everyday context, and by talking them out of the context of portentous, pure talk, Wittgenstein wants to show us that such words can also exert very different influences on us, different influences in different situations. Especially in the realm of pure talk, words functioning as *names* can, in particular, exert a powerful influence on us. But again, as Wittgenstein (1953) remarks: "Naming is so far not a move in the language-game – any more than putting a piece in its place on the board is a move in chess. We may say: nothing has so far been done, when a thing has been named. It has not even got a name except in the language-game. This was what Frege meant too, when he said that a word had meaning only as part of a sentence" (no. 49). Although words play a crucial role in our meaning something to each other, they have no meaning in themselves.

Poetic expression

> "Philosophy ought really to be written only as a *poetic composition*" (1980a, p.24).

Wittgenstein's (1953) work, then, does not provide us with some ready-made conclusions, some new answers to old problems that no one had managed previously to solve. His work, unexpectedly, confronts us with a new set of difficulties, with difficulties of the will rather than of the intellect, difficulties which, if we are to overcome them, require us to work on ourselves, to work on our ways of seeing things, on what we expect of them. For, as he makes clear to us, every question we pose to ourselves orients us in the form in which it is posed toward answering it in a certain way: our ends are in our beginnings. Our ways of talking can exert powerful effects on us unconsciously, without our being easily able to deliberate on how we might in the course of our thought and talk take alternative paths, how we might 'go on' in different ways.

To sum up his endeavours in his own words: "I have been trying in all of this," he says, "to remove the temptation to think that there '*must* be' what is called a mental process of thinking, hoping, wishing, believing, etc., independent of the process of expressing a thought, a hope, a wish, etc... If you are puzzled about the nature of thought, belief, knowledge, and the like, substitute for the thought the expression of the thought, etc... the expression of belief, thought, etc. is just a sentence [utterance]; – and the sentence only has sense as a member of a system of language; as one expression within a calculus... [Thus]: If we scrutinize the usages which we make of such words as 'thinking', 'meaning', 'wishing' etc., going through this process rids us of the temptation to look for a peculiar act of thinking, independent of the act of expressing our thoughts, and stowed away in some peculiar medium. We are no longer prevented by the established forms of expression from recognizing that the experience of thinking *may* be just the experience of saying, or may consist of this experience plus others which accompany it" (pp.41-43).

In working on the edge, in struggling always to break new (common) ground, we have always in the past looked for patterns, for forms, for rules, laws, or principles, as pointing to way forward for us to 'go on' in ways that would make sense for us, and were not *mere random groping*. In other words, we have sought explanations. Wittgenstein (1953), however, suggests to us that "we must do away with all explanation, and description alone must take its place" (no.109). And he goes on again to outline a temptation we often fall prey to trying to describe the 'open', 'incomplete' nature of actual human situations: "Mere description is so difficult," he says, "because one believes that one needs to fill out the facts in order to understand them. It is as if one saw a screen with scattered colour-patches, and said: the way they are here, they are unintelligible; they only make sense when one completes them into a shape. – Whereas I want to say: Here *is* the whole. (If you complete it, you falsify it)" (1980b, I, no.257). Indeed, traditionally in our inquiries, "we are under the illusion that what is sublime, what is essential, about our investigation consists in its grasping *one* comprehensive essence" (1981, no.444). We seek a single order of connectedness – a theory of everything – that will bring all the complexity apparent to us in our daily human affairs into a single, comprehensive perspective, so that everything will be related to everything else in a single orderly fashion. That is our dream, or according to Wittgenstein, our delusion.

So how can a mere description be of help, if it doesn't provide us with such a perspective? Well, it can exert its orienting influence upon us in a person's very speaking of it, if it is an appropriately detailed description. For it can exert its influence in arousing in us the appropriate expectations and anticipations as to how to find our 'way about' and to 'go on' in the circumstance in question. This is where Wittgenstein's (1980a) suggestion that philosophy should only be written *as* one writes poetry becomes relevant: for it is not a matter of giving information, but of arousing certain 'inner callings' in ourselves and others by the use of certain words, or combinations of words. But let us be quite clear here, Wittgenstein did not say that philosophy should be written only *as poetry*, but that one should write it *as one writes* when writing poetry, i.e., with some of the same attitudes to the working of words in arousing quite specific expectations. It is the poetic 'calling out' of certain further expectations of further experiences in us, to move us on beyond solely representational uses of language, that is at issue.

Indeed, with respect to the way in which our voicing (intoning) of our words matters here, Wittgenstein (1953) describes some of the things that can go wrong in reading a poem: "'When I read a poem or narrative with feeling, surely something goes on in me which does not go on when I merely skim the lines for information'. – What processes am I alluding to? – The sentences have a different ring. I pay careful attention to my intonation. Sometimes a word has the wrong intonation, I emphasize it too much or too little. I notice this and shew it in my face. I might later talk about my reading in detail, for example about the mistakes in my tone of voice. Sometimes a picture, as it were an illustration, comes to me. And this seems to help me to read with the correct expression. And I could mention a good deal more of the same kind. – I can also give a word a tone of voice which brings out the meaning of the rest, almost as if this word were a picture of the whole thing. (And this may, of course, depend on sentence-formation.)" (p.214). In other words, "understanding a sentence is much more akin to understanding a theme in music than one may think" (1953, no.527), as we explored in Chapters 6 and 8. And it is in this orientational sense that we can think of a description working to help us to know both our 'way around' and how to 'go on' in a particular circumstance in which we are involved.

In other words, the words in a *poetically structured* text are working like a set of 'signposts' staking out a 'journey' over a shared landscape of possible places to go. But in working in this way, our words are doing something very much more than merely 'picturing' or representing such a landscape: like signposts, they are pointing to publicly shared (possible) realities *beyond themselves*. How can our words works like this?

In discussing how our use of words can work like this, as an aid in our knowing our 'way about' within a landscape of possibilities, Wittgenstein (1953) discusses the importance to us of being struck by the particular use of a word, and how by remembering that use, we can go on to make that same use of it in other similar such circumstances. He begins this discussion by noting the differences between our first being 'struck' by a word, and then by describing what can happen afterwards. He starts this discussion by asking a comparative question: "Can one keep hold of an understanding of meaning as one can keep hold of a mental image? That is, if one meaning of a word suddenly strikes me, – can it also stay there in my mind?" (p.176). He then goes on to explore the issue further by, characteristically, inventing an unusual occurrence, a person saying unusually or oddly: "The whole scheme presented itself to my mind in a flash and stayed there like that for five minutes." He then goes on to ask, rhetorically: "Why does this sound odd?" It sounds odd because it seems that what occurred in a flash cannot be the whole scheme, in detail. Surely, the detail must have been got or developed later. But it is often the case that we do, nonetheless, give a start and go on to exclaim: 'Now I've got it!', and go on to demonstrate the fact that we've 'got it' by setting forth the whole scheme in detail. But about that occurrence, Wittgenstein 91953) asks: "What is supposed to have stayed in this case? A picture, perhaps" (p.176). But 'Now I've got it!' cannot mean simply having a picture, for what one has grasped is very much more than simply a picture of something. If the particular meaning of a word is its use in a particular circumstances, and: "If a meaning of a word has occurred to you, and have not *forgotten* it again, you can now use the word in such-and-such a way" (p.176).

In other words, when one is seemingly 'struck by' a word and can remember being so struck, what one remembers here is not primarily its representational use. It is its relational or orientational use within the whole circumstance that is being remembered; and it is in recalling its unfolding time-contour that can it can again 'point beyond itself' to draw attention again to otherwise unnoticed aspects in our shared activities.

Thus, by the use of poetic forms of talk and writing in our inquiries, by juxtaposing ordinary words in extraordinary combinations, for instance, we can 'arrest' our routine forms of 'reality-talk' and to put them on '*freeze frame*', so to speak. We might then have the possibility of being able to search over that *freeze frame* for alternative ways in which we might relate ourselves responsively to aspects of the situation represented in it that we might not otherwise have noticed. The kind of writing which can achieve this, is writing about concrete details, quoting actual voiced utterances, using metaphors, making comparisons, in short, writing in such a way that, in juxtaposing one's words in unconventional ways, writers create occasions in which readers must creatively complete – dialogically, not cognitively – the process of understanding. Thus poetic forms can work noncognitively, for, as long as the 'gaps' created by us juxtaposing our words in unusual ways are not too great, our bodies will responsively create {Gr: poiesis = creation, making} ways of bridging them. Indeed, we can now begin to see, perhaps, how each word in a text, just as each point we look at in a visual scene, can – due to the *action guiding anticipations* it arouses – send us on to the next with certain tasks already in hand.

Conclusions

What Wittgenstein (1953) wants to bring to our attention is that, besides our representational use of words, our words work both on those around us as well as ourselves, to arouse in us, spontaneously, various attitudes of expectancy, even when no definite pictorial image is aroused in us or definite object is before us. In previous chapters we have called these arousals transitory understandings and action guiding anticipations. Above, I suggested that our task in many spheres of human inquiry, instead of having the form of intellectual problems which can be solved by appropriate ways of thinking, our task is a much more practical one of continually *struggling* to 'break new (common) ground' on the edge or on the horizon of our living out our lives together.

To the extent that we cannot rely on already established conventions or rules, to the extent that we cannot plan our next step ahead of time, we must find the relevant features influencing our next step in what becomes present to us as we take each step. Only as we actively engage, as we bodily move around within our surroundings, do these influences become known to us. If we cease our active involvement, they cease. Hence we must always create the relevant, sequentially unfolding *ways of relating* ourselves to events in our circumstances, for another next first time, in the very course of our involvements.

Clearly, then, to repeat. Wittgenstein does not want in every case to *replace* scientific inquiries with his own philosophical/grammatical ones. But what he does want to do is to bring us to a realization that we almost always at the moment think, in every case, that our difficulties are scientific ones, or have the form of scientific problems, when in fact they are not. To insist that there must be 'hidden' processes or things of some kind to be discovered when we face an orientational or relational difficulty, and that we can only do something relevant to overcoming our difficulty by discovering it, is to seriously mislead ourselves. As I noted above, misunderstanding the kind of difficulty we face can not only divert our attention away from the kinds of inquiry that might help us resolve appropriate lines of action, it can also very easily orient us toward enormously expensive projects which, even if enormously interesting in their own right, can still leave us no less bewildered as before as to how to act for the best in a disorienting circumstance.

Notes:

1. A good deal of emotion is associated, not so much with the use, as with the maintaining of our 'basic' ways of speaking in existence. It is encountered during those times when an attempt is made to change them in some way. Thus, as Foucault (1972) points out, although speech may not seem to be a very powerful activity in itself "the prohibitions surrounding it soon reveal its links with power and desirability... speech is not merely the medium which manifests – or dissembles – desire; it is also the object of desire. Similarly, historians have constantly impressed upon us that speech is no mere verbalization of conflicts and systems of domination, but that it is the very object of man's conflicts" (p.216).

2. The term "specifically vague" appears in the following quotation from Garfinkel (1967), in discussing a husband's account of a conversation he and his wife had about events occurring when he brought their young son home from nursery school one afternoon: "The events that were talked about were specifically vague. Not only do they not frame a clearly restricted set of possible determinations but the depicted events include as their essentially intended and sanctioned features an accompanying 'fringe' of determinations that are open with respect to internal relationships, relationships to other events, and relationships to retrospective and prospective possibilities" (pp.40-41).

3. A fact, perhaps, reflected in the number of books about "chaos theory" and similar matters (e.g., Prigogine and Stengers, 1984; Bohm, 1985; Gleik, 1987; Peat, 1990).

4. It is the kind of knowledge one has, not only *from within a social situation*, a group, or an institution, and which thus takes into account (and is accountable within) the social situation within which it is known. It is also knowledge that one has *from within oneself as a human being and as a socially competent member of a culture* – hence I know 'from the inside', so to speak, what it is like to be involved in conversation (see my Chapter 2 epigraph quote from Garfinkel, 1967, p.40). So, although I may not able to reflectively contemplate the nature of that knowledge as an inner, mental representation, according to the questions asked me, I can nonetheless call upon it as a practical resource in framing appropriate answers.

5. This is why I cannot agree with those who, like Gergen (1999), suggest that joint action is best understood in terms of "the form of coordination we achieve" (p.146). As I see it, one of its major features is the creation of unique, once-occurrent outcomes, *unintended* by any of the participants. Thus joint action is just as liable to create misunderstandings as understandings. Indeed, this is the power of Wittgenstein's (1953) whole later philosophy: to bring to our attention the fact that many of our 'coordinations' are one's in which we have 'bewitched' ourselves by our own misleading use of words.

6. Below, what Rorty (1979) calls a 'normal discourse', i.e., a discourse which *dominates* our talk in the sense of providing the basic or the final unquestioned terms in which we make sense of things, I shall call a 'basic' way of talking.

7. "I have been urging in this book that we try *not* to want something which stands beyond history and institutions" (Rorty, 1989, p.189).

8. He wants to offer "my account of intellectual progress as the literalization of selected metaphors" (p.44).

9. "At the basis of the modes of linguistic thought that lead to the postulation of language as a system of normatively identical forms lies a *practical and theoretical focus of attention on the study of defunct, alien languages preserved in written monuments*... We can state outright: *linguistics makes its appearance wherever and whenever philological need has appeared*...Guided by philological need, linguistics has always taken as its point of departure the finished monologic utterance – the ancient written monument, considering it the ultimate realium... Any utterance – the finished, written utterance not excepted – makes response to something and is calculated to be responded to in turn. It is but one link in a continuous chain of speech performances. Each monument carries on the work of its predecessors, polemicizing with them, expecting active, responsive understanding, and anticipating such understanding in return... The philologist-linguist tears the monument out of that real domain and views if as if it were a self sufficient, isolated entity. He brings to bear on it not an active ideological understanding but a completely passive kind of understanding, in which there is not a flicker of response, as there would be in any authentic kind of understanding" (Voloshinov, 1986, pp. 71-73).

10. "In point of fact," says Voloshinov, 1986, "word is a *two-sided act*. It is determined equally by *whose* word it is and *for whom* it is meant... it is precisely *the product of the reciprocal relationship between speaker and listener, addresser and addressee*. Each and every word expresses the 'one' in relation to the 'other'. I give myself verbal shape from another's point of view, ultimately, from the point of view of the community to which I belong" (p.86).

11. As Foucault (1972) points out, disciplinary discourses lay down rituals that those participating in them must observe: "it lays down gestures to be made... it lays down the supposed, or imposed significance of the words used, their effect upon those to whom they are addressed, the limitations of their supposed validity" (p.225).

12. As Dreyfus and Rabinow (1982) say in discussing Foucault's (1972) exposure of the illusion of autonomous, decontextualized, discourse: "This exotic form of speech act flourished in especially pure form in Greece around 300 B.C., when Plato became explicitly interested in the rules that enabled speakers to be taken seriously, and, by extrapolating the relative context independence of such speech acts to total independence, invented pure theory... This systematic, institutionalized justification of the claim of certain speech acts to be true of reality takes place in a context in which truth and falsity has serious social consequences" (p.48).

13. "Demonstrably he [a speaker] is responsive to this background [in terms of various expectancies], while at the same time he is at a loss to tell us specifically of what the expectancies consist. When we ask him about them he has little or nothing to say" (Garfinkel, 1967, pp.36-37). As Garfinkel suggests, some of these expectancies will depend upon *prior* agreements and will be according to agreed practices or 'methods', but others, I claim, due to the intrinsic properties of joint action, will emerge out of the immediate and local practical circumstances of the conversation in question.

14. The idea that language works in terms of a set of pre-established, basic meanings, has long been a commonplace of academic linguistics. Witness Jakobson's (1956) claim that "the speaker and the listener have at their disposal more or less the same 'filing cabinet of prefabricated representations': the addresser of a verbal message preselects one of these 'preconceived possibilities' and the addressee is supposed to make an identical choice from the same assembly... Thus the efficiency of a speech event demands the use of a common code by its participants" (p.71).

15. "The outwardly actualized utterance is an island rising from the boundless sea of inner speech..." (Voloshinov, 1973, p.96).

16. As Wittgenstein (1980a) notes: "Perhaps what is inexpressible (what I find mysterious and am not able to express) is the background against which whatever I could express has its meaning" (p.16). While Raymond Williams (1977, p.132) uses the term "structures of feeling" to characterize the usually taken for granted meanings and values as they are actively lived and felt in the moment of our acting together with the others around us. Vico (1968) says about our common sense, our "sensus communis" as he calls it, that it is "judgement without reflection, shared by an entire class, an entire people, an entire nation, or the entire human race" (para.142).

17. I am hesitant about the word 'normative' here. I do not want to suggest that there are, in general, any pre-established normative conventions ruling conversational moves or responses; the forming of a felicitous response, is a matter of 'fitting' it into the momentarily available conversational context at the time. Its 'fittingness' is a matter, not of it according with prior norms, but of it as a `sensible` response to a previous speaker's utterance, in the developing development of the conversation.

18. Where, as Wittgenstein (1953) noted, it is seemingly impossible to "weld" such investigations into "a natural order without breaks," i.e., to form a coherent 'picture' of the terrain as such: "And this was, of course, connected with the very nature of the investigation. For this compels us to travel over a wide field of thought criss-cross in every direction. - The philosophical remarks in this book are, as it were, a number of sketches of landscapes which were made in the course of these long and involved journeyings" (p.ix).

19. "The real foundations of his enquiry do not strike a man at all. Unless *that* fact has at some time struck him" (Wittgenstein, 1953, no.129).

20. Wittgenstein (1953, p.227) formulated the difficulty here as follows: it is "... to put all indefiniteness, correctly and unfalsified, into words." This is why there is a "... difficulty of renouncing all theory: One has to regard what appears so obviously incomplete, as something complete" (I, 1980, no.723).

21. *Entanglement*: "When two systems, of which we know the states by their respective representation, enter into a temporary physical interaction due to known forces between them and when after a time of mutual influence the systems separate again, then they can no longer be described as before, viz., by endowing each of them with a representative of its own. I would not call that *one* but rather *the* characteristic trait of quantum mechanics" (Erwin Schroedinger, "Discussion of probability relations between separated systems," *Proc. Camb. Phil. Soc*, 31, p.555, 1935).

22. "Ahead of what I can see and perceive, there is, it is true, nothing more actually visible, but my world is carried forward by lines of intentionality which trace out in advance at least the style of what is to come..." (Merleau-Ponty, 1962, p.416).

23. Later, in Chapters 5 and 6, when we discuss Merleau-Ponty's (1968) notions of the *chiasmic* further, and the *poetic* nature of Wittgenstein's (1953) methods, we shall see that this idea, not of matching a state of affairs with one or another picture or representation in terms of its fittingness, but of viewing it *through* or *in accord with* a 'way of looking' acquired by coming to embody a familiarity with a paradigmatic exemplar, is crucial. It gives us a way, in practice, of relating or of placing the unknown event or state of affairs before us in relation to what is already familiar to us – in short, it is an orientational aid in our efforts to 'know our way around'.

24. Some here may want to speak of 'landscapes with their horizons', but this seems to me to be too static a metaphor. Drawing upon my own experiences sailing, I prefer talk of 'seascapes'.

25. Basic, that is, in a political-moral (and methodological) sense if not the ontological sense: thus I want to argue that, even if there is no already fixed *basis* in terms of which to 'root' or to 'ground' our claims, we can still none the less identify the 'place' or 'sphere of activity' within which the *judging* of people's claims can be located. The 'grounds' for settling arguments are to be found within the argumentative activities themselves, not outside them, and hence, the moment when politics is at its most intense is to be found there too. A lack of 'foundations' is not a lack of bases for judgment. This is not to say, however, that it is in the sphere of verbal interaction that, ontologically, we should seek the developmental *origins* of all our verbal formulations.

26. Although I have not the space available to discuss the matter at length here, conversational realities should be sharply distinguished from disciplinary (academic) discourses (Foucault, 1972). In open conversation, one switches from metaphor to metaphor as one pleases, according to the requirements of the conversation. In a disciplinary discourse, certain metaphors are literalized into 'pictures' or 'models', and talk within them is disciplined by the 'order' required to sustain such a 'picture' within one's talk (Shotter, 1991b, in press). A 'basic' way of talking is sustained (at least at first), not so much by a 'picture' as by certain institutionalized practices.

27. Here we might also talk of formative or architectonic tendencies... a bit of extra vocabulary is always useful.

28. That is, the complex affective and communicational intentionalities in actual acts of speaking, intentionalities which change and 'temporally develop' as an utterance is executed, must be replaced by something merely imaginable: an already completed, spatialized image.

29. In this view, the emergence of "representation" is due to the fact that, as linguistic competency increases, one becomes more adept in constructing a network of *intralinguistic* references to function as a context into which to direct one's utterances. In other words, there is a move away from a reliance upon the sense of one's speech, i.e., a reliance upon a referent in the immediate, shared context, and a move toward a reliance

upon meaning and syntax, i.e., upon links within what has already been, or, with what might be, said. In essence, this is a decrease of reference to what 'is' with a consequent increase of reference to what 'might be', an increased reference to an hermeneutically constructed imaginary (or theoretical) world.

As a result, what is said requires less and less grounding in an extralinguistic context - for it can find its supports almost wholly within a new, intralinguistically constructed context. Thus one can tell people about (represent to them or give them an account of) situations not actually at the moment present. Such a consequence requires, however, the development of methods for *warranting* in the course of one's talk (i.e., giving support to) one's claims about what 'might be' as being in fact what 'is' - one must learn to say, for instance, when making a claim about a state of affairs, that others saw it that way too, and so on. By the use of such methods and procedures, adults can construct their statements as factual statements, and adult forms of speech can thus come to function with a large degree of independence from their immediate context.

30. This, as we shall discover, is the wrong term, if 'express' is taken to mean representing in an order of words the supposed order of one's thoughts (the 'picture theory'). "Experience teaches us that thought does not express itself in words, but rather realizes itself in them" (Vygotsky, 1986, p.251).

31. Vygotsky (1986) distinguishes between words as in a dictionary (which have a *meaning*) and words in use in a context (which have a *sense*). "A word acquires its sense from the context in which it appears; in different contexts, it changes its sense. Meaning remains stable throughout the changes of sense. The dictionary meaning of a word is no more than a stone in the edifice of sense, no more than a potentiality that finds diversified realization in speech" (p.245).

32. Vygotsky (1986, pp.240-2) illustrates this with an anecdote from Dostoevsky's *The Diary of a Writer*, in which Dostoevsky relates a conversation between six drunks, who traverse over an intricate landscape of positions and evaluations in their utterances in turn, of the same unprintable word with six different intonations.

33. "The idea of the *conventionality, the arbitrariness of language*, is a typical one for rationalism as a whole, and no less typical is the *comparison of language to the system of mathematical signs*. What interests the mathematically minded rationalist is not the relationship of the sign to the actual reality it reflects not to the individual who is its originator, but the *relationship of sign to sign within a closed system* already accepted and authorized. In other words, they are interested only in *the inner logic of the system of signs itself*, taken, as in algebra, completely independently of the ideological meanings that give the signs their content" (Voloshinov, 1973, pp.57-58). See also Wittgenstein (1953, no.81).

34. "...when I was in Norway during the year 1913-14 I had some thoughts of my own, or at least it seems to me now. I mean I have the impression that at the time I brought to life new movements in thinking (but perhaps I am mistaken). Whereas now I seem just to apply old ones.." (Wittgenstein, 1980a, p.20).

35. "Our language can be seen as an ancient city: a maze of little streets and squares, of old and new houses, and of houses with additions from various periods; and this surrounded by a multitude of new boroughs with straight regular streets and uniform houses"

(Wittgenstein, 1953, no.17) – with, perhaps, the maze of little streets as the currently unacknowledged background to our more 'official' forms of academic and intellectual forms of talk, represented by the new boroughs with straight and regular streets.

36. "A record of natural speech will show numerous false starts, deviations from rules, changes of plan in mid-course, and so on" (Chomsky, 1965, p.4). Thus, in Chomsky's view, it is necessary – if one's aim is to discover the ideal syntactical rules, the linguistic *competence* underlying actual speech *performances* – then we cannot attribute much importance to actual linguistic performances. Wittgenstein's (1953) and Bakhtin's (1981, 1984, 1986, 1993) view is the exact opposite, of course.

37. "There is no reason for saying that meaning belongs to a word as such. In essence, meaning belongs to a word in its position between speakers; that is, meaning is realized only in the process of active, responsive understanding... meaning is the effect of interaction between speaker and listener produced via the material of a particular sound complex" (Voloshinov, 1973, pp.102-3).

38. Although, here too, Bakhtin points out that other 'voices' are at work: "The word cannot be assigned to a single speaker. The author (speaker) has his own inalienable right to the word, but the listener has his rights, and those whose voices are heard in the word before the author comes upon it also have their rights (after all, there are no words that belong to no one)" (Bakhtin, 1986, pp.121-122).

39. Rorty (1989, p.19) approves of "the Davidson claim that metaphors do not have meanings...," and takes it as implying that we cannot therefore *argue* for new ways of talking, for meanings as such, he claims, can only come "from the interior of a language game" (p.47). Thus all we can do is to try to make vocabularies we don't like "look bad" (p.44). If Vico and Grassi are right, this is nonsense; the presentation of a new metaphor *is* an argument.

40. Grassi notes that the term 'metaphor' is itself a metaphor, as it is derived from the verb *metapherein* 'to transfer' which originally described a concrete activity.

41. As C.W. Mills (1940) said, now more than 50 years ago, "the differing reasons men give for their actions are not themselves without reasons... What we want is analysis of the integrating, controlling, and specifying functions a certain type of speech fulfills in socially situated actions" (p.439).

42. The view that *proper* theory should provide a foolproof method, a mathematical formula, leading to the prediction and control of behavior, is a product of modern philosophy. As Grassi (1980, p.20) makes clear – see quote in text – this is not the original sense of what is involved in speaking theoretically.

43. See also Wittgenstein (1953, nos.131, 132, and 133).

44. I should have called it this in line with the whole "practical-descriptive" approach I outlined earlier (Shotter, 1984, p.xii), in line with my essentially Wittgensteinian project there. For, as Wittgenstein (1953) sees it: "We must do away with all *explanation*, and description alone must take its place" (no.109). For our task is not that, as individuals, of

gaining control or mastery over a process that is out of our control; but that of looking into the workings of our dialogically-structured activities that we rely on in making sense to each other in such a way as to make us recognize their actual workings. And we must do this *in spite of an urge to misunderstand* them, due to our taken-for-granted commitments to a natural scientific way of conducting our inquiries. The temptation is always to try to dig deeper, to go beyond (or behind) immediate appearances – but there is no need go beyond one's present circumstances – the way to 'go on' can be found 'there', within them.

45. In a recent book, Geertz (2000) remarks: "If it is true, as has been argued, that writers are willing to call master are those who seem finally to be saying what we feel we have long had on the tip of our tongue but have ourselves been quite unable to express, those who have put into words what are for us only inchoate motions, tendencies, and impulses of mind, then I am more than happy to acknowledge Wittgenstein as my master" (p.xi).

46. "The ethnographer does not, and, in my opinion, largely cannot, perceive what his informants perceive. What he (sic) perceives, and that uncertainly enough, is what they [his informants] perceive 'with' – or 'by means of', or 'through'... whatever the word should be" (Geertz, 1983, p.58).

47. See in this connection the 'circular' process diagrammed as Fig.1 in Chapter 2.

48. A task, as we shall see, that can only be achieved *dialogically* (see Chapter 5).

49. Or better, the 'becoming' of both ourselves and our social worlds.

50. Others, no doubt, contesting my version of joint action, will be a case in point.

51. Most current texts in psychology place the reader in the position of the Saussurian, passive recipient of the author's ideas – quite literally, we cannot find ourselves in such texts (Shotter, 1991).

52. Later, we shall want to say that being able to 'follow' someone's meaning, in fact involves our being able to 'anticipate' their 'point', i.e., the overall whole they are aiming at in their talk that *in-forms* its 'parts'.

53. "... it is not that before you can understand it you need to be specially trained in abstruse matters, but the contrast between understanding the subject and what most people *want* to see. Because of this the very things which are most obvious may become the hardest of all to understand. What has to be overcome is a difficulty having to do with the will, rather than with the intellect" (Wittgenstein, 1980a, p.17).

54. Vygotsky (1966) has discussed these issues in a most useful manner, suggesting that we can describe them as having to do with "... [the] *mastery of one's own process of behavior*. It is surprising to us that traditional psychology has completely failed to notice this phenomenon which we can call mastering one's own reactions. In attempts to explain this fact of 'will' this psychology resorted to a miracle, to the intervention of a spiritual factor in the operation of nervous processes..." (pp.33-34).

55. "I would be at great pains to say *where* is the painting I am looking at. For I do not look at it as I look at a thing; I do not fix its place. My gaze wanders in it as in the halos of Being. It is more accurate to say that I see according to it, or with it, than that I *see it*" (Merleau-Ponty, 1964, p.164)...

56. How it comes to be a shared grammar is a question for later consideration.

57. See also Heidegger (1977), *The age of the world picture*. As Heidegger remarks there, the term "world picture, when understood essentially, does not mean a picture of the world but the world conceived and grasped as a picture" (p.129).

58. In actual vision, we do not see *separate, independent, elements of reality*; in fact, in 'pointillism', dynamic *chaismic* relations emerge as we look over the points of paint to create a 'luminous' effects.

59. An early (1969) unpublished, mimeographed paper of mine was called: "Objections to the idea that everything essential to the understanding of human behavior can be formalized" (available on my website: http://pubpages.unh.edu/~jds/OBJECTIONS.htm)

60. In *Journal for the Theory of Social Behaviour*, *26*, pp.293-311.

61. All date only references are to Wittgenstein's works.

62. Genova (1995) points out that "style or how something is said determines for Wittgenstein what is said. The relationship is implicit in his practice and explicit in his ideas on the connection between form and content" (p.xiv). For example: "... there is no sharp boundary between methodological propositions and propositions within a method" (1969, no.318). "Writing in the right style is setting the carriage straight on the rails" (1980b, p.39). I will explore these issues further in Chapter 9.

63. Bourdieu (1977), in his theory of the "*habitus*," has of course already offered an extensive characterization of our embedding in such a flow of activity. As he sees it, the habitus consists in "systems of durable, transposable *dispositions*, structured structures predisposed to function as structuring structures, that is, as principles of the generation and structuring of practices and representations... collectively orchestrated without being the product of the orchestrating action of a conductor" (p.72). But such *theoretical* characterizations (representations) are beside the point, in that not only do they leave our own practices as social theorists untouched, but they hide from us the details of the particular forms of life from within which our talk makes sense. They are also after the fact, in that they divert attention away from the changing character of the moment by moment struggles between (and within) people as they 'orchestrate' their practices. As Wittgenstein sees it, in human affairs, all theoretical pictures divert our attention away from what is in fact before our eyes, by standing in the way of us seeing crucial details.

64. In posing this question like this, I have been very influenced by Johnston (1993).

65. Wittgenstein (1953) distinguishes between an *experience of meaning* we have when we just say a word out of any context of use, and the practical meaning of our words in

their use: "The meaning of a word is not the experience one has in hearing or saying it, and the sense of sentence is not a complex of such experiences" (p.181). Such "experiences of meaning" are, mostly, irrelevant to our employment of our words in us shaping our actual, practical exchanges with each other. Indeed, as we have seen, our utterances may make an almost negligible contribution to the momentary meaning of a person's action in a situation.

66. Here, we are not concerned either with *episteme* (knowing-that) or *techne* (knowing-how), but with a third kind of knowing *sui generis*, an ethical know-how, to do with our way of being in the world, our stance in relating ourselves to our surroundings: "What makes a subject hard to understand... is not that before you can understand it you need to be specially trained in abstruse matters, but the contrast between understanding the subject and what most people *want* to see. Because of this the very things which are most obvious may become the hardest of all to understand. What has to be overcome is a difficulty having to do with the will, rather than with the intellect" (1980b, p.17).

67. Here he quotes Goethe, *Faust*, PartI (In the Study).

68. In discussing the place of pictures in our mental processes, Wittgenstein comments that, even if we were to possess a faithful picture of an intention, say, it would still not be enough. "When one has the picture in view by itself it is suddenly dead, and it is as if something had been taken away from it, which had given it life before.. it remains isolated, it does not point outside itself to a reality beyond" (1981, no.236).

69. The difficulty here, however, is always to remind oneself of the backgrounded surroundings to which a foregrounded point is related, i.e., that here, one's unique, momentary, inessential special expressions must be accountable if one's use of them is challenged by others.

70. This is not to say that he is not interested in what is common to all of humanity: "The common behavior of mankind is the system of reference by means of which we interpret an unknown language" (1953, no.206). And we find him assuming that all peoples of the world relate themselves to each other in language intertwined forms of life, that they have beliefs, hopes, and wishes, make judgments, grieve, trust and distrust each other, enact rituals, bury their dead, sexually couple, educate their young, have disputes and ways of settling them, and so on.

71. See the remarks in Chapter 1 about Garfinkel's 'breaching' experiments.

72. Ochs, Jacoby, and Gonzales (1994) discuss what they call the momentary "liminal worlds" constructed by research physicists in their weekly, blackboard mediated, discussions of work-in-progress. Besides the central use of dynamic gestures in constructing such worlds, gestures that both point to a process statically portrayed on the blackboard, and pantomime its unfolding, they also point to another phenomenon of interest: the lack of sharp linguistic boundaries between subject and object, i.e., between the researcher and the physical phenomenon under study. The researcher says such things as, "I can't just hop over" (while gesturing toward a boundary depicted on the blackboard) or, "If I go below in temperature (gestures at a crucial point in a diagram)... the domain structure is gone." They call the momentary worlds constructed liminal

worlds, as they seem to hover between the visual display on the blackboard, and the imaginary world constructed in the physicist's discussions.

73. In this respect, Wittgenstein (1965) suggests that "the psychoanalysts... were misled by their own way of expression into thinking that they had done more than discover new psychological reactions; that they had, in a sense, discovered conscious thoughts which were unconscious" (p.57).

74. Vygotsky's (1986) influence is at work here, as it is in fact in much of this manuscript. The use of speech to 'direct', 'instruct', and 'organize' both the practical activities of others, as well as our own activity, is, of course, central to his whole approach. His 'voice', in fact, is a part of the 'hidden dialogicality' at work in much of this manuscript - as are the 'voices' of Bakhtin and Volosinov, though to document that fact would make an already overlong manuscript even longer.

75. Our 'inner', 'mental' lives are not, so to speak, geographically within us; they are grammatically *in* the way in which we live out our lives. The complex 'shape' of our activities and their relation to their circumstances, occasions our talk of mental states. As Volosinov (1973) puts it: "It is not experience that organizes expression, but the other way around - *expression organizes experience*. Expression is what first gives experience its form and specificity of direction" (p.85). Thus, "It is misleading to talk of thinking as 'mental activity'. We may say that thinking is essentially the activity of operating with signs" (Wittgenstein, 1965, p.6). Wittgenstein's stance toward our mental activities is clearly shared by Vygotsky, Bakhtin, and Volosinov. There is not space here to pursue this most important point (but see Shotter, in press).

76. Of course, this is also precisely what concerns Vygotsky (1986) in his studies: "The general law of development says that awareness and deliberate control appear only during an advanced stage in the development of a mental function, after it has been used and practiced unconsciously and spontaneously. In order to subject a function to intellectual and volitional control, we must first possess it" (p.168). Like Vygotsky, Wittgenstein also seeks to give us a deliberate, intellectual grasp on our otherwise spontaneous, responsive activity.

77. Here, we should note the two senses of the word picture. For, we only too easily think of a picture as simply depicting the structure of state of affairs in some way. Whereas, if we think of a picture as displaying a *scene* (as if in a play), in which an action is taking place within a setting, then we can get a grasp of the actions' relation to its surroundings. And our *use* of such a picture as this, is entirely different from our use of it in the first sense: "One says: How can these gestures, this way of holding the hand, the picture, be the wish that such and such were the case? It is nothing more than a hand over a table and there it is, alone and without a *sense*. Like a single bit of scenery from the production of a play, which has been left by itself in a room. It had its life only in the play" (1981, no.238).

78. Rose (1991), in discussing the anthropological poetry of Stanley Diamond (1982), quotes the following example from his "Shaman's Song." Diamond begins the poem as shaman (implied narrator) and then moves beyond the shaman to the Bear (character):

> What do you know of the Bear
> His body, my spirit

where, by juxtaposing *his body* immediately with my spirit, the two become one and we sense the shaman's relation to the bear. While Geertz (1983) suggests that anthropologists should tack "between the most local of local detail and the most global of global structure in such a way as to bring them into simultaneous view" (p.69), the dialogical juxtapositions of Diamond (and Wittgenstein) give us more than just an interpretation; they give "a sense of a new way to relate to meanings inherent in another cultural system" (Rose, 1991, p.232). Such juxtapositions, then, introduce a new intellectual 'movement', a new way of grasping the character of others who are 'placed' or 'positioned' differently from ourselves.

79. Kenny (1973) notes that "the *Investigations* contains 784 questions. Only 110 of these are answered; and seventy of the answers are meant to be wrong" (p.20).

80. "'Farewell!' 'A whole world of pain is contained in these words'. How *can* it be contained in them? – It is bound up with them. The words are like an acorn from which an *oak* tree can grow" (1980b, p.52).

81. See the comments in the previous chapter on Wittgenstein's (1953) use of *objects of comparison* – to establish "an order in our knowledge of the use of language: an order with a particular end in view; one of many possible orders; not *the* order" (no.132).

82. Here is an alternative formulation of the relativity thesis: "... users of markedly different grammars are pointed by their grammars toward different types of observations and different evaluations of externally similar acts of observation, and hence are not equivalent as observers but must arrive at somewhat different views of the world" (Whorf, 1956, p.221).

83. "Hopi," he says (1956, p.216), "may be called a timeless language. It recognizes psychological time, which is much like Bergson's 'duration', but this 'time' is quite unlike mathematical time, T, use by our physicists. Among the special properties of Hopi time are that it varies with each observer, does not permit of simultaneity, and has zero dimensions; i.e., it cannot be given a number greater than one [talked of as split into numbered parts]".

84. Whorf characteristically capitalized words he wanted to be especially noticed.

85. This is the last time I shall self-consciously mark the importance of our vocabulary here. For, I cannot wholly purge my writing of visual metaphors, it would make my writing even more tortured, peculiar and multivoiced (i.e., full of qualifications and 'second thoughts'), than it already is. But nonetheless, readers should remain vigilant in noticing their pervasive presence.

86. Whorf's statement here clearly resonates closely with Wittgenstein's (1953) claim that: "For a large class of cases – though not for all – in which we employ the word 'meaning' it can be defined thus: the meaning of a word is its use in the language" (no.43).

87. Goffman talks of the context of self-presentation as having a *moral* nature, in terms of involving different rights and duties for speakers and listeners.

88. "A picture held us captive. And we could not get outside it, for it lay in our language and language seemed to repeat it to us inexorably" (Wittgenstein, 1953, no.115).

89. In his original chapter, Whorf (1956) provides a diagram depicting the relations between a speaker, hearer, and the speech situation. Hence my need to replace his reference to aspects of it which the words in square brackets.

90. Intensity factors are denoted by "a special part of speech, the 'tensors', a huge class of words, [that] denote only intensity, tendency, duration, and sequence," says Whorf (1956). "The function of the tensors is to express intensities, 'strengths', and how they continue or vary, their rate of change... Tensors convey distinctions of degree, rate, constancy, repetition, increase and decrease of intensity, immediate sequence, interruption or sequence after an interval, etc., also QUALITIES of strengths, such as we should express metaphorically as smooth, even, hard, rough. A striking feature is their lack of resemblance to the terms of real space and movement... There is not even more than a trace of apparent derivation from space terms. So, while Hopi in its nouns seems highly concrete, here in the tensors it becomes abstract almost beyond our power to follow" (pp.146-147).

91. See quote from Max Scheler (1954, p.153) on page 158 of this book. Sacks, clearly, was responding to what Dr.P still could be that were merely hinted at in his daily coping with his life.

92. Therapists, if they are to adopt the "not-knowing" position, they must adopt a position which is very frightening to those of us trained as academics. For they must think of communication as working, not as primarily in terms of shared understandings, but – in rhetorical terms – as originating in vague, not-yet-cognitively-formulated *feelings*, of 'sensed movements' or 'sensuous re-positions', to which, as a recipient, they must reply in some way, but in what way, if it is not to do with trying to establish what they think life *ought* to like? Whatever they answer, it is their task to 'feel' in the course of it, the unique other who confronts them, what it is like to be him or her. Thus, as well as re-thinking the nature of communication, they must also re-think the nature of their knowledge (of the other) as beginning with a whole sequence of vague, fragmentary feelings that, over time, they must integrate into a 'felt' totality, a whole which functions as a 'basis' in terms of which a linguistic formulation of its nature can be judged for its adequacy. Thus, in switching to a language of 'feeling', they must stop thinking in terms of visually 'seeable things', in terms of patterns, structures, or systems as spatially *complete* entities, with all their parts simultaneously present. They must begin to think of 'experiencing historical events', which develop, of course, over time, and whose 'parts' at one moment in time, owe their character to what has happened in the past, and what might happen in the future. Hence, they can no longer think of them as primarily spatial, but they must think of them as having primarily a temporal existence, as like conversations, which are almost always incomplete until the last words are said, and which even then may be resumed the next day. And perhaps what will be most difficult for them, trained as they have been to a high degree as academics, to think and to act

autonomously, with a 'plan' or 'picture' in mind, they must grasp what it is like, just to 'feel one's way forward,' to just creatively respond to their circumstances - as we do in fact do it all the time, in sensing, say, the 'shape' of a problem in something that someone has just said, and in formulating a question which we hope will clarify things, But it is still not something we make rationally-visible to ourselves in our explicit accounts of what we think our knowledge is.

93. Sir Frederick Bartlett (1932) talks of all remembering as beginning with "very largely a matter of feeling, or affect" (p.206).

94. In their search for 'it' – the single, proper, accurate narrative – therapists ask clients, what the client of Anderson and Goolishan's (1992) I mentioned earlier, called "conditional questions." These are questions, the client felt, that functioned to check out whether the client knew what he was *supposed* to know (on the basis of the therapist's theory). This client became very sensitive to such questions; hence his characterization of them. But let me also repeat here, Wittgenstein's (1980b, I) warning against filling in the 'missing' fragments: "Mere description is so difficult because one believes that one needs to fill out the facts in order to understand them. It is as if one saw a screen with scattered colour-patches, and said: the way they are here, they are unintelligible; they only make sense when one completes them into a shape. – Whereas I want to say: Here *is* the whole. (If you complete it, you falsify it.)" (no.257).

95. First draft of a paper to be given at the Taos Institute Conference: Social Construction: A Celebration of Collaborative Practices, Oct 6th - 9th, 2005.

96. Here are some types of adjacency pairs that have been extensively studied: assertion-assent/dissent; question-answer; summons-answer; greeting-greeting; apology-acceptance/refusal; compliment-acceptance/rejection; threat-response; challenge-response; assessment/agreement; accusation-denial/confession; boasting-appreciation/derision (see Nofsinger, 1991).

97."One cannot... understand dialogic relations simplistically or unilaterally, reducing them to contradiction, conflict, polemics, or disagreement. *Agreement* is very rich in varieties and shadings. Two utterances that are identical in all respects ("Beautiful weather!" – "Beautiful weather!"), if they are really *two* utterances belonging to *different* voices and not one, are linked by dialogic *relations of agreement*. This is a definite dialogic event, agreement could also be lacking ("No, not very nice weather," and so forth)" (Bakhtin, 1986, p.125).

98. "Speaking as a true researcher-clinician, Jim's [Dr James Alexander] suggestion was that we must integrate rigor and sensitivity, and not allow these to become poles around which we organize our practice with any particular family, or our profession. With ample data demonstrating the superior clinical efficacy and cost effectiveness of his Functional Family Therapy approach over other approaches, he convincingly argued that manualized, researchable interventions can also respond and adapt to the particular cultural dimensions of each family's experience and style." (From: Kids on the Brink of Disaster: Research on Family-Centered Interventions, by Peter Fraenkel. The AFTA 2000 Research Plenary. In the Newsletter of the American Family Therapy Academy, Issue #80)

99. "What we find out in philosophy is trivial; it does not teach us new facts, only science does that. But the proper synopsis of these trivialities is enormously difficult, and has immense importance. Philosophy is in fact the synopsis of trivialities" (Wittgenstein, 1980b, p.26) – a synopsis that can be expressed in a moving portrayal of the circumstance(s) in question.

100. Earlier, in this connection, I quoted Vygotsky's (1978) remark that, in learning to coordinate their actions linguistically with the actions of those around them, "the child begins to perceive the world not only through his eyes but also through his speech" (p.32).

References:

Amrine, F. (1998) The metamorphosis of the scientist. In D. Seamon and A. Zajonc (Eds.) *Goethe's Way of Science: a Phenomenology of Nature*, pp.33-54. Albany, NY: State University of New York Press.

Andersen, T. (1995) Language is not innocent. In F. Kaslow (Ed.)*The Handbook of Relational Diagnosis*. New York: John Wiley and Sons.

Anderson, H. and Goolishan, H. (1992) The client is the expert: a not-knowing approach to therapy. In S. McNamee and K.J. Gergen (Eds.) *Therapy as Social Construction*. London: Sage.

Anderson, H. (1998) Collaborative learning communities. In McNamee, S. & Gergen, K.J. (Eds.), *Relational responsibility: Sources for sustainable dialogue.* (pp. 65-70). Thousand Oaks, CA: Sage Publications.

Bachelard, G. (1992) *The Poetics of Space*, trans. by Maria Jolas. Boston, MA: Beacon Press.

Bakhtin, M.M. (1981) *The Dialogical Imagination*. Edited by M. Holquist, trans. by C. Emerson and M. Holquist. Austin, Tx: University of Texas Press.

Bakhtin, M.M. (1984) *Problems of Dostoevsky's Poetics*. Edited and trans. by Caryl Emerson. Minnieapolis: University of Minnesota Press.

Bakhtin, M.M. (1986) *Speech Genres and Other Late Essays*. Trans. by Vern W. McGee. Austin, Tx: University of Texas Press.

Bakhtin, M.M.(1990) *Art and Answerability: Early Philosophical Essays by M.M. Bakhtin*. Edited by Micheal Holquist and Vadim Liapunov. Translation and Notes by Vadin Liapunov. Austin, Tx: Univerity of Texas Press.

Bakhtin, M.M. (1993) *Toward a Philosophy of the Act*. Trans by Vadim Liapunov and M. Holquist. Austin, Tx: University of Texas Press.

Barthes, R. (1983) *A Lover's Discourse*. New York: Hill and Wang.

Bartlett, Sir F.C. (1932) *Remembering: a Study in Experimental Psychology*. London: Cambridge Univ. Press.

Bateson, G. (1972) *Steps Toward an Ecology of Mind*. London: E.P. Dutton.

Bateson, M.C. (1990) *Composing a Life*. New York: (Plume) Penguin Books.

Bergson, H. (1911) *Creative Evolution*. London: Macmillan.

Bernstein, R.J. (1983) *Beyond Objectivism and Relativism*. Oxford: Blackwell.

Bernstein, R.J. (1992) *The New Constellation: the Ethical-Political Horizons of Modernitv/Postmodernity*. Cambridge, MA: MIT Press.

Billig, M. (1985) Prejudice, categorization and particularization: from a perceptual to a rhetorical approach. *European Journal of Social Psychology, 15*, 79-103.

Billig, M. (1986) Thinking and arguing: an inaugural lecture. Loughborough: University of Loughborough.

Billig, M. (1987) *Arguing and Thinking: a Rhetorical Approach to Social Psychology*. Cambridge: Cambridge University Press.

Billig, M. (1991) *Ideology, Rhetoric and Opinions*. London: Sage.

Billig, M., Condor, S., Edwards, D., Gane, M., Middleton, D. and Radley, R. (1988) *Ideological Dilemmas*. London: Sage Publications.

Bohm, D. (1965) Appendix: physics and perception. In *The Special Theory of Relativity*. New York:Benjamin.

Bohm, D. (1980) *Wholeness and the Implicate Order*. London: Routledge and Kegan Paul

Brady, R.H. (1998) The idea in nature: rereading Goethe's organics. In D. Seamon and A. Zajonc (Eds.) *Goethe's Way of Science: a Phenomenology of Nature*. Albany, NY: State University of New York, pp.83-111.

Capek, M. (1961) *The Philosophical Impact of Contemporary Physics* New York: Van Nostrand.

Cassirer, E. (1951) *The Philosophy of the Enlightenment*, trans by Fritz C.A. Koelin and James P. Pettegrove. Princeton, NJ: Princeton University Press.

Cavell, S. (1969) *Must We Mean What We Say?*. London: Cambridge University Press.

Chomsky, N. (1965) *Aspects of the Theory of Syntax*. Cambridge, Mass.: M.I.T. Press.

Cottrell, A.P. (1998) The resurrection of thinking and the redemption of Faust: Goethe's new scientific attitude. In Zajonc, A. and Seamon, D. (Eds.) *Goethe's Way of Science: a Phenomenology of Nature*. Albany, NY: State University of New York Press, pp.255-276.

Coulter, J. (1979) *The Social Construction of Mind*. London and Basingstoke: Macmillan.

Coulter, J. (1983) *Rethinking Cognitive Psychology*. London and Basingstoke: Macmillan.

Coulter, J. (1989) *Mind in Action*. London and Basingstoke: Macmillan.

Crites, S. (1986) Storytime: recollecting the past and projecting the future. In T.R. Sarbin (Ed.) *Narrative Psychology: the Storied Nature of Human Conduct*. New York: Praegar.

Descartes, R. (1968) *Discourse on Method and Other Writings.*Trans. with introduction by F.E. Sutcliffe. Harmondsworth: Penguin Books.

Descartes, R. (1986) Meditations on First Philosophy: with Selections from Objections and Replies. *Translated by J. Cottingham. with an introduction by B. Williams.* Cambridge, UK: Cambridge University Press.

Diamond, S. (1982) *Totems.* Barrytown, NY: Open Books/Station Hill.

Edwards, J.C. (1982) *Ethics Without Philosophy: Wittgenstein and the Moral Life.* Tampa, FL: University of South Florida Press.

Einstein, A. (1979) On the method of theoretical physics. In A.P. French (Ed.) *Einstein: a Centenary Volume*, London: Heinemann.

Fleck, L. (1979) *The Genesis and Development of a Scientific Fact.* Chicago: Chicago University Press

Foucault, M. (1970) *The Order of Things: an Archaeology of the Human Sciences.* London: Tavistock Publications.

Foucault, M. (1972) *The Archaeology of Knowledge.* trans. A.M. Sheridan, London: Tavistock.

Foucault, M. (1979) *Discipline and Punishment: the Birth of the Prison.* trans. A.M. Sheridan, Harmondsworth: Penguin Books.

Fraser, R. (1984) *In Search of a Past: the Manor House, Amnersfield, 1933-1945.* London: Verso.

Gadamer, H-G (1975) *Truth and Method.* London: Sheed and Ward.

Gadamer, H-G (1989) *Truth and Method*, 2nd revised edition, trans J. Weinsheimer & D.G. Marshall. New York: Continuum.

Garfinkel, H. (1956) Conditions for successful degradation ceremonies. *American Journal of Sociology*, 61, 101-105.

Garfinkel, H. (1967) *Studies in Ethnomethodology.* Englewood Cliffs: Prentice-Hall.

Garfinkel. H. (2004) *Seeing Sociologically: the Routine Grounds of Social Action.* Boulder, CO: Paradigm Press.

Geertz, C. (1983) *Local Knowledge: Further Essays in Interpretative Anthropology.* New York: Basic Books.

Geertz, C. (1986) Making experiences, authoring selves. In V. Turner and E. Bruner (eds.) Anthropology of Experience. Chicago: Univ of Illinois Press.

Genova, J. (1995) *Wittgenstein: a Way of Seeing.* New York and London: Routledge.

Gergen, K.J. (1999) *An Invitation to Social Construction.* London: Sage.

Gergen, K.J. (1982) *Toward Transformation in Social Knowledge.* New York: Springer.

Gergen, K.J, (1985) The social constructionist movement in modern psychology. *American Psychologist*, 40, 266-275.

Gergen, K.J. (1989a) Social psychology and the wrong revolution. *European Journal of Social Psychology, 19*, 463-484.

Gergen, KJ. (1989b) Warranting voice and the elaboration of self. In J. Shotter and K.J. Gergen (Eds.) *Texts of Identity*. London: Sage.

Gergen, K.J. (1990a) Social understanding and the inscription of self. In J.W. Stigler, R.A. Shweder, and G. Herdt (Eds.) *Cultural Psychology: Essays on Comparative Human Development*. Cambridge: Cambridge University Press

Gergen, K.J. (1990b) If persons are texts. In S.B. Messer, L.A. Sass and R.L. Woolfolk (Eds.) *Hermeneutics and Psychological Theory*, New Brunswick: Rutgers University Press

Gergen, K.J. (1991) *The Saturated Self: Dilemmas of Identity in Contemporary Life*. New York: Basic Books.

Gergen, K.J. and Morowski, J.G. (1980) An alternative metatheory for social psychology. In L.Wheeler (Ed.) *Review of Personality and Social Psychology*. Beverley Hills: Sage.

Gergen, K.J. and Gergen, M. (1987) Narratives of relationship. In R. Burnett, P. McGee, and D. Clarke (Eds.) *Accounting for Personal Relationships: Social Representations of Interpersonal Links*. London: Methuen.

Gibson, J.J. (1979) *The Ecological Approach to Visual Perception*. London: Houghton Mifflin.

Giddens, A. (1979) *Central Problems in Social Theory: Action, Structure and Contradiction in Social Analysis*. London: Macmillan.

Giddens, A. (1984) *The Constitution of Society*. Cambridge: Polity Press.

Giddens, A. (1991) *Modernity and Self-Identity: Self and Society in the Late Modern Age*. Stanford, CA: Stanford University Press.

Goethe, Johann Wolfgang von (1995). *Scientific Studies* (vol. 12 of *Collected Works*). Princeton: Princeton University Press.

Goffman, E. (1959) The presentation of self. *The Presentation of Self in Everyday Life*. New York: Doubleday.

Goffman, E. (1972) *Relations in Public*. Harmondsworth: Penguin.

Goffman, E. (1967) *Interaction Ritual*. Harmondsworth: Penguin.

Grassi, E. (1980) *Rhetoric as Philosophy*. University Park and London: Pennsylvanni State University Press.

Gustavsen, B. (1992) *Dialogue and Development: Theory of Communication, Action Research and the Restructuring of Working Life*. Van Assen, Netherlands: Gorcum.

Harré, R. (1970a) *The Principles of Scientific Thinking*. London: Macmillan.

Harré, R. (1970b) Powers. *Brit. J. Philos. Sci., 21*, 81-101.

Harré, R. (1972) *Philosophies of Science*. Oxford: Oxford University Press.

Harré, R. (1979) *Social Being: a Theory for Social Psychology*. Oxford: Blackwell.

Harré, R. (1983) *Personal Being: a Theory for Individual Psychology*. Oxford: Blackwell.

Harré, R. (1986a) The step to social constructionism. In M.P.M. Richards and P. Light (Eds.) *Children of Social Worlds*. Oxford: Polity Press.

Harré, R. (1986b) *Varieties of Realism*. Oxford: Blackwell.

Harré, R. (1986c) Social sources of mental content and order. In J. Margolis, P.T. Manicas, R. Harré and P.F. Secord (Eds.) *Psychology: Designing the Discipline*. Oxford: Blackwell.

Harré, R. (1986d) The social construction of selves. In K. Yardley and T. Honess (Eds.) *Self and Identity*. Chichester: John Wiley.

Harré, R. (1986e) An outline of the social constructionist viewpoint. In R. Harré (Ed.) *The Social Construction of Emotions*. Oxford; Blackwell.

Harré, R. (1990) Exploring the human Umwelt. In R. Bhaskar (Ed.) *Harré and his Critics: Essays in Honour of Rom Harré with his commentary on them*. Oxford: Blackwell.

Harré, R. and Secord, P.F. (1972) *The Explanation of Social Behaviour*. Oxford: Blackwell.

Harré, R. and Madden, E.H. (1975) *Causal Powers: a Theory of Natural Necessity*. Oxford: Blackwell.

Harré, R., Clarke, D. and De Carlo, N. (1985) *Motives and Mechanisms: an Introduction to the Psychology of Action*. London: Methuen.

Harris, R. (1980) *Language-Makers*. London: Duckworth

Harris, R. (1981) *The Language Myth*. London: Duckworth

Heidegger, M. (1977) The age of the world picture. In Heidegger, M. *The Question Concerning Technology and Other Essays*, trans. W. Lovitt. New York and London: Garland Publishing, Inc.

Hoffman, L. (2002) *Family Therapy: an Intimate History*. New York: Norton.

Jakobson, R. (1956) Two aspects of language and two types of aphasic disturbance. In R. Jakobson and M. Halle, *Fundamentals of Language*. The Hague: Mouton, pp.115-133.

Johnston, P. (1993) *Wittgenstein: Rethinking the Inner*. London and New York: Routledge.

Kant, I. (1970) *Critique of Pure Reason,* translated by Norman Kemp Smith. London: Macmillan's St Martin's Press.

Katz, A.M. and Shotter, J. (1996) Hearing the patient's 'voice': toward a social poetics in diagnostic interviews. *Social Science and Medicine, 46.* pp.919-931.

Katz, A.M. and Shotter, J. (2004) One the way to 'presence':methods of a 'social poetics'. In D.A. Pare & G. Larner (Eds.) *Collaborative Practice in Psychology and Psychotherapy*. New York: Haworth Clinical Practice Press.

Katz, A.M., Shotter, J. and Seikkula J. (2004) Acknowledging the otherness of the other: peotic knowing in practice and the fallacy of misplaced systematicity. In T. Strong & D.A. Pare (Eds.) *Furthering Talk: Advances in the Discursive Therapies*. New York: Kluwer Academic/Plenum Press.

Kenny, A. (1973) *Wittgenstein*. London: Allen Lane.

Kuhn, T.S. (1962) *The Structure of Scientific Revolutions*. Chicago: University of Chicago Press.

Lakoff, G. and Johnson, M. (1980) *Metaphors We Live By*. Chicago: University of Chicago Press.

Lienhardt, G. (1961) *Divinity and Experience: the Religion of the Dinka*. New York and Oxford: Oxford University Press.

Lowe, R. (2005) Structured methods and striking moments: using question sequences in 'living' ways. *Family Process, 44(1)*. pp.65-75.

MacIntyre, A. (1981) *After Virtue*. London: Duckworth.

MacIntyre, A. (1988) *Whose Justice? Which Rationality?*. London: Duckworth.

MacIntyre, A. (1990) *Three Rival Versions of Moral Enquiry: Encyclopaedia, Genealogy, and Tradition*. Notre Dame, IA: University of Notre Dame Press.

Malcolm, N. (1994) *Wittgenstein: a Religious Point of View*. Ithaca, NY: Cornell University Press.

Maturana, Humberto. & de Rezepka, S.N. (1997) Human awareness: Understanding the biological basis of knowledge and love in education. University of Chile, Santiago, Chile http://members.ozemail.com.au/~jcull/articles/bol.htm

Mead, G.H. (1934) *Mind, Self and Society*. Chicago: University of Chicago Press.

Merleau-Ponty, M. (1962) *Phenomenology of Perception* (trans. C. Smith). London: Routledge and Kegan Paul.

.Merleau-Ponty, M. (1964) *Signs,* translated by Richard M. McCleary. Evanston, Il: Northwestern University Press.

Merleau-Ponty, M. (1968) *The Visible and the Invisible.* Evanston, Il: Northwestern University Press.

Merleau-Ponty, M. (1970) *Themes from the Lectures at the College de France* (trans. John O'Neill). Evanston: North-Western University Press.

Mills, C.W. (1940) Situated actions and vocabularies of motive. *American Sociological Review, 5,*. 904-913.

Mills, C.W. (1940/1975) Situated actions and vocabularies of motive. In D. Brisset and C, Edgley (Eds.) *Life as Theater: a Dramaturgical Sourcebook.* Chicago; Aldine Publishing Company, 1975.

Monk, R. (1990) *Ludwig Wittgenstein: the Duty of Genius.* New York: Free Press.

Mooney, M. (1985) *Vico and the Tradition of Rhetoric.* Princeton: Princeton University Press.

Ochs, E., Jacoby, S., and Gonzales, P. (1994) Interpretative journeys: how physicists talk and travel through graphic space. *Configurations*, *1*, 151-171.

Ossorio, P. G. (1981) Ex post facto: the source of intractable origin problems and their resolution. Boulder, Colorado: Linguistic Research Institute report No. 28.

Parker, I. (1992) *Discourse Dynamics: Critical Analysis for social and Individual Psychology.* London: Routledge.

Parker, I. (1998) *Social Constructionism, Discourse and Realism.* London: Sage.

Peat, F.D. (1990) *Einstein's Moon: Bell's Theorem and the Curious Quest for Quantum Reality.* Chicago: Contemporary Books.

Penn, P. and Frankfurt, M. (1994) Creating a participant text: writing, multiple voices, anrrative multiplicity. *Family Process, 33(3).*

Polanyi, M. (1958) *Personal Knowledge: Towards a Post-Critical Philosophy.* London: Routledge and Kegan Paul, also New York: Harper and Row Torchbook, 1962.

Prigogine, I. (1980) *From Being to Becoming: Time and Complexity in the Physical Sciences.* San Fransisco: Freeman

Prigogine, I. and Stengers, I. (1984) *Order out of Chaos: Man's New Dialogue with Nature.* New York: Bantam Books.

Rorty, R. (1980) *Philosophy and the Mirror of Nature.* Oxford: Blackwell.

Rorty, R. (1982) *The Consequences of Pragmatism.* Minneapolis: University of Minnesota Press.

Rorty, R. (1989) *Contingency, Irony and Solidarity*. Cambridge, UK: Cambridge University Press.

Rose, D. (1991) In search of experience: the anthroplogical poetics of Stanley Diamond. In Ivan Brady (Ed.) *Anthroplogical Poetics*. Savage, MD: Rowan and Littlefield.

Ryle, G. (1949) *The Concept of Mind*. London: Methuen.

Sacks, O. (1985) *The Man Who Mistook His Wife for a Hat*. London: Duckworth.

Sampson, E.E. (1988) The debate on individualism: indigenous psychologies of the individual and their role in personal and societal functioning. *American Psychologist*, 43, 1203-11

Sampson, E.E. (1990) Social psychology and social control. In I. Parker and J. Shotter (Eds.) *Deconstructing Social Psychology*, London: Routledge.

Sampson, E.E. (1993) *Celebrating the Other: a Dialogic Account of Human Nature*. Boulder, CO: Westview Press.

Sarbin, T. R. (1986) Narrative Psychology: the Storied Nature of Human Conduct. New York: Praegar.

Saussure, F. de (1960) *Course in General Linguistics* (Eds. C. Bally and A. Sechehaye). London: Peter Owen, first pub.1911.

Schaeffer, J.D. (1990) *Sensus Communis: Vico, Rhetoric, and the Limits of Relativism*. Durham, NC: Duke University Press.

Scheler, M. (1954) *The Nature of Sympathy*. trans. Peter Heath. London: Routledge and Kegan Paul.

Schön, D. (1983) *The Reflective Practitioner: How Professionals Think in Action*. London: Maurice Temple Smith.

Schutz, A. (1964) *Collected Papers II: Studies in Social Theory* The Hague: Martinus Nijhoff

Scott, M.D. and Lyman, S. (1968) Accounts. *American Sociological Review*, 33. 46-62.

Searle, J. (1983) *Intentionality: an Essay in the Philosophy of Mind*. Cambridge: Cambridge University Press.

Seikkula, J. (2002) Open dialogues with good and poor outcomes for psychotic crisis: examples from families with violence. *Journal for Marital and Family Therapy, 28(30)*. pp.263-274.

Seikkula, J. and Arnkil, T. (2005) *Network Dialogues* London: Karnac Books.

Sheehy, G. (1976) *Passages: Predictable Crises of Adult Life*. New York: Dutton.

Shields, P.R. (1994) *Logic and Sin in the Writings of Ludwig Wittgenstein*. Chicago and London: University of Chicago Press.

Shotter, J. (1969) A note on a machine that 'learns' rules. *Brit.J. Psychol.,59,* 173-177.

Shotter, J. (1970) Men, the man-makers: George Kelly and the psychology of personal constructs. D. Bannister (Ed.) *Perspectives in Personal Construct Theory*. London and New York: Academic Press.

Shotter, J. (1973a) The transformation of natural into personal powers. *J. Theory Soc. Behav., 3*, 141-156.

Shotter, J. (1973b) Prolegoma to an understanding of play. *J. Theory Soc. Behav., 3*, 47-89.

Shotter, J. (1974a) The development of personal powers. In M.P.M.Richards (Ed.) *The Integration of a Child into a Social World.* Cambridge: Cambridge University Press.

Shotter, J. (1974b) What is it to be human?. N. Armistead (Ed.) *Reconstructing Social Psychology*. Harmondsworth:Penguin Books.

Shotter, J. (1975) *Images of Man in Psychological Research*. London: Methuen.

Shotter, J. (1980) Action, joint action, and intentionality. M. Brenner (Ed.) *The Structure of Action*. Oxford: Blackwell.

Shotter, J. (1984) *Social Accountability and Selfhood.* Oxford: Blackwell.

Shotter, J. (1986a) Realism and relativism; rules and intentionality; theories and accounts: a reply to Morss. *New Ideas in Psychology, 4*, 71-84.

Shotter, J. (1986b) A sense of place: Vico and the social production of social identities. *British Journal of Social Psychology, 25,* 199-211

Shotter, J. (1987a) The social construction of an 'us': problems accountability and narratology. In R. Burnett, P. McGee, and D. Clarke (Eds.) *Accounting for Personal Relationships: Social Representations of Interpersonal Links*. London: Methuen.

Shotter, J. (1987) The rhetoric of theory in Psychology. In W.J. Baker, M.E. Hyland, H.V. Rappard and A.W. Staats (Eds.) *Current Issues in Theoretical Psychology*. Proceedings of the first International Conference of the Society for Theoretical Psychology. Amsterdam: North Holland, pp.1-14.

Shotter, J. (1989a) Vygotsky's psychology: joint activity in a developmental zone. *New Ideas in Psychology*, 7, 185-204.

Shotter, J. (1989b) Rhetoric and the recovery of civil society. *Economy and Society, 18*, 149-166.

Shotter, J. (1989c) The social construction of 'you'. In J. Shotter and K.J. Gergen (Eds.) *Texts of Identity*. London: Sage Publications.

Shotter, J. (1990a) Underlabourer's for science, or toolmakers for society . Review essay on R. Bhaskar, *Reclaiming Reality: a Critical Introduction to Contemporary Philosophy*, 1989. *History of the Human Sciences*, 3, 443-457.

Shotter, J. (1990b) Wittgenstein and psychology: on our 'hook up' to reality. In A. Phillips-Griffiths (Ed.) *The Wittgenstein Centenary Lectures*. Cambridge: Cambridge University Press.

Shotter, J. (1990c) Social individuality versus possessive individualism: the sounds of silence. In I. Parker and J. Shotter (Eds.) *Deconstructing Social Psychology*. London: Routledge.

Shotter, J. (1991) A poetics of relational forms: the sociality of everyday social life. Special issue on "Evolutionary models in the Social Sciences," edited by T. Ingold. *Cultural Dynamics*, 4, 379-396.

Shotter, J. (1992a) Is Bhaskar's realism only a theoretical realism? Review essay on R. Bhaskar, *Philosophy and the Idea of Freedom*, 1991. *History of the Human Sciences*, *5*, 175-182.

Shotter, J. (1992b) 'Getting in touch': the metamethodology of a postmodern science of mental life. In Steiner Kvale (Ed.) *Psychology and Postmodernism*. London: Sage Publications.

Shotter, J. (1993a) *Cultural Politics of Everyday Life: Social Constructionism, Rhetoric, and Knowing of the Third Kind.* Milton Keynes: Open University Press.

Shotter, J. (1993b) *Conversational Realities: Constructing Life through Language*. London: Sage.

Shotter, J. (1995) In conversation: joint action, shared intentionality, and conversational ethics. *Theory and Psychology*, *5*, 49-73.

Shotter, J. (1998) Telling of (not about) other voices: 'real presences' within a text. *Concepts and Transformations*, *3*, pp.77-96.

Shotter, J. (2000) Seeing historically: Goethe and Vygotsky's 'enabling theory-method'. *Culture and Psychology*, *6(2)*, pp.233-252.

Shotter, J. (2005) Goethe and the refiguring of intellectual inquiry: from 'aboutness'-thinking to 'withness'-thinking in everyday life. *Janus Head: Journal of Interdisciplinary Studies in Literature, Continental Philosophy, Phenomenological Psychology and the Arts*, 8(1), pp.132-158.

Shotter, J. (2006) Moving on by backing away. In George Yancy and Susan Hadley (Eds.) *Narrative Identities: Psychologists Engaged in Self-Construction*. London: Jessica Kingsley, pp.150-171.

Shotter, J. and Gergen, K.J. (1989) *Texts of Identity*. London: Sage.

Shotter, J. and Lannamann, J. (2002) The situation of social constructionism: its 'imprisonment' within the ritual of theory-criticism-and-debate. *Theory & Psychology*, 12(5), pp.577-609.

Spellmeyer, K. (2003) *Arts of Living: Reinventing the Humanities for the Twenty-first Century*. Albany, NY: State University of New York Press.

Spence, D.P. (1986) Narrative smoothing and clinical wisdom. In T.R. Sarbin (Ed.) *Narrative Psychology: the Storied Nature of Human Conduct*. New York: Praegar.

Spinosa, C., Flores, F. and Dreyfus, H.L. (1997) *Disclosing New Worlds: Entreprenueurship, Democratic Action, and the Cultivation of Solidarity*. Cambridge, MA: MIT Press.

Staten, H. (1984) *Wittgenstein and Derrida*. Lincoln and London: University of Nebraska Press.

Steiner, G. (1989) *Real Presences*. Chicago, Ill: University of Chicago Press.

Stolzenberg, G. (1978) Can an inquiry into the foundations of mathematics tell us anything interesting about mind? In G.A. Miller and F. Uenneberg (Eds.) *Psychology and Biology of Language and Thought: Essays in Honour of Eric Lenneberg*. New York: Academic Press.

Tannen, D. (1989) *Talking Voices: Repetition, Dialogue, and Imagery in Conversational Discourse*. Cambridge: Cambridge University Press.

Tharp, R.G. & Gallimore, R. (1988) *Rousing minds to life: Teaching, learning, and schooling in social context*. New York: Cambridge University Press.

Toulmin, S (2001) Return to reason. Cambridge, Mass. : Harvard University Press.

Vico, G. (1944) *The Autobiography of Giambattista Vico*, trans. by M.H. Fisch and T.G. Bergin. Ithaca: Cornell University Press.

Vico, G. (1965) *On the Study Methods of Our Time*, trans Elio Gianturco. New York: Bobbs-Merrill.

Vico, G. (1968) *The New Science of Giambattista Vico*. Ed. and trans. by T.G. Bergin and M.H. Fisch. Ithaca, N.Y.: Cornell University Press.

Vico, G. (1988) *On the Most Ancient Wisdom of the Italians*, trans. Lucina Palmer. Ithaca: Cornell University Press.

Voloshinov, V.N. (1973) *Marxism and the Philosophy of Language*. Trans. by U. Matejka and I.R. Titunik. Cambridge, Mass.: Harvard University Press.

Voloshinov, V.N. (1976) *Freudianism: a Critical Sketch*. Bloomington and Inianapolis: Indiana University Press.

Vygotsky, U.S. (1962) *Thought and Language*. Edited and translated by E. Hanfman and G. Vakar. Cambridge, MA: MIT Press.

Vygotsky, U.S. (1966) Development of the higher mental functions. In A.N. Leont'ev, A.R. Luria and A. Smirnov (Eds.) *Psychological Research in the USSR* Moscow: Progress Publishers.

Vygotsky, U.S. (1978) *Mind in Society: the Development of Higher Psychological Processes*. M. Cole, V. John-Steiner, S. Scribner, and E. Souberman (Eds.) Cambridge, MA: Harvard University Press.

Vygotsky, U.S. (1987) *Thinking and Speech*. In *The Collected Works of L.S. Vygotsky: Vol.1* Edited by R.W. Rieber and A.S. Carton, and translated by N. Minick. New York: Plenum Press..

Vygotsky, U.S. (1986) *Thought and Language*. Translation newly revised by Alex Kozulin. Cambridge, MA: MIT Press..

Wertsch, J.V. (1991) *Voices of the Mind: a Sociocultural Approachto Mediated Action*. London: Harvester Wheatsheaf.

White, M. and Epston, D. (1990) *Narrative Means to Therapeutic Ends*. New York: Norton.

Whitehead, A.N. (1975) *Science and the Modern World*. London: Fontana.

Williams, R. (1977): Ch.9 "Structures of feeling," in *Marxism and Literature*. Oxford: Oxford University Press, pp.128-135.

Wittgenstein, L. (1922) *Tractatus-Logico-Philosophicus*. London: Routledge and Kegan Paul.

Wittgenstein, L. (1953) *Philosophical Investigations*. Oxford: Blackwell

Wittgenstein, L. (1965) *The Blue and the Brown Books*. New York: Harper Torch Books.

Wittgenstein, L. (1966) *Lectures and Conversations on Aesthetics, Psychology, and Religious Belief.* Edited by Cyril Barrett. Oxford: Blackwell.

Wittgenstein, L. (1969) *On Certainty*. Oxford: Blackwell.

Wittgenstein, L. (1980a) *Remarks on the Philosophy of Psychology*, vols.I and II. Oxford: Blackwell.

Wittgenstein, L. (1980b) *Culture and Value,* introduction by G. Von Wright, and translated by P. Winch. Oxford: Blackwell.

Wittgenstein, L. (1981) *Zettel*, (2nd. Ed.), G.E.M. Anscombe and G.H.V. Wright (Eds.). Oxford: Blackwell.

Index of Subjects

Index of Names (writers mentioned on almost every page of the book, i.e., Wittgenstein and Bakhtin, have not been indexed)

Printed by BoD™ in Norderstedt, Germany

9 780971 231252